The Importance of Fathers

It is widely acknowledged that children need structure, security, stability and attachment to develop and flourish. However, many changes have occurred in society which have changed the traditional family structure, including high divorce rates, increased mobility and women's liberation. This book sets out to explore what has happened to men and to fathers during all these changes and transitions.

Judith Trowell and Alicia Etchegoyen, along with an array of renowned contributors, consider a variety of topics, including:

- The role of the father at different stages of children's development
- The missing father
- Loss of a father
- Grandfathers.

It is argued that the father is important, not only to support the main carer (usually the mother), but also to provide a caring, thinking, comfortable, confident presence.

Judith Trowell is a Psychoanalyst and Child Analyst. She is Consultant Child and Adolescent Psychiatrist at the Tavistock Clinic, London.

Alicia Etchegoyen is a Psychoanalyst and Child Analyst. She is a Consultant and Child Adolescent Psychiatrist at Chelsea and Westminster Hospital, London.

THE NEW LIBRARY OF PSYCHOANALYSIS

The New Library of Psychoanalysis was launched in 1987 in association with the Institute of Psycho-Analysis, London. Its purpose is to facilitate a greater and more widespread appreciation of what psychoanalysis is really about and to provide a forum for increasing mutual understanding between psychoanalysts and those working in other disciplines such as history, linguistics, literature, medicine, philosophy, psychology and the social sciences. It is intended that the titles selected for publication in the series should deepen and develop psychoanalytic thinking and technique, contribute to psychoanalysis from outside, or contribute to other disciplines from a psychoanalytical perspective.

The Institute, together with the British Psycho-Analytical Society, runs a low-fee psychoanalytic clinic, organizes lectures and scientific events concerned with psychoanalysis and publishes the *International Journal of Psycho-Analysis*. It also runs the only UK training course in psychoanalysis which leads to membership of the International Psychoanalytical Association – the body which preserves internationally agreed standards of training, of professional entry, and of professional ethics and practice for psychoanalysis as initiated and developed by Sigmund Freud. Distinguished members of the Institute have included Michael Balint, Wilfred Bion, Ronald Fairbairn, Anna Freud, Ernest Jones, Melanie Klein, John Rickman and Donald Winnicott.

Volumes 1–11 in the series were prepared under the general editorship of David Tuckett. Volumes 12–39 appeared under the general editorship of Elizabeth Bott Spillius. Subsequent volumes are under the general editorship of Susan Budd. Ronald Britton, Egle Laufer, Donald Campbell, Michael Parsons, Rosine Jozef Perelberg, David Taylor and Stephen Grosz have acted as associate editors for various periods.

ALSO IN THIS SERIES

THE NEW LIBRARY OF PSYCHOANALYSIS
42

General Editor: Susan Budd

The Importance of Fathers

A Psychoanalytic Re-evaluation

Judith Trowell and Alicia Etchegoyen

BRUNNER-ROUTLEDGE
Taylor & Francis Group

First published 2002
by Brunner-Routledge
27 Church Road, Hove, East Sussex BN3 2FA

Simultaneously published in the USA and Canada
by Taylor & Francis Inc.,
29 West 35th Street, NY 10001, USA

Brunner-Routledge is an imprint of the Taylor & Francis Group

Typeset in Bembo by Keystroke, Jacaranda Lodge, Wolverhampton
Printed and bound in Great Britain by TJ International Ltd, Padstow, Cornwall

British Library Cataloguing in Publication Data
A catalogue record for this book is available from the British Library

Library of Congress Cataloging-in-Publication Data
Trowell, Judith.
The importance of fathers / Judith Trowell and Alicia Etchegoyen.
p. cm.
Includes bibliographical references and index.
ISBN 1–58391–173–1—ISBN 1–58391–174–X (pbk.)
1. Fatherhood—Psychological aspects. 2. Father and child.
3. Psychoanalysis. I. Etchegoyen, Alicia, 1944– II. Title.

HQ756 .T76 2001
306.874′2—dc21
2001035815

ISBN 1–58391–173–1 (hbk)
ISBN 1–58391–174–X (pbk)

Father's Day 2000 finds fatherhood in a curious state akin to the current position of the monarchy:

Hovering somewhere between unlikely trendiness and utter redundancy. Fathers are said to be more important than they once were, but their exact role remains unclear. When men talk about what it means to be a modern father, we are generally pretty vague, preferring to remark on how it changes your priorities or the focus of your existence.

Tim Dowling, The Telegraph, 17 June 2000

Contents

Contents

Contributors

Martin N. Baily, PhD, was formerly an Economics Professor at Maryland University, USA and more recently has been Chair of the Economics Council, US Administration in Washington, DC. He is a partner in Mackenzie Associates and currently at the Institute for International Economics, Washington, DC.

Kate Barrows is a Member of the British Psycho-Analytical Society. She also trained in Child Psychotherapy at the Tavistock Clinic. She works in private practice in Bristol and teaches, lectures and writes on a variety of psycho-analytic topics.

Paul Barrows is Principal Child and Adolescent Psychotherapist with the United Bristol Healthcare (NHS) Trust and has a particular interest in work with parents and infants, and the role of the father. He is author of a leaflet on fathers for the Child Psychotherapy Trust.

Dr Suzanne Blundell was born and educated in Basel, Switzerland, and studied Special Education and Psychology at the University of Fribourg. She then trained as a Child and Adolescent Psychotherapist at the Tavistock Clinic in London. She now works in the Inpatient Unit at Alder Hey Children's Hospital, Liverpool as well as in London.

Dr Abraham Brafman is a Psychoanalyst of children and adults. He worked in the NHS as a Consultant Child and Adolescent Psychiatrist. While recognizing the significance of a person's early experiences and the value of focusing on the 'internal world' of the patient, he stresses the importance of taking into account the patient's conscious experience of his present life.

Dr Ronald Britton, FRCPsych., is well known internationally as a psycho-analytic writer and teacher. He is a Training Analyst of the British Psycho-Analytical Society, a Vice President of the International Psychoanalytical

Association, and was Chair of the Department for Children and Parents, Tavistock Clinic. He is married with three children and five grandchildren.

M. Fakhry Davids is an Associate Member of the British Psycho-Analytical Society and a Member of the Tavistock Society of Psychotherapists. He is Honorary Consultant Psychologist at the London Clinic of Psychoanalysis, and is in full-time private practice. He has supervised and taught in a number of different settings.

Ricky Emanuel is a Consultant Child and Adolescent Psychotherapist trained at the Tavistock Clinic and working at the Department of Child and Adolescent Psychiatry at the Royal Free Hospital, London. He is also Head of Child and Adolescent Psychotherapy Services for Camden and Islington Community Health Services NHS Trust. He teaches at the Tavistock Clinic including Infant Observation. He was a contributor to *Closely Observed Infants*.

Dr Alicia Etchegoyen is a full member and child analyst of the British Institute of Psychoanalysis. She is also a Consultant Child and Adolescent Psychiatrist and Clinical Director of the Perinatal Mental Health Service at the Chelsea and Westminster Hospital, London. Publications include papers on the analyst's pregnancy, latency, infant observation and childcare.

Denis Flynn is an Associate Member of the British Psycho-Analytical Society. He trained in Philosophy, then at the Tavistock Clinic as a Child and Adolescent Psychotherapist. He is Head of the Inpatient Adolescent Unit at the Cassel Hospital and a Psychoanalyst in private practice. He has written mainly on child abuse and borderline adolescents.

Professor Peter Fonagy, PhD FBA, is Freud Memorial Professor of Psychoanalysis and Director of the Sub-Department of Clinical Health Psychology at the University College London. He is Director of the Clinical Outcomes Research and Effectiveness Centre and the Child and Family Centre both at the Menninger Foundation, Kansas. He is also Director of Research at the Anna Freud Centre, London.

Dr Marcus Johns is a Psychiatrist and Psychoanalyst. He was Chairman of the Child Guidance Training Centre, Tavistock Centre, with responsibility for the Day Unit for Seriously Disturbed Children. He is Deputy Director of the London Clinic of Psychoanalysis.

Dr Maureen Marks is a member of the British Psycho-Analytical Society, Senior Lecturer at the Institute of Psychiatry and Senior Clinical Tutor, Perinatal and Psychotherapy Services, South London and Maudesley NHS Trust.

Anton Obholzer, BSc, MB, CHB, DPM, FRCPsych., is a Consultant Psychiatrist at the Tavistock Clinic, London. He is a Psychoanalyst and Child

Analyst and is an Honorary Senior Lecturer at the Royal Free Hospital, University College London Medical School. He is also the Chief Executive, Tavistock and Portman NHS Trust.

Dr Mary Target, PhD, is a Senior Lecturer in Psychoanalysis at University College London, an Associate Member of the British Psycho-Analytical Society and Deputy Director of Research, Anna Freud Centre. She is a member of the Curriculum and Scientific Committees, Chairman of the Research Committee of the British Psycho-Analytic Society, and Chairman of the Working Party on Education of the European Psychoanalytic Federation.

Dr Judith Trowell, MBBS, DCH, DPM, FRCPsych., is a Consultant Child and Adolescent Psychiatrist at the Tavistock Clinic, Honorary Senior Lecturer, Royal Free and University College Hospital School of Medicine. She is a Psychoanalyst, child analyst, and Chairperson and Co-Founder of Young Minds, now Vice-President. She is Vice-Chair of Camden Area Child Protection Committee, an Expert Witness, and has undertaken Part 8 Reviews. Currently, she is Treasurer for the Association of Child Psychology and Psychiatry College as well as being a member of the President's Inter-disciplinary Committee, Family Law. Her research includes Psychotherapy Outcome Studies, Adult Mental Health and Child Protection, and Comparative Studies. Her training interests include court work and Psychodynamic Psychotherapy and she has an MA and PhD in child protection and family support.

Dr Clifford Yorke, FRCPsych., is an Honorary Fellow of the American College of Psychoanalysts, and a Training Analyst and Child Analyst for the British Psycho-Analytical Society. Formerly, he was Director and Psychiatrist In-Charge at the Anna Freud Centre, London. He is the author of many professional papers and three books.

Biddy Youell is a Child and Adolescent Psychotherapist at the Child and Family Department of The Tavistock Clinic and at the Monroe Young Family Centre. She has been involved in teaching on a number of courses and has a particular interest in the application of psychoanalytic thinking to non-clinical settings.

Foreword

Dr Anton Obholzer

It is now approximately a hundred years since Freud expressed his seminal views on the role of fathers. The time is ripe for a revisiting of the topic. Freud's views had a major influence on the psychological and sociological frameworks in which the roles of men and fathers were seen in the twentieth century. His ideas in turn were based on the cultural values of late-nineteenth-century Central Europe.

In the latter half of the twentieth century, Freud's ideas were largely overtaken by the writings of psychoanalysts such as Melanie Klein, Donald Winnicott and John Bowlby in the United Kingdom and by Margaret Mahler and others in the United States. The emphasis in this work inexorably, and rightly, tilted in the direction of the importance of mothers and of early bonding relationships.

From the 1960s onwards, the women's liberation movement steered a difficult path between, on the one hand, stressing the equality and importance of women, and, at the same time on the other hand, seeing motherhood as a potentially disadvantageous role in the battle for equality. There is little doubt that the new ideas on the importance of women – whether these were based on psycho-analytic ideas, on aspects of the women's liberation movement, or on changes in the profile of the workforce (which now drew in many more women) – had the result that, in the second half of the twentieth century, there was an increasing loss of confidence in the value of the received sense of manhood and of fatherhood.

Increased divorced rates and the inexorable rise in single-parent families have contributed to a social climate in which fathers, as consistent and stable role models, are increasingly unavailable to the next generation. Even unstable fathering role models are in short supply.

The acceptance of a whole new mode of procreation, ranging from 'do it yourself turkey-baster' interventions to sophisticated *in vitro* conception techniques, has contributed to the appearance that fathers are redundant beyond donating sperm. Cloning and surrogate mothering seem to make the connection between two parents and a birth still more distant.

The picture is not necessarily one of doom and gloom but can be seen as part of a gradual psychosocial development process from a primal-horde structure to a social configuration that emphasises the autonomy of the individual.

There is substantial research evidence coming from psychoanalytic, psychological, social and brain developmental perspectives which shows that early child-rearing patterns do have lifelong consequences both positive and negative. There are enough educational, social and psychological studies available to show that the way in which men's roles in the family have been modified over the last few generations is related to a significant increase in emotional casualties. These findings are confirmed by the World Health Organization's prediction that mental health problems are going to feature increasingly in the health profile of the twenty-first century.

It is therefore appropriate that, alongside the studies of mothering and of early bonding relationships that are a hallmark of late-twentieth-century research, there should be a reviewing and rethinking of the role of fathers. This is important both from the perspective of child development (assessing the component ingredients necessary for the raising of the next generation) and from the perspective of adults' development as fathers and mothers. Fathering and mothering are important biological, psychological and societal stimuli that foster the further development of adults as they work their way through their own developmental milestones.

Ideas of fathering and mothering go beyond child rearing. As states of mind at both the conscious and unconscious level, they have general application. Such parenting states of mind influence management and leadership styles in all organisations, even extending to the politics of nations and the relationships between nations. Fathering and mothering is thus not only a matter affecting those who choose to embark on the procreative process, it is of supreme importance to how all of us on this planet conduct our relationships.

Introduction

---- 1 ----

SETTING THE SCENE

Judith Trowell

Introduction

Fatherhood and fathering have recently become interesting again for psycho-analysts after a long period of preoccupation with mothers and mothering. Our overall aim in this book is to convey how fathers are important in the internal and external world of children. They always exist in the internal world just as the centrality in the internal world of the Oedipus complex is one of the facts of life. We want to consider ordinary fathers, good or bad, and ordinary developmental and psycho-pathological issues. We are aware that we have omitted two particular current social concerns: assisted parenting and gay/lesbian parents. Both merit in-depth consideration and, after considerable thought and discussion, we have decided to include them in a subsequent publication.

This book develops two strands: Mainly Theoretical, followed by Mainly Clinical, with two introductions by Judith Trowell and Alicia Etchegoyen. Fakhry Davids explores some of the changes in the internal world of the man on becoming a father. Mary Target and Peter Fonagy look at the impact of fathers in child development, Maureen Marks writes on the impact of severe maternal mental illness on the baby and the father, and Ronald Britton considers the impact on our understanding of fathers from ancient and modern father/daughter relationships. Abraham Brafman then contributes some thoughts on the role and impact of grandfathers for the child and family.

In the second section, Mainly Clinical, Ricky Emanuel explores what can be understood and learnt about fathers from observation. Clifford Yorke considers child development and the implications of a disability in a child or parent. Denis Flynn explores some of the complex issues that arise when foster or adoptive parents raise children. Suzanne Blundell presents an account of the impact on boys of their father being intermittently or permanently absent within the

3

context of domestic violence. Biddy Youell explores the impact on a mother of her own absent and then abusive father on her capacity to parent and make relationships. Paul and Kate Barrows write about the effects of loss in one generation on those trying to parent their own children, and Marcus Johns explores the impact of emerging sexuality in adolescence on the father/child relationship.

Fathers and their older adolescent children is an area that we regretfully were not able to cover in depth. This book has focused on the early years and the experiences of fathers and their children, to try and contribute to an understanding of the intrapsychic as well as social forces that men must negotiate in the transition to fatherhood and fathering.

Becoming and being a father

Becoming a parent may be unexpected, but for most people there comes a time during adult life when they wish for babies or children. Not everyone can become a parent. Many do, but others become step-parents or adoptive parents. Parenting is an ordinary everyday activity, and yet it is also one of the most skilled, difficult and demanding tasks an adult is called upon to perform. The paradox of ordinariness and yet complexity is perhaps why there are so many problems for fathers and mothers and for society (Greenberg 1985).

When a man becomes a father, it is not only biological issues that are involved. Becoming a father involves psychological and emotional changes; the child's interests have to take precedence over one's own. In order to be mentally and emotionally ready for this, the man needs to have had reasonably satisfactory childhood experiences. He needs to have in his internal world internalised carers who were able to meet his emotional, psychological, physical and social needs well enough, most of the time. They must also have been able to manage his and their own anger and envy appropriately. If not, then he needs to have had subsequent relationships that ameliorated early adverse experiences. The individual man needs to have a good sense of his identity, and also a sense of self – 'this is what I am good at; these are my faults or weaknesses' – so that he feels confident and worth while as a person. This sense of a secure base is important if he is to withstand the emotional highs and lows that are an inevitable part of parenthood. It is developed when an individual has had experience of another who is reliably and consistently available, who can contain and process their own and their child's thoughts and feelings. Fathers who have had this then have the capacity to sustain commitment; caring for a child depends more on commitment and containment than having glowing feelings. A screaming, vomiting, soiling child in the middle of the night needs committed parents.

Fathers need to have a good sense of their own sexual identity, their maleness. This is both a valuing and appreciation of their physical attributes, body, hair, strength, voice and genitalia, but also an appreciation of their emotional, intellectual and creative attributes. This has little to do with the roles and tasks of parenthood and how they will be shared by the adults. It has more to do with the capacity to value and tolerate sexual difference. The recognition and acceptance of these differences lead on to a recognition of a need for another so that there can be a parental couple capable of creativity both in the mind of the individual and in creating the baby. This recognition of being equal, but different, is key to becoming a parent. If male and female differences can be accepted and valued, then generational differences follow more easily: the acceptance by the man that he is an adult, and that his offspring is a child or a baby. These facts of life and acceptance of them are at the core of becoming a parent. Many men find this transition from carefree young man to fatherhood − becoming one of the parental generation − particularly painful and difficult, and some try hard to avoid it. Another linked developmental step is the capacity to make and sustain satisfying intimate relationships. Whether the parents' relationship has been externally confirmed by society in 'marriage' may not be important (it may), but what certainly is important is that the father has attained the capacity to manage the emotional demands of an intense relationship.

Theoretical considerations

Psychoanalytic theory is discussed in Alicia Etchegoyen's chapter and in many of the other chapters. However, we briefly allude here to attachment theory, given its increasing prominence in our understanding of relationships.

John Bowlby, as were most psychoanalysts of the early post-war period (Winnicott, Bion, Klein), was particularly concerned with the mother/child relationship, with the mother as the child's attachment figure and as providing the secure base. The father was seen as protecting the mother–child relationship as it developed, but then needed to intervene to make his own relationship with the child and to encourage healthy separation. He needed to go off with the child, with the child knowing that the mother can be returned to as a secure base. Bowlby sees the paternal function as preventing the mother from feeling overwhelmed by the needs and demands of the child; this can lead to rejection of the child or the mother's wish to remove herself by leaving or suicide. Bowlby was interested in the child's security of attachment: the differences in the child's development where a child had a secure relationship with both parents, a secure relationship with neither, or who had a secure relationship with either mother or father. A secure attachment seemed to lead to confidence and competence in the child and so father's contribution was recognised as important. Recent work looking at children with divorced parents confirms this (Solomon and George 1999).

Building on the contributions of John Bowlby, Mary Ainsworth devised the Strange Situation Test to explore systematically the child's relationship with its mother, father or any other key figure. The crucial component of this is the observation by the assessors of the child's and adult's reactions and responses to separation and reunion. Children can be securely attached to their mother or father or both; that is, they can explore and play creatively in the adult's presence, can tolerate separation, or, if tearful, can fairly quickly regain their equilibrium and continue to play and explore once the adult returns.

Insecure children find separations difficult. Their play prior to separation may be exploratory and creative, or may not, but after separation they respond in two main ways. The anxious children become very distressed on separation and when the adult returns cling and are very slow to regain composure. They are then very reluctant to resume play, remaining preoccupied with the adult. Some may show ambivalence and may attempt to approach and then withdraw, and some may hurt the adult. The avoidant child may not appear distressed on separation and may not need much consoling when the adult returns, but their energies appear to be focused on holding themselves together, so there is little left to really play and the toys are often used in a repetitive way that lacks creativity, curiosity and enjoyment. These children have marked physiological changes with raised cortisol level and blood pressure during separation.

Some children behave in a confusing and bewildered way when they are separated. They may engage in odd body movements or repetitive stereotypes, they may back away when the adult returns, or run forward, stop and lie face down on the floor. These children are classified as disorganised, disorientated children and there is a strong link between these behaviours and unresolved loss or abuse in the parents. The behaviours are thought to relate to fear, the parent may have been frightened or frightening previously, which has left the child confused and uncertain.

How children react to separation at one year old indicates a great deal and seems to be a means of obtaining an understanding of some aspects of their internal world. The secure child goes on to develop socially, cognitively and emotionally to achieve his or her potential. Insecure children and disorganised children have difficulties with relationships, become aggressive or vulnerable, have problems with concentration and learning and may have emotional difficulties and various psychopathologies. What is the relevance of all these developments, as well as the increasing use of the Adult Attachment Interview developed by Mary Main from the Strange Situation Test and the Reflective Function Scale developed by Fonagy *et al.* (1997)? They all indicate that attachments in childhood shape and influence adult relationships, and that how adults make sense of their experiences influences their thinking and their emotional and psychological development.

The facilitating and protective importance of early experiences has been confirmed in a measurable way, and fathers, as secure attachment figures, can be demonstrably confirmed as of great importance alongside or independent of the mother (Ainsworth *et al.* 1971; Bowlby 1988; Main and Goldwyn 1994; Fonagy 1997).

Why do men become fathers?

Many men find fatherhood thrust upon them, but others choose to become or not to become fathers. Why embark on a course of action that usually involves self-sacrifice for the rest of one's life? There are the drives, powerful emotional forces which fuel the desire for a sexual relationship, and the wish to have a product of this relationship, the longing men and women have to have children. Then, there is a longing for the relationship with the child itself, arising from previous experience of relationships, both with real external people but also intrapsychically. Inside each individual adult's internal world there are relation-ships, and also many phantasies. These may be about the self, in relation to the mother, or the father, a sibling, an extended family member or current and past sexual partners; all these phantasies can be focused on and invested in the conception and birth of a baby. The baby carries many hopes, expectations and fears. These may be conscious, but many of them are likely to be deeply unconscious and the father and child may never be aware of them. Giving an account of his family, one father described how his mother as a child had lost a younger sibling when she was about eight years old and the dead child was three. His own anxieties about this forthcoming child and its survival were hard to link in the mass of concerns about the birth and external world dangers, but it became apparent that the father's presenting anxieties about the child were strongly linked to the father's experience of his mother's preoccupation with her dead younger sibling, the fear, the rivalry and the anxiety about murderous rage. Most of these hopes, fears and phantasies are likely to have a considerable influence on the relationship between the father and child.

Many men become fathers for reasons they are not consciously aware of, the force of the drive to impregnate must never be underestimated. Men can consciously decide the time is right now, but it is usually driven by unconscious need as well; they may suddenly become anxious about infertility and fear the ageing process. Others may have had a bereavement, and creating a new life redresses the balance between life and death. Many pregnancies that are apparently unplanned may in fact happen because of some unconscious need or wish of one or other partner. For men, all pregnancies, whether consciously planned or unplanned, are the outcome of both unconscious drives and internal object relationships. A young couple were in conflict because of a third 'unwanted' pregnancy. The situation had become so fraught that termination or separation were seen as the options. Both parents explained their views and then were encouraged to listen to each other's account of early and past experiences.

The man's close but ambivalent relationship with his mother and her lengthy illness emerged. On the anniversary of her death he had needed support and reassurance, which involved considerable sexual activity. It seemed the baby had been conceived at this time. Understanding the baby as a replacement life helped the couple think about a way forward together.

Becoming a father

For the woman, becoming a parent is a massive physiological, physical and hormonal transformation. The pregnancy is a time when slowly, psychologically, the woman adapts to and develops a relationship with the baby, the baby in her mind and in her body, the unseen, the 'phantasy baby'. Pregnant women arouse very strong feelings: the envy of other women and men, shame and disgust (because to be pregnant declares to the world you are having a sexual relationship), and a wish to possess and take over the baby. The woman herself is having to deal with her own ambivalence: the longing for the baby, the fear of the birth and the anxiety about the child. She may be fearful about what the baby will be like, and there may be her own envy of the baby who will have a better life than she did. The baby may also represent many other of her internal objects: dead babies, dead, loved or hated parents, siblings.

Becoming a father lacks such physical underpinnings. Having impregnated the woman, a man has to manage his own internal conscious and unconscious hopes, fears and phantasies. Many men feel enormous pride and relief at having managed the task of conceiving a baby, although there may be lurking doubts as to whether it is 'my baby'. Unconscious phantasies are generally more ambivalent; the man both wanting the baby and feeling threatened by it. The father, whilst receiving affirmation intrapsychically of his masculinity, may find the identification with his own father provokes anger, rejection or guilt that may not be consciously available to work through. The loss of freedom and the need to care for his wife is often linked with unconscious envy of the woman, a feeling of being displaced. The father may be aware of his own mother, and her subsequent pregnancies when he was displaced as a child. (The father also has to review and reflect upon his relationship with his own father, Greenberg 1985.)

Consciously, the man thinks about what he wants to do in relation to his own father; he will have to consider what he wants to emulate and what he wants to do differently. Unconsciously, his internalised experiences of his own fathering and mothering influence and shape his attitudes. Many fathers find discipline a particular problem. If they were physically chastised or hit severely they may be determined to be different. Provoked by his son, a father said, 'I was so determined not to use physical punishment and there I was hitting him and I suddenly thought what am I doing? I did try to stop but I'm afraid it could easily happen again.'

A conception followed by a spontaneous abortion or a termination has frequently been dismissed as not having any effect on becoming a father. There is some clinical evidence that even where the pregnancy was relatively brief physiologically, emotionally the work of adapting to the presence of a new person had begun (Bourne 1991). The next pregnancy will be altered by this failed pregnancy, and there are emotional implications that need to be acknowledged.

As they approach fatherhood men can welcome the move to adulthood and the parental generation. But many of them slip into a state of terror and persecutory anxiety, consciously overwhelmed by a sense of responsibility, unconsciously confronted with unresolved Oedipal issues, so that the move from a two-person to three-person relationship feels unmanageable. They can become quite depressed or they can escape in manic flight, which leads to activity, including sexual affairs, and denial (Gurwitt 1989). Some men react by becoming overanxious, overprotective, which can be emotionally suffocating for the woman. The man who has fathered a child has to struggle to find a new balance: there is hope and love, but also his anger and envy of the mother's role and the need to share his partner's affection. The mother and father have to deal with the intrusion into their relationship of a third person. Both of them have to allow the idea of a baby, a child, to grow in their minds at the same time as it is literally growing in the woman's body. The father very easily can feel pushed out or left out or exclude himself. Fathers have to emotionally and psychologically undertake this transition without the overwhelming hormonal and body changes to impel them. The need for this intrapsychic work may be avoided or reluctantly undertaken. As a boy, working through, coming to terms with the Oedipal conflict, he had to let go of the special relationship with his mother and be left out, the third person. Now there is an opportunity for the man to identify with and make the connection (which may occur only unconsciously), to see the repetition of the triangle in the present generation, his mother (now his baby's mother), his father (now himself), and himself as small boy (now the baby). The man's identifications with and internalisations of the father leading to the internal object father have also shaped and continues to shape the internal object self (the man). The conception and birth of the baby cause considerable turmoil in the internal world. Hopefully, the father can accept and own his psychic potency, his physical and psychic sexuality and his partner's loving acceptance of him, her sexuality. The result of this is their baby. If this can develop, then a fluidity and strength permeates the relationships between the father, his parents, the mother and their baby (Berman and Pederson 1987).

Fathering and particular issues for some fathers

Conceiving a baby produces very powerful emotional reactions, primarily in the two participants. Conception can confirm and consolidate a person's view of their own sexuality, but it can also feel very threatening, as unconscious phantasies are stirred up. Alongside the pride and loving feelings there may be unconscious hate, fear and guilt. The castrating father who had to be placated in childhood may be re-evoked unconsciously so that retaliation is anticipated. The mother and father have to work out, preferably together, how they will manage the practical and emotional needs of the child. Gender roles are not as fixed as they were, and with more women working it is necessary to consider whether the father or mother will be the primary carer. The mother needs to retain some independence and personal authority and not become swamped in the physical and emotional caring; she needs another, usually the father, to support her as she finds her role as mother. Sometimes, one or other parent wants to possess the child and exclude the other parent. Or one parent cannot bear the time and energy needed by the baby and feels excluded. If the father's experience has been that there was never enough love and attention, then the prospect of sharing what there is is difficult. As well as the rivalry that can occur there can also be envy: the father may envy the mother and baby and their feeding intimacy; the mother may envy the father his freedom to come and go; grandparents, friends and relatives may envy the couple's new baby.

The issues are complex for anyone becoming a father, but there are particular issues for teenage fathers and older fathers. *Teenage pregnancy* means that the parents may have only just reached adulthood physically and psychologically. They will almost certainly be maturing and 'growing up' emotionally whilst the baby is also growing up. This does mean there is an even greater need to hold on to the view of the baby as a small dependent being rather than a rival for attention. Where the father is struggling to come to terms with some painful issues in his own childhood, only recently lived through, the baby can all too easily become identified with one of the protagonists, seen as provoking or hating the father like a sibling or, like his own mother or father, not loving the father enough.

When *older adults become parents* they can have problems with the flexibility required by a baby or child. If a lifestyle has been established and relationships have settled, dramatic changes are more difficult. The internal changes needed to one's sense of self are even more threatening because they can reawaken the fear of psychic catastrophe – the fear of falling to pieces because the adult over the years has consolidated defensive mechanisms; with the passage of time these tend to ossify so that change is felt to be dangerous. Many older couples are settled into a lifestyle with an established pattern of sexual relationship, work and social life. An older father may struggle with his partner's bodily changes, and as the pregnancy progresses he may himself be facing decreasing sexual arousal, a decline in physique and hair, and increasing girth. Active involvement with the baby may then feel like further decline and ageing, as the older father realises how much time and energy the baby needs, and the response can be a flight into relationships with young women who can restore the confidence and excitement of the man without so many apparent emotional needs. Conflicts and problems in current or past relationships that could be left well alone may be re-opened and need resolution. A first-time father in his fifties was initially very excited when his partner in her forties conceived, but as she became less active, and after the birth was preoccupied and frequently tired, he became restless. Family life left him feeling trapped. He found sharing his wife's attention was unbearable. His own limitations were also apparent to him and he took flight into a passionate affair with a much younger woman. Since he did not want to leave his wife and child he sought help.

Whilst all these emotional issues are going on for the new parents, they may also be required to *support their own parents*. Becoming a grandparent is also a developmental step in the life cycle; there is pleasure and delight, but also the need to come to terms with ageing and being a part of the senior generation. If there have been many frustrations and disappointments in their own lives, this is not easy, and potential grandparents may look to their children to support them through this without recognising all the emotional work the new parents have to do alongside the physical demands of parenthood.

Having a baby, becoming a father, requires the acknowledgement of difference. Fundamentally, the difference between men and women. However, there may well be other *differences* that need work and thought: skin colour, hair colour and texture, physical attributes, how the baby will look, how others will react. This is particularly so where there is a racial mix. Grandparents, family and friends may react quite strongly and the father will be very aware of this. Cultural differences can have a large impact in child-rearing practices. How children are brought up is decided by their parents, but each parent tends to draw on their own race, class, culture and ethnic background. Sorting all these out and arriving at an agreed way forward is not easy, particularly if the dynamic in the father's internal world includes feelings of loyalty, betrayal, envy and rivalry, part conscious and part unconscious.

Disability in a child may need to be faced and arrangements made to facilitate the child's maximum development. But the anxiety on possibly becoming a father of a disabled child needs to be worked with in anticipation. Shock, distress, guilt, blame, can too easily become overwhelming and destructive – both to the baby and to the parents – if the baby is born with a disability or chronic illness (Yorke, Ch. 14 this volume).

Being a father

After months of thinking, feeling and planning, the baby arrives and a man becomes a father with a real live baby – but also a family. For many men this is the culmination of something that has been longed for, but others can feel trapped and resentful. Natural parents have had the period of the pregnancy to prepare themselves, but parents wanting to adopt a child have to prepare in hope, and then have only a brief time when they know a child is actually coming. Parents who act as foster carers or adoptive parents may only have a few hours' warning (Flynn, Ch. 13 this volume).

When the baby arrives, what it needs is a carer who, for a while, can devote themselves to the child. The carer is usually the mother, but it can be an adoptive mother, grandmother or aunt, and can also be the father. Whoever takes on the role should, if possible, have a state of mind encompassing several aspects, described by Winnicott as 'primary parental preoccupation', by Bion as 'reverie'. An adult in this state has unconsciously opened themselves up to the baby in a way that enables them to be deeply responsive to the baby's communications. The baby has physical needs and a range of emotions and feelings, as well as physical sensations. Psychoanalysts believe that the baby has powerful loving feelings but also powerful negative feelings of hate, rage and envy. The baby is believed to fear falling to pieces, or being attacked and destroyed (Klein 1945; Bion 1967). The baby cannot speak, so communicates by sounds, cries, squeals and other non-verbal signals, eyes, hands, body posture and movements, and by unconscious communication, mainly understood via projective identification. In order to be open to these communications and become attuned to the baby, the primary carer needs to be a little detached from ordinary everyday relationships and interactions. During this phase, the primary carer will therefore be rather vulnerable and need the protection of another. If the mother is in this state of reverie, she needs another, usually the father, to manage the practical external demands and to act as a protector so that, for example, the mother is not too exhausted by relatives and friends or by her own anxieties about the baby. Father can settle the baby to sleep, change the baby, give a bottle so that the mother can rest and recover, encourage visitors to stay for a short while only, and contain and help think about the mother's and baby's emotional responses. The concepts of 'holding in mind' and 'containment' are both vital aspects of the relationship between child and father.

All these influences affect how fathers can manage the emotional roller coaster between pleasure and delight at some times and exhaustion and despair at others. It is, of course, difficult for mothers too, but fathers frequently find the emotional turmoil more difficult. A young father said 'I feed him, change him, play rough and tumble, I can't take any more.' The mother was more in touch with the baby and could hold him and accept his distress. Father had to act to make it better and couldn't tolerate the distress. The presence of a small person who is vulnerable and so dependent, but who is also something of a demanding tyrant, can seem to take over. This does vary considerably with the personality and temperament of the baby. It used to be thought that babies could be moulded and had no innate attributes or capacities, but it is now known that from the start babies play an active role in any relationship and bring their own unique constellation of personality variables into a relationship (Dunn and Polmin 1990; Belsky *et al.* 1995).

After the birth, fathers have to rediscover their own sexuality. The sexual relationship will have been interrupted and changed, since for the mother to rediscover her own sexual body and what is pleasurable and what is not, takes time. Fathers have to rediscover themselves as men and fathers in the changed relationship with their child's mother. The sex of the baby can influence this rediscovery. A male child can consolidate the father's masculine identity and he can feel supported, endorsed and validated by his son. The intrapsychic implications of this father–son birth and subsequent relationship are explored in this book, both when it goes well and when it does not. The father's relationships with his own father and now with his son are a mixture of friendship, love and support, but also rivalry and envy. One father, who had had a difficult relationship with his own father who had been frequently absent, was delighted and proud of his son, but later had immense difficulties when the boy, who was obviously a very bright able child and who was particularly good with words, started to challenge him. The son displaces the father and, in his turn, is displaced. The father also has to understand his partner, the mother's response to the boy baby. A mother was entranced by her son since her own father had died of cancer early in her life; the young boy was an unconscious replacement. The father found it hard to understand and tolerate. The father may feel displaced with his female partner, she preferring his son to the father; women may be excited by the birth of a son or resentful. The birth of a daughter can be supportive for a woman but also arouse rivalry, as there is recognition that this young girl will have the attention of the father and leave her as a mature woman no longer in the bloom of youth. The father has to enjoy and take pleasure in his daughter, whilst at the same time managing his emotional and physical longings and needs.

A current challenge

Fathers face an additional dilemma at present because of the increased awareness of the physical and sexual abuse of children. The abusers are usually men, whereas neglect usually involves mothers; emotional abuse can be by either parent. In the context of this book, sexual abuse would be incest, or a father–child sexual relationship. If a stepfather or adoptive father or foster father has cared for the child for many years and is in the fathering position as a trusted supportive adult, then abuse is psychological incest even if the biological link is not there.

How can we think about and understand the issues? Infantile and childhood sexuality is a reality and children can be charming, seductive and provocative. Children need parents who are aware and appreciative of their children's sexuality. Boys and girls need a father whose eyes light up with pleasure, admiration and some arousal when the child is dressed up, or displaying some physical prowess or flirting. But they also need fathers who can manage their own sexual feelings, needs and longings, and can control the situation so that

13

they do not enact the sexual urge. The child and the father may, for example, make eyes at each other, play a tickling game, have a cuddle while watching a television programme. But the father needs to control himself in a situation which, if they were potential sexual partners, would lead on to further intimacy. The appropriate limits must be imposed by the father.

Fathers' capacity to respond appropriately is rooted in their own early experiences and their negotiation of the Oedipal complex, and then its reworking in adolescence. Many men who sexually abuse children were physically or sexually abused themselves as children (30–90 per cent, according to the studies of Freeman-Longs (1986) and Briggs and Hawkins (1996)). The emotional impact of the sexual abuse on the boy is complex and still not fully understood. There are some common features, regardless of the relationship with the abuser, such as the shock and trauma, the sense of being damaged and dirty, and the loss of the ability to concentrate. Children and adults talk of being changed, of feeling that their personality has been altered – and not only in relation to sexual awareness. They feel bad, no good, unable to concentrate and hopeless about the future. They complain they can no longer trust, have lost their sense of humour, and feel hollow and empty inside.

Abuse leads to intrapsychic change resulting in confusion, distress and disorientation. It alters relationships between internal objects and the internal object themselves. The abuser uses the child as a sexual object, losing sight of the child as a person and as someone who needs care and protection. During the sexual contact, whilst aroused and climaxing, the adult has split off his own contact with reality, with his adult responsible aspects. These may be projected into the child and into society, the police and their partners. The child, the victim, is therefore the recipient not only of the bodily intrusion and the painful and pleasurable sensations, but also of the manic/triumphant/sadomasochistic/psychotic projections of the abuser. The child's internal world is invaded as his or her body is invaded. If these sexual contacts are frequent and accompanied by violence, and therefore the child is also fearful, then the internal chaos is even greater.

A boy's response to these experiences is always considerable, but does vary. The quality of the relationship has an effect. If the sexual abuse was in the context of a friendly loving relationship or involved minimal force or restraint it seems to be less traumatising, but the intrapsychic changes seem to be similar.

How children respond is influenced by where they were in their psychosexual development. The small child who has had little experience of containment and so has not internalised any secure containing function will be left in a chaotic state, with fragmented and fractured early internal objects resembling Bion's 'bizarre objects'. It is unclear when a young lad of seven had been first abused, but it was probably when he was about three years old. White and shaking in the consulting room, he could do almost nothing, his drawings were marks on the paper or else he stabbed holes in the sheet of paper. His language was very limited and he had no sense of time, he kept either aimlessly wandering in the room or sitting immobile and frozen. Where the child has begun to work on the Oedipal issues and has already developed an internal world with internal objects – mother, father, self – then the abusive experiences can be split off.

Where the abuser is the father, or father figure, the core of the internal object relationship world is threatened with destruction. The primary object relationship is still with the mother, and if this is good enough then the child has some resources to draw upon. But the significance of the father means that internally the extent of the splitting, the denial, the introjective and projective indentifications can leave the child, as one described, with the following thoughts: 'I feel as though there is only an outer shell that is me. I feel taken over in my head. My own thoughts, my own feelings are only there on the edges.' Over time, these split-off experiences may be processed and reduced, but they may remain as denied, split-off disavowed aspects. This is usually so when the abuse is by the father or father figure. Gradually, over time, the inner chaos becomes less obvious. This may be because the child was offered therapy and the emotional conflict and turmoil could be addressed, but more usually the passage of time leads to extensive splitting with a superficial functioning veneer of normal behaviour. Then if the veneer breaks down the extent of the paranoid–schizoid state is revealed. If the abuser was a grandfather, uncle or brother, the impact can be rather different. The child may have an intact live internal world based on good experiences with his parents. The sense of self is of course changed but the internal parental couple may be more of a resource. As with abuse by the father, where the impact varies with the mother's external and internal response, so with the abuse by the extended family, the response varies acccording to how the parents respond unconsciously and consciously. Instead of the chaos and fragmentation, there can be splitting and a paranoid–schizoid state from the start; the hatred and the rage can feel intractable as well as the rather cut-off detached state. A child whose older brother had been the abuser stated coldly of the excluded brother 'I wish he was dead, he is evil, he should be got rid of', and a child who had been abused by grandfather remarked 'He doesn't exist'. Where the abuser was a family friend, a neighbour, baby sitter or stranger, the effects are similar but not as fixed and intransigent. The confusion, distress and emotional pain are more available.

If the man who is now a father has had any of these experiences, and if they are still present as split-off, denied aspects in the unconscious, his capacity to manage his aggression and sexuality may be problematic. He may also, if the abuse continued over time, be introjectively identified with the abuser during adolescence and early adulthood. He may then function with his child, unconsciously projectively identifying with the father. His rage, hate and envy of the child who is innocent, and has not been abused as he was, may be overwhelming. An abused father was shocked that his child had been abused; it felt too cruel. But when the child was offered intensive therapy and the parents only once-weekly sessions, it became clear that the father repeatedly sabotaged the child's treatment. He was unable to tolerate the child being believed and offered help when he had not been, and he was given much less therapy than the child. When sexual thoughts and feelings arise in the abused father, both the splitting and denial, the internal chaos and the projective identification may prevent adult thought and awareness inhibiting their enactment in the sexual relationship with the child.

Fathering as the child grows up

During all these changes and developments, there is another process that must be recognised. The adults who have to totally readjust their lives and their identities must then be prepared to let the child go. As well as all the gains of parenthood, there are losses; the loss of independence, freedom, a higher standard of living and, for the primary carer, possibly loss of career and professional development. The baby needs total care early on, but then steadily moves towards separateness, a wish to be alone and then to leave. This process means parents have, to some extent, to be left behind, discarded. For those adults who were uncertain of themselves, or who found in the baby an intense relationship they have had with no one else, there is a dread of losing the child and a painful wish to hold on. It is difficult but important to recognise that the child is not to be possessed or owned by the parent. To give the love and commitment required, knowing that what you want is that the child to whom you have given so much can confidently walk away, is one of the most impressive aspects of parenting. Fathers have to both accept this themselves and help the mother separate and relinquish the child.

Conclusion

And yet all of this does not capture what it means to be a father, which is the most challenging and yet elusive task a man can undertake. There are all the practical tasks: the education, the stimulation that the young child needs, the protection from dangers, the provision of warmth and a home. But for the baby or child to develop, they need much more: the richness of a lively creative self-confident father who can enjoy them, respond sensitively, say no and mean it and encourage the child. This means drawing on past and current relationships, having overcome adversity and internal and external conflicts, and managing their own unconscious phantasies. As well as all this, they need to be able to sustain their intimate relationship with their partner and support and facilitate her, and, when possible, the extended family.

The task of this book is to focus in detail on what is happening to fathers. Fathers feel uncertain and threatened, and yet their role is vital. Whatever the needs or the demands in the external world, their role in the internal world is of central importance in the child's development of the Oedipus complex. The child in the development of his or her internal world will be preoccupied with 'mother' and 'father', the rivalry for and the wish to possess and partner each of them, the wish to triumph over each and to destroy and to separate them. One of the major developmental tasks is to come to terms with being a third, being left out and allowing one's 'mother' and 'father' to be a creative couple who mutually enjoy a relationship. How this is understood and worked through intrapsychically is crucial. What is not clear is how the historical changes in the external world and family structure affect this profound intrapsychic development. Resolution of the Oedipal conflict is essential to free intrapsychic energy to embark on an engagement with life, creativity, relationships, learning. Whether social changes have made this more difficult is something this book will attempt to explore. What seems certain is that a father is essential biologically and intrapsychically, but the role and place of actual fathers in families and in Western society is currently changing. The hope is that this book will provide some ideas, some insight into this area.

We are all aware of the increase in marital breakdown, single-parent families and the dramatic change in women's position in society – all of which reduce the significance of fathers. The increased awareness of the extent of traumatic experiences, domestic violence, and all the forms of child abuse which usually involve men have also challenged men's behaviour and their role. Nonetheless, we believe that good fathers are profoundly important for the child's development and the establishment of sound mental health. We suggest that the reduction in the significance of fathers and their exclusion in reality or from our thinking, the lack of recognition of their significance, may be a factor in the current apparent increase in mental distress and the more severe mental and psychological problems. We hope that this book will throw light on the role, function and importance of fathers.

References

Ainsworth, M.D.S., Bell, S.M. and Stayton, D.J. (1971) Individual Differences in Strange Situation Behaviour of one year olds. In H.R. Schaffer (ed.) *The Origins of Human Social Relations*, London: Academic Press, pp. 17–57.

Belsky, J., Rosenberger, K. and Crinc, K. (1995) The Origins of Attachment Security: 'Classical' and Contextual Determinants. In S. Goldberg, R. Muir and J. Kerr (eds) *Attachment Theory, Social Developmental and Clinical Perspectives*, Hillsdale, NJ: The Analytic Press, pp. 153–185.

Berman, P. and Pederson, F. (1987) Research on Men's Transition to Parenthood: An Integrative Discussion. In P. Berman and F. Pederson (eds) *Men's Transition to Parenthood*, Hillsdale, NJ: Lawrence Erlbaum Associates, pp. 217–242.

Bion, W. (1967) *Second Thoughts. Selected Papers on Psychoanalysis*, New York: Aronson.

Bourne, S. (1991) The Psychological Sequelae of Perinatal Death and Fetal Malformation. In *Clinics in Developmental Medicine*, Volume 122. London: MacKeith Press.

Bourne, S. (1992) *Delayed Psychological Effects of Perinatal Deaths, the Next Pregnancy and the Next Generation* (Tavistock pamphlet).

Bowlby, J. (1982) *Attachment*, Vol. 1 of *Attachment, Separation and Loss*, London: Hogarth Press.

Bowlby, J. (1988) *A Secure Base, Clinical Applications of Attachment Theory*, London: Routledge.

Brayelton, T.B. and Cramer, B. (1990) *The Earliest Relationship*, Reading, MA: Addison-Wesley Lawrence.

Briggs, F. and Hawkins, R. (1996) Molesters Compared with Non Offenders, *Child Abuse and Neglect 20*: 221–233.

Britton, R. (1989) The Missing Link: Parental Sexuality in the Oedipus Complex. In R. Britton, M. Feldman and E. O'Shaughnessy (eds) *The Oedipus Complex Today*, London: Karnac, pp. 83–103.

Britton, R. (1998) Subjectivity, Objectivity and Triangular Space. In *Belief and Imagination*, New Library of Psychoanalysis 31, London: Routledge, pp. 41–58.

Dunn, J. and Polmin, R. (1990) *Separate Lives*, London: New York: Basic Books.

Fonagy, P., Steele, M. and Target, M. (1997) *Reflective Functioning Manual* (June), London: Psychoanalysis Unit UCL.

Freeman–Longs, R.E. (1986) The Impact of Sexual Victimization on Males, *Child Abuse and Neglect 10*: 411–414.

Freud, S. ([1905] 1953) Three Essays of the Theory of Sexuality, *Standard Edition* 7, Hogarth Press, pp. 125–243.

Freud, S. ([1923] 1961) The Ego and the Id, *Standard Edition* 19, London: Hogarth Press, pp. 3–66.

Freud, S. ([1924] 1961) The Dissolution of the Oedipus Complex, *Standard Edition* 19, London: Hogarth Press, pp. 172–179.

Greenberg, M. (1985) *The Birth of a Father*, New York: The Continuum Publishing Company.

Gurwitt, A. (1989) Flight from Fatherhood. In S. Cath, A. Gurwitt and L. Gunsburg (eds) *Fathers and Their Families*, Hillsdale, NJ: The Analytic Press, pp. 167–188.

Klein, M. ([1932a] 1986) Early Stages of the Oedipus Conflict and Super Ego Formation, in Vol. II of *Writings of Melanie Klein. The Psychoanalysis of Children*, London: Hogarth Press.

Klein, M. ([1932b] 1986) The Effects of Early Anxiety Situations on the Sexual Development of the Girl, in Vol. II of *Writings of Melanie Klein. The Psychoanalysis of Children*, London: Hogarth Press.

Klein, M. ([1932c] 1986) The Effects of Early Anxiety Situations on the Sexual Development of the Boy, in Vol II of *Writings of Melanie Klein. The Psychoanalysis of Children*, London: Hogarth Press.

Klein, M. ([1945] 1975) The Oedipus Complex in the Light of Early Anxieties, in Vol. I of *Writings of Melanie Klein. Love, Guilt & Reparation*, London: Hogarth Press.

Main, M. and Goldwyn, R. (1994) *Adult Attachment Scoring and Classification Systems*, London: UCL.

Main, M., Kaplan, N. and Cassidy, J. (1985) Security in Infancy, Childhood and Adulthood: A Move to the Level of Representation. In I. Bretherton and E. Walters (eds) *Growing Points of Attachment Theory and Research*, Child Development publications: University of Chicago Press.

Solomon, J. and George, C. (1999) The Development of Attachment in Separated and Divorced Families: Effects of Overnight Visitation Parents and Couples Variables. In *Attachment & Human Development*, Vol. I, pp. 2–33.

Winnicott, D.W. (1951) *Transitional Objects and Transitional Phenomena*. In D.W. Winnicott *Collected Papers*, London: Tavistock Publications, 1958.

Winnicott, D.W. (1956) *Primary Maternal Preoccupation*. In D.W. Winnicott *Collected Papers*, London: Tavistock Publications, 1958.

Winnicott, D.W. ([1969] 1993) The Building Up of Trust. In C. Winnicott, C. Bollas, M. Davis and R. Shepherd (eds) *Talking to Parents*, Reading, MA: Addison-Wesley, pp. 121–135.

Winnicott, D.W. (1971) *Playing and Reality*, London: Tavistock Publications.

2

PSYCHOANALYTIC IDEAS ABOUT FATHERS

Alicia Etchegoyen

Introduction

The first psychoanalysts viewed the father as the central figure in mental life. Early formulations by Freud, Ferenczi, Abraham and others focused on the major role of the castration complex as the major organiser for emotional growth. Their theoretical outlook was patrocentric and phallocentric, with relative neglect of the significance of mothering and nurturing in human development.

After the Second World War, there was a shift in perspective. The evolution of psychoanalytic knowledge, including object relations theories and direct observational studies on child development, resulted in an increased interest in the mother–child dyad in the 1940s and 1950s, and in the study of motherhood as a developmental phase. Melanie Klein, Anna Freud and Margaret Mahler wrote about the baby's early dependence on the mother and conflicts over separation and individuation. In the 1960s, Bion, Winnicott and Bowlby made further contributions to the significance of the early mother–baby relationship/ attachment as the bedrock of mental health. This emphasis on the role of the mother was balanced most recently by Lacan's "return to Freud" which emphasised the role of the father (the Law of the Father) in structuring the unconscious.

Until the early 1970s there has been very little psychoanalytic literature about fathering, the father–child bond and fatherhood from a developmental viewpoint. As will be discussed later, Lacan used a structuralist model, based on language, and was not concerned with development. Ross (1979: p. 317) wrote that "until recently the father has been the forgotten parent in the psychoanalytic and psychological literature".

Slowly a number of papers and books, mainly from America, began to emerge: Cath *et al.* (1982, 1989), Lamb (1976), Abelin (1971, 1975). These studies use observation of actual fathers and an attempt to conceptualise the father's direct relationship with the child, as well as the father's role outside the mother–child dyad.

The reasons for this apparent "paternal deprivation" (Biller 1974) are unclear. Lansky (1992) suggested that the relationship to the mother and father is not symmetrical. The close emotional bond and caretaking functions involved in mothering are most easily apprehended. Fathering, instead, is "more context – and system dependent" (Lansky 1992: p.4). In other words, mothering may be connected with the biological immaturity and dependency of the newborn. Fathering may be more culture-dependent and be mediated by the mother's relationship to the father.

Benedek suggests that

the psychobiology of fatherhood seems to have evaded investigation; as if it were hidden by the physiology of male sexuality and by the vital socio-economic functions of fathers as providers. While biology defined the role the male invariably plays in the propagation of the species, the role of fathers as providers changes with cultural and socio-economic conditions.

(Benedek 1970: p. 167)

Kraemer (1993) points out that primate and pre-agricultural societies accentuate the role of the mother regarding the caretaking and food-gathering functions. In these societies the father's role is relegated to conception. He has no special relationship with his offspring. By the time of classical Greece this conception has radically changed: the mother is seen as the nurse looking after the seed planted (and owned) by the father, as described in Aeschylus' *The Oresteia*. This social definition of parental roles remained basically unchallenged until recently. We have now come full circle: the feminist movement, improved earnings and assisted conception techniques make it possible for woman to decide to have a child/children on her own.

The social changes which might lead to dispensing with the role of the father altogether are connected with clinical developments in the fields of family therapy, child abuse, trauma and borderline conditions. The realities of the modern family in Western society, often with absent or abusive fathers, give indirect impressive evidence of the psychological damage which occurs when there is not a "good enough loving father" (Layland 1985) around.

Psychoanalytic ideas about fathers can be broadly grouped under three headings: the role of the father in the Oedipus complex, the father as an intrapsychic construct (the "internal father"), and the role of the father in child development. The concepts interrelate, but will be described separately for the sake of clarity.

In this chapter I shall look at the intrapsychic and developmental aspects of the role of the father by way of a historical overview. I will concentrate on the ideas of some classical and contemporary psychoanalytic writers.

The Oedipus complex

Freud: the Oedipus complex and the primal father

Freud discovered the Oedipus complex through his own self-analysis, as recorded in his letters to Fliess (Freud 1950). In letter 69, Freud wrote "the possibility remained open that sexual phantasy invariably seized upon the theme of the parents" (Standard Edition Volume 1: 260) and in letter 71 (Vienna 15 October) he says "I have found, in my own case too, falling in love with the mother and jealousy of the father" (Standard Edition Volume 1: 265).

He thought it to be a universal intrapsychic conflict, a nuclear organising phantasy in sexual development, and of great significance to emotional growth: "Every new arrival on this planet is faced by the task of mastering the Oedipus complex; anyone who fails to do so falls a victim to neurosis" (1905, p. 171).

The concept and relevance of the nuclear complex are present from the beginning of Freud's work, though the term "Oedipus complex" only appears in the 1910 paper "A special type of choice of object made by men". The essay on Leonardo, of the same year, referred to the important role of the father, whether present or absent in the family, in helping the child to modulate his or her libidinal impulses towards the mother. He considered that the Oedipus complex arose around the age of three years out of the child's awareness of a libidinal relationship between the parents. The child wishes to have an exclusive relationship with the parent of the opposite sex, which places him/her in a position of rivalry with the parent of the same sex.

Freud argued that the recognition of sexual difference had significant, though not identical, consequences for the boy and the girl. In his paper "On the sexual theories of children" (1908) Freud argued that children of both sexes believed that both men and women have a penis. "Little Hans" (1909) describes the clinical application of this theory and with it the significance of the castration complex as the inevitable outcome of the Oedipus complex. From then on, the castration complex becomes an established idea referred to in "The infantile genital organisation" (1923), "The dissolution of the Oedipus complex" (1924) and "Some physical consequences of the anatomic distinction between the sexes" (1925).

Freud revised his theory of infantile sexuality in the 1920s. In addition to the oral and anal organisation of the libido there is also a genital infantile organisation (1923), characterised by "the fact that, for both sexes, only one genital, namely the male one, comes into account. What is present, therefore, is not a primacy of the genitals, but a primacy of the *phallus*" (p. 142, italics in the original). He referred to the importance of the phallic phase, which undergoes repression due to the castration threat: "Now it is my view that what brings about the destruction of the child's phallic genital organisation is the threat of castration" (1924: p. 175). In the same paper, he argued that there was a difference in the sexual development of the boy and the girl: "the girl accepts castration as an accomplished fact, whereas the boy fears the possibility of its occurrence" (p. 178).

The castration threat terminates the Oedipal conflict for the boy who is forced out of fear to abandon the wish to possess the mother in rivalry with father. He abandons the wish to possess the mother, in rivalry with the father. For the girl, the awareness of castration (the lack of a penis) confirms the threat of castration and initiates the Oedipus complex. She is forced to give up the wish for a penis in relation to the mother as the first love object. Instead the little girl turns to the father as her love object, wishing for babies as a substitute for the penis. Eventually, this wish is given up, leading to the resolution of the Oedipal situation for the girl.

In his paper "Female sexuality" (1931) Freud discovered the importance of the pre-Oedipal phase for both sexes. He described in greater detail the vicissitudes of sexual development in the girl, which began with an intense and prolonged pre-Oedipal attachment to the mother, to be followed by the phallic phase and penis envy. The girl's disillusionment with the mother not giving her a penis determines her move towards the father and initiates her Oedipus complex. Freud thought that the resolution of the Oedipus complex consisted in giving up the claim to possess the parent of the opposite sex (which under-goes repression) and in identifying with the parent of the same sex. The impetus for resolution was that of underlying anxiety and fear (the castration complex, penis envy).

The relation to the Oedipal father occupied a central place in Freud's most philosophical and anthropological writings over three decades, from "Totem and taboo" (1913) and "Civilisation and its discontents" (1930), to "Moses and monotheism" (1939). The notion of the primal father described the inherent violence and ambivalence in the relationship between the father and the son and the guilt that ensued. He used the hypothesis of the primal horde and murder of the primal father by the sons to explain the origins of exogamy and the incest taboo. The central theme of "Civilisation and its discontents" is that of the inevitable opposition between the demands of the instincts and the renunciations imposed by civilisation. He discussed in detail the origins of the sense of guilt arising from the killing of the primal father and also as a expression of "the conflict due to ambivalence, of the eternal struggle between Eros and the instinct of destruction of death" (p. 132). In the same paper, Freud refers to the infant's helplessness and the longing for the father: "I cannot think of any need in childhood as strong as the need for the father's protection" (p. 72).

In another paper, "The return of totemism in childhood" (1913), Freud writes about the importance of the father within the social order:

The totemic system was, as it were, a covenant with their father, in which he promised them everything that a childish imagination may expect from a father – protection, care and indulgence – while on the other side they undertook to respect his life, that is to say, not to repeat the deed which had brought destruction on their real father.

(Freud 1913: p. 144)

"Moses and monotheism", written towards the end of his life, developed further the idea of a phylogenetically inherited sense of guilt dating from the parricide of primitive men. Freud refers to the essential ambivalence in relation to the father, expressed in the Judas-Christian tradition by the allegiance to God the Father and the sense of guilt (the bad conscience of the original sin, the hostility against the father). The theme of prohibition and threat emanating from the father is fundamental to Freud's thinking. Freud's relationship to his own father (Ross 1979), and his family dynamics (Reder 1989), may have shaped his views on the subject.

Freud placed less emphasis on the positive relation to the father, described as the ego ideal. The nucleus of the superego consists of the prohibitions and their outcome of hatred and rivalry with the father. The primary relation to the mother, the "oceanic feeling" of primary narcissism referred to in "Civilisation and its discontents" (1930: p. 72) is submerged under the conflict with the father, representing external reality, which directed against the gratification of libidinal wishes towards the mother. The theory of penis envy and the castration complex place more significance on the role of the father in the Oedipal drama. Early psychoanalytic thinking emphasised a phallocentric view of the Oedipal struggle.

Loewald (1951) suggested that the resolution of the Oedipus complex and the castration threat represent the demands of reality on the ego. For Freud "the concept of reality is bound up with the father" (p. 7). The father appears mainly as a powerful figure to be fought or to whom we must submit. Religious feelings, the creation of father gods, the longing for the father are to be understood as defensive compromises to cope with castration anxiety. Loewald's own view (1951) is that the Oedipus and castration complex described by Freud should be thought of as part of a lengthy process. (Loewald postulates a direct positive relationship and a defensive one towards each parent.) There is a positive relationship to the mother, a development from the primary narcissistic phase and a defensive one against the threat of a return to the original undifferentiated state (the dread of the womb). He suggests an early positive identification with the father, which acts as a powerful force against the danger of engulfment with the mother. This identification takes place before the Oedipus complex. The defensive relationship to the father occurs later, in response to the castration threat.

Loewald concluded that the Oedipal situation was wider than the original castration complex. It included the libidinal relationship to the mother and the dread of the womb, the early positive identification with the father (the "ego

24

ideal") and the defences against castration anxiety. These components are not the result of the castration threat but are independent and interconnected.

Melanie Klein and early development

Melanie Klein focused on the significance of the child's primary relationship to the mother's body or womb. She described the early pregenital phases of the Oedipus complex and of superego formation as well as a dyadic relationship between the mother and child in the first months of life. In "Early stages of the Oedipus conflict" ([1928] 1975) Klein postulated that the Oedipal situation starts at weaning. She described an early harsh and cruel superego battling against the infant's weak ego, overwhelmed by persecution and guilt. Klein thought that the Oedipus complex was triggered by the mother's body and its contents. (She called this the feminine phase.) During the anal-sadistic stage of libidinal development, in the second year, she believed that both the boy and girl showed an interest in the mother's body and its contents – initially faeces, but later on differentiated as other part-objects, such as babies, breast, penis, etc.

In this feminine phase the child fantasises the mother's body as full of richness and identifies with it. The child's awareness of the father's penis as a special content inside the mother is part of the Oedipus complex. The boy wishes to destroy the father's penis to take possession of the mother's body. The girl identifies with the mother's body to receive the father's penis. The combined parental figure (the fantasy is of the mother containing the father's penis, in permanent intercourse) is a source of anxiety for both sexes. The early Oedipal configuration is thus related to the mother's body and its fantasised contents (such as milk, food, the father's penis, and babies) as part-objects.

In "The Psychoanalysis of children" ([1932] 1975) Klein placed greater significance on the relationship to the breast, which was further formulated in her theory of the depressive position (1935–1940). She considered that the child's early relation to the breast primarily shapes the Oedipal conflict. It is the frustration at the breast (paranoid anxiety) and the wish to spare and repair it (depressive anxieties) that bring about the infant's turning to the father's penis and with this the Oedipal triangular situation. (She called this the "passage from the breast to the penis".) Klein contended that the basic anxiety situation for both the boy and the girl is that of persecution and guilt, the result of the child's fantasised attacks on the mother's body and breast, the father's penis and their sexual relation (the primal scene). As development proceeds and the father is perceived more as a separate person, this primitive fantasy changes to that of the classic configuration which Freud had described. She argued that castration anxiety in the boy and the fear of loss of love in the girl are secondary derivatives from the primitive anxiety about attacks on the child's insides, by the hostile mother or by the parental couple as a combined figure. This early Oedipal situation is suffused with anxiety, pain and guilt stemming from the early superego. Resolution of the conflict is shaped by oral, anal and urethral sadism and by hatred and fear towards the parental couple.

A later paper "The Oedipus complex in the light of early anxieties" ([1945] 1975), shows some modification in Klein's views. She came to believe that loving feelings and the wish for reparation towards the parents were as important as hostile impulses in the resolution of the Oedipal situation. (She abandoned the notion that the frustration of weaning initiates the Oedipus complex with oral sadism in ascendant.) She now held that the development of the depressive position and the Oedipus complex were interlinked. The fundamental anxiety is not only persecutory in nature but that of concern and guilt towards the parents as good objects. The gradual recognition of the mother as a whole object includes awareness of separation between mother and infant and of the existence of other relationships such as those with father and siblings.

Klein wrote about the sexual development of the girl and the boy in "The Psychoanalysis of children" ([1932] 1975). She thought that children of both sexes turn away from the frustrating breast to the father's penis as an object of desire. Providing that anxieties about damage to the mother's body and breast are not excessive, a resolution of this early Oedipal configuration will take place. In the little boy the identification with the penis will lay the basis for heterosexuality, whilst turning to the father's penis as an object of desire will contribute to homosexual trends. In the little girl the identification with the father's penis will contribute to homosexual developments, whilst the turning to the father's penis as an object of desire will prepare the way for later genital receptivity.

As we have already seen, Freud in 1925 thought that the little girl's sexual development was different from that of the little boy because of anatomical differences (anatomy is destiny). Over the next few years, he revised his theories on infantile sexuality, including a growing awareness of the importance of the pre-Oedipal stage of development. He thought that before genitality, both the girl and the boy took the mother as the primary object of desire. When the Oedipal complex starts around the third year, the girl turns away from the mother in anger in discovering she has not got a penis. She turns to the father and substitutes for her desire for a penis the wish for a baby. The girl's genital sexuality remains dormant until puberty, when she becomes aware of the vagina as her sexual organ. Klein thought that the father is at the same time an object of desire and of rivalry for both sexes. The early oral relation to the penis, as described by Jones (1927), paved the way for genital development later on. Together with Jones and others, Klein argued for an early awareness of the vagina for both sexes. She rejected Freud's view of female sexuality as a castrated configuration of male sexuality. (She described female sexuality as having a separate existence.)

For Klein the pregenital stages of the Oedipus complex were "mother centred". The relationship to the father, as part-object, emphasised the jealousy and rivalry that both the boy and the girl felt for the possession of the mother. The wish or need for a relationship with the father as separate and distinct from the mother was not clearly delineated. The working through of the Oedipus complex at whole-object level still emphasises the fundamental importance of the early relationship to the breast, and the interconnection between the resolution of the depressive position and the Oedipus complex.

Bion: psychic truth, knowledge and the Oedipus complex

After Klein, Wilfrid Bion extended the classical concept of the Oedipus conflict in two directions. First, he referred to the significance of the Sphinx in the myth ([1959] 1961: p. 162), as representing man's curiosity about himself, a precursor of psychoanalytic insight (under the k [knowledge] link). Second, he thought that arrogance underlay the problem of incest represented by Oedipus' boast to pursue the truth at all costs. Bleandonu (1994) called this reconfiguration "the intellectual Oedipus". He argued that

> Bion's little Oedipus has a very different experience from Freud's; whereas the latter feels sexual desire towards his mother and death wishes towards his father, the former becomes the intractable enemy of an envied couple and an arrogant investigator. The latter was the royal hero of a family tragedy involving three people; the former is a solitary incarnation of an intellectual odyssey.
>
> (Bleandonu 1994: p. 135)

In "Elements in Psychoanalysis" ([1963] 1977) Bion used the Oedipus myth to describe different elements of the Oedipal situation: the sexual dimension and an emotional pre-conception which bound "the various components in the story in a manner analogous to the fixation of a scientific deductive system by their inclusion in the system" (p. 45). This preconception present in the baby's mind will be realised by coming into contact with parental figures, real or substitute. This "private Oedipus myth" is a precursor of knowledge of psychic reality. It enabled the infant to understand his relationship to the parental couple and to adapt to reality.

If this knowledge cannot be tolerated, a destructive link, under the sway of constitutional envy, greed and sadism, will precipitate destructive attacks on the parental couple. As a consequence the parental preconception will suffer fragmentation and dispersion. Bion found his psychotic and severely borderline patient lacked an inner model of the Oedipal couple, which seriously impaired the capacity to learn from experience and to think.

Winnicott and the independent tradition

Winnicott's contributions to psychoanalysis centred on infant development and the fundamental role of the mother. He argued that "the infant and the maternal care together form a unit" ([1960] 1990: p. 39). For Winnicott the concept of the mother as the facilitating environment is fundamental to the baby's development. Good enough mothering ([1968] 1991: p. 141): "includes fathers, but fathers must allow me to use the term maternal to describe the total attitude to babies and their care. The term paternal must necessarily come a little later than maternal". Winnicott held that the father's role in early infancy was to support the mother in her state of primary maternal preoccupation, to enable her to provide a holding environment and to avoid unnecessary impingements on the baby. In his paper "The capacity to be alone" ([1958] 1990), he suggested that when the infant is in the state of absolute dependency on the maternal holding, the father is not known to the infant. As development progressed, emotional separation from the mother eventually led to the infant being able to move from a two- to a three-person relationship. The chronology is similar to the classical Oedipal conflict. In his interesting paper "Contemporary concepts of adolescent development" ([1968] 1991), Winnicott argued that (p. 144): "If, in the fantasy of early growth, there is contained death, then at adolescence there is contained murder." Adolescent growing up means taking the parents' place in reality, and this is experienced in unconscious fantasy as an aggressive act. Winnicott commented on the importance of both parents surviving the adolescent's murderous wishes and feelings of personal triumph on taking the parents' place. The parents' role in adolescence is to provide a containing, non-retaliatory, non-vindictive environment which allows confrontation and rebellion. If the parents survive the adolescent's aggression, and are able to remain as an intact Oedipal couple, this allows for identification with the existence of their sexual relationship.

Like Klein, though with a different theoretical framework, Winniccott's model is "mother centred", in that there does not appear to be a role for the father as separate and independent from the mother in infancy and childhood. (His theory of human development centres on the role of the mother as the infant's first environment.) The baby depends on the mother's attentiveness, on her active and sensitive adaptation to his needs, in order to survive. The mother depends on the father and a supportive environment to carry out her tasks. (There seems to be a more distinct role of the father, as part of the Oedipal couple in adolescence, when the father is experienced as providing a model for identification.)

Phillips (1988) suggested that the father, in his own right, was generally absent in Winnicott's writing. (What is pivotal to Winnicott is the mother and baby couple, not the parental couple.) He quoted several examples from Winnicott's papers: the seminal paper "The capacity to be alone" ([1958] 1990) argued that the capacity to be alone depends on the child's experience of being alone in the presence of the mother. No mention is made on the significant experience of being alone in the presence of the father. "Reparation in respect of mother's organised defence against depression" ([1948] 1982) discussed how the child might develop a lively false self to support the mother, whilst identifying with the mother's depression. There is no role for the father as an alternative figure for identification for the child and for support for the mother. The notions of the transitional space ([1951] 1982), progressive disillusionment and acceptance of the "not me" experience does not include a picture of the father coming in between and separating the nursing couple. Phillips concluded that there is very little direct or implied acknowledgement in Winniccott's work on fathering and what it means for the baby and child to be fathered.

Lacan and the "Law of the Father"

The main cause of the reappearance of the father as a specific presence in psychoanalytic theory is due to the influence of Jacques Lacan. The complexity of his views and the controversy that surrounds them go well beyond the scope of this chapter. Lacan returned to the early Freud of the *Interpretation of Dreams* (1900) and *The Psychopathology of Everyday Life* (1901), works which described the language of the unconscious and the role of language as the "talking cure". There are, however, important theoretical differences between Freud and Lacan. For Lacan the unconscious is structured as a language and it is the father who introduced the "law of the language system", fracturing the illusory link between mother and child. Language is what distinguishes the Subject from the Other.

Lacan was concerned with the study of unconscious language structures, not with instincts or with the development of the ego as an organ of adaptation to internal and external reality. He argued that the function of the ego is totally imaginary, resulting in the alienation of the subject. For Lacan the individual's sense of self is not firmly anchored in early-internalised experiences. It is rather in a permanent state of flux, which is dependent on the Other, as a signifier. Mitchell (1982: p. 5) suggested that: "Lacan's subject is a being that can only conceptualise itself when it is mirrored back to itself from the position of another's desire." In that sense psychoanalysis is about unconscious desire, which by definition cannot be satisfied in reality.

Lacan shared Freud's view that the Oedipus complex is of fundamental importance in the structuring of the personality and of human desire. Castration is a privileged moment of psychic restructuring, inextricably linked with the development of language. There is therefore no room in his theory for preverbal, pre-Oedipal experiences. (Lacan wrote about his views on the Oedipus complex from the mid-1950s to the early 1960s.) In 1936, he described the "mirror stage" (see [1949] 1966) as a formative moment in the development of the ego. It occurs between the ages of 6 and 18 months, when the infant is able to recognise his image in a mirror. Although the mirror stage is prior to the Oedipus complex, Lacan's theories are not developmental. Birksted-Breen (1993: p. 17) refers to the cultural divide between the diachronic (mainly Anglo-Saxon) and synchronic (French) perspectives. The diachronic approach is concerned with the development of the child into the adult. It relies on observational and biological data, including the concept of the ego as an organ of adaptation to the environment. The synchronic approach focuses on the structures of the mind and how they interrelate. It is not concerned with a genetic viewpoint; that is, with the historical past and notions of causality.

The mirror stage is Freud's primary narcissism redescribed in structural terms. The child's sense of identity develops from seeing himself reflected in the other – the mother. This is a dyadic, imaginary relationship in which both the object and subject mirror each other and are, in essence, the same. In this imaginary situation the child identifies with the mother's desire for what she lacks – the penis. The child becomes the desire (the penis) of the mother's desire. At some point in the mirror stage brothers appear, which precipitates primitive aggression and jealousy. The father is seen as another brother wishing to take the child's place with the mother.

Lacan describes three stages in the development of the Oedipus complex. In the first (mirror stage) the father does not appear as a distinct structure. He is experienced as a brother competing for the dyadic relationship with Mother. In the second stage, the father intervenes: he becomes a castrator by cutting the imaginary link between the mother and child. The father appears as an omnipotent figure (a castrating superego) who prohibits the desire of the mother and makes the child realise he is not the mother's penis. Lacan considers that this cut is necessary to constitute the subject as a separate structure. The absence of castration precipitates psychoses. In the third stage the father facilitates a positive identification with himself (the ego ideal) and this is the moment when the child recognises that he is not the phallus and that the father has the phallus. He renounces the wish to be the father. Instead he wishes to be like the father.

The symbolic castration constitutes the "Law of the Father". It represents a momentous change in psychological organisation, a passage from the Imaginary (dyadic) to the Symbolic order where the presence or absence of the phallus determines the difference between the sexes. When it has occurred, the child painfully accepts that he is not the phallus and that the mother has no phallus. This realisation establishes the phallus as a symbol, the first signifier. It implies a substantial structural change: a shift from an empirical fact, the lack of a penis, to a signifier, the phallus as a symbol of the differences between the sexes. Lacan calls this mental structure "The name of the Father" (*nom-du-père*) or the "paternal metaphor". This metaphor is the "Law of the Father", which binds the individual to the symbolic order. In other words, the father's role in rupturing the mother–child union is to introduce the law of the language system, under which the child becomes a subject and enters culture.

The acquisition of the "Law of the Father" is not dependent on the presence of the real father. The mother's relationship to her own symbolic father and how she mediates her relationship with the child's actual father may be as significant. The "Law" represents an internal structure, which defines the subject in relation to the other. The first "law" is that of symbolic castration. For Lacan the Symbolic order is conveyed by the "law" of the language system, which structures the unconscious. The "paternal metaphor" refers to the separation of the subject from the object of desire.

In summary: Lacan's structural linguistic approach goes back to Freud's theories of phallic monism. Castration becomes the organising mental event, which places the individual in the Symbolic order. The role of the father is of prime significance for mental health and for the insertion of the individual in the human order and in culture. For Lacan the father's symbolic castration and prohibition against incest transcends individual experience. It belongs to the human order and separates humans from the animal kingdom.

Recent developments

In recent British and American psychoanalytic thinking, fathers appear in different ways but remain important. The Oedipus complex changes its meaning and is seen "not so much as the nucleus of the neuroses as the nucleus of normal character structure and as the basis of mature life" (Gitelson 1952: p. 354).

There is a general recognition of the importance of the early relationship to the father, both in his direct relationship with the child and indirectly through his relationship to the mother. Tyson (1986) referred to the non-defensive pre-Oedipal relationship to the father from an ego psychology perspective. Greenson (1968) and Glasser (1985) emphasised the role of the boy's positive relationship to the pre-Oedipal father, which encouraged his disengagement (disidentification) from the Oedipal mother.

Abelin (1971, 1975) expanded Mahler's ideas about the positive role of the father in early development as a facilitator in the separation/individuation process. Mahler suggested that the father provided a stimulus for the child's development of early exploration and phallic attitude during the practising subphase, and also protected the child against the regressive symbiotic pull to the mother during the rapprochement subphase. Abelin postulated an additional role for the father during the rapprochement subphase: he suggested that the child begins to notice the existence of the parental couple, at around 18 months. This experience of "early triangulation" is both traumatic and organising, which encourages a developmental move from a one-to-one mirror type (dyadic) relationships to a symbolic representation of the parental couple and the self.

Drawing on Klein and Bion, Meltzer (1973) elaborated on the inner world of the primal scene and the difference between infantile and adult sexuality. He thought that infantile sexuality is based on projection, whilst adult sexuality is connected with the introjection and identification with the parental couple in coitus. Meltzer described the reparative functions of the penis in relation to the three zones (the geography) of the mother's body: feeding in relation to the mouth, cleaning in relation to the anus, and generative of babies in relation to the vagina. For Meltzer the penis, as a part-object in the depressive position, included the notion of the phallus and of the testicles carrying functions both of reparation and creation.

Following a similar line of thought, Resnik (1989) referred to the significance of the good combined parental figure as a structuring agent for the ego. The combined good parents constitute a model of psychic structure which has the mother as the container and the father as the agent that constructs and organises. Resnik referred to Lacan's ideas on the "Law of the Father" in suggesting that the structuring function of mental life pertains to the phallus, internalised as a psychological "spine".

In a recent paper Steiner (1996) questioned the classical notion (Freud 1924) that the resolution of the Oedipus complex was propelled by castration anxiety and suggested that the child's awareness of the father coming in between his exclusive relationship with the mother is experienced as a traumatic injury. One outcome, (the "paranoid solution") consists in the child submitting and identifying with a father who is experienced as a powerful figure motivated by hatred and envy. The child renounces his claim on the mother out of fear and the reality of the parental relationship in its own right is evaded. Omnipotence and hidden idealisation of the mother take over and the underlying feelings of grievance and resentment against the father become a "psychic retreat", which prevents the development of true emotional autonomy. The "depressive solution" begins from the recognition of the reality of the parental relationship which carries the acceptance of the generation gap (the parents prefer each other as sexual partners) and of separation from the mother. Steiner suggested that in this situation the hatred and aggression shift from the castrating father to both parents. The working through of the murderous and loving feelings mobilised towards the parental couple will facilitate emotional growth.

Some contemporary Kleinian writers have described early Oedipal phenomena and fantasies and the effect that these have on perception and thinking. There has been a conceptual shift over the nature of the Oedipal conflict and its resolution. What is seen as central is the recognition and acceptance of the creative, sexual relationship of the parental couple, which produces a baby, with the accompanying feelings of envy and jealousy provoked. Britton (1989a) suggested that the internalisation of the Oedipal triangle creates a mental space where the child is able to have differentiated relations with each parent whilst recognising their relation to each other which excludes him. This developmental move results in a capacity for self-reflection and for seeing ourselves in interactions with others. Britton went on to argue that if the internalisation of the primal family triangle miscarries, the Oedipal situation appears in analysis in primitive form. In this situation there may be a profound split between the ideal breast/mother and the persecuting penis/father.

Another Kleinian author, Feldman (1989) described how primitive Oedipal fantasies affect thinking. He suggested that the capacity to make links include the link between the parents. If the Oedipal situation cannot be tolerated creative thinking is not possible. Temperley (1992) discussed the role of the father from a feminist Kleinian perspective. She argued that Freud's and Lacan's theories, which made the penis/phallus the signifier, resulted in women being placed in a disadvantageous and relatively powerless position, "rendering them 'objects' in a world of male signification" (p. 274). She contended that what the child had to come to terms with is not the prohibition of his incestuous longings but the "reality of his position in relation to the parents' sexual relation" (p. 271). She thought that both Klein and Lacan agree on the significance of the father and his penis to bring about a separation in the mother and baby dyad, but suggested that Lacan's view on the ultimate authority and power of the father could be redefined to describe the father's use of his authority to preserve a creative relationship with the mother as an equal partner. In this situation it is the child who has to relinquish the fantasy of omnipotent control of the mother (the imaginary order), and this is what Temperly believes is the genuine "realisation of castration" (p. 273).

Overall, modern Kleinian thinking focuses on the significance of the parental couple as a complementary pair and as an organiser of perception and thinking. The role of the father as a separate, significant figure is not discussed in detail. Britton's papers on "Projective identification: communication and evasion" (1989b) and "Keeping things in mind" (1992), where he comments on the direct and indirect role of the father, are exceptions. The indirect role is that of the father's capacity to contain the mother's anxieties to help her to respond to the infant's projections and needs. The direct role is that of the father as a figure for identification to help or sabotage the mother–infant relationship. Birksted-Breen's recent paper (1996) distinguished between "penis as link" and phallus: "the phallus as representative of omnipotence and completion and the unconscious significance of the penis as linking" (p. 651). The latter implied a recognition of the parental relationship and Oedipal situation, which structures mental space and thinking.

Fatherhood and "the internal father"

In spite of some contemporary interest on fatherhood (Cath *et al.* 1982, 1989; Samuels 1985), there is very little work in comparison with the wealth of research and writing on the mother–child relationship. There is no comprehensive and cohesive body of theory about fatherhood in the psychoanalytic literature.

(The subject may be studied from a variety of angles, including socio-cultural developments.) It is beyond the scope of this introduction to consider the impact of the decline of patriarchal society and rise of feminism on the concept of fatherhood.

In contemporary society, fathers may be absent following conception or from some point onwards in the young child's life. There are many causes, including advances in fertility treatment and changes in the stability of the nuclear family. There are an increasing number of one-parent families, because of marital breakdown or because women choose to have a child without the father's involvement. Psychoanalytic theory assumes that despite the physical and emotional absence of a real father, there is always some kind of internal picture or representation. Father exists as an object in the internal world.

How this "internal father" is construed is a complex matter. Bion ([1962] 1977) and Money-Kyrle ([1971] 1978) suggested a priori knowledge of the breast, penis and the parental couple, analogous to Jung's description of an innate imprint, "The Archetypal Father". These inborn dispositions operate like a basic structure, a preconception that will be filled in and shaped by actual relationships. The experience of having or not having a father is clearly important. Neubauer (1989) found that children fill the void of the absent father with an omnipotent picture of an ideal or an all-punishing father. The need is not just to fill a psychological void but to find a father as a real significant figure, described by Herzog (1982) as "father hunger". The internalisation of the experience of having a father is not only the result of the child's direct relationship with him but is also influenced by the mother in several ways. Marks and Lovestone (1995) argued that the child perceives the father directly, but also through the eyes of the mother. The mother's conscious and unconscious expectations and fantasies about the role of the father will shape the father's representation. These in turn will have been created in part by the mother's present relationship with her partner.

We are therefore thinking of a three generation pattern, mediated by mother. To Winnicott's dictum "there is no such thing as an infant" ([1960] 1990: p. 39) referring to the nursing couple, we may add that there is no such thing as a father without the mother's relationship to the father. There is also an internal mother, and similar identifications apply. But perhaps there is a difference, this having to do with the more direct, physical nature of the relationship between the baby and the mother. The baby grows inside the mother and is generally utterly dependent on her at first for feeding and overall care. The direct experience of the mother–child relationship may be more direct, at least in early infancy, than the more indirect father–child relationship mediated through the mother.

The apparent absence of an "internal father" has been noted in the studies of psychopathology. Limentani (1991) noticed, in a reassessment of his work with sexual deviants, the relative absence of the father in the material in the trans-ference. Chasseguet-Smirgel (1985) suggested that the sexual pervert denies the difference between generations and minimises the role of the father, in the belief that he can be the object of the mother's sexual desire. Lacan argued that the lack of internalisation of the father results in psychosis. Such a lack of internalisation may be due to a deficit in mental development or to a defensive repudiation of this "fact of life", part and parcel of the reality of the parental relationship.

Juliet Mitchell (1998) recently argued that there have been important social changes in family structure in the last 40 years, including an increased rate of divorce, single-mother families and paternal absenteeism. She considered that the relative absence of the father in contemporary Western society was mirrored in the relative absence in object relations theory of the castration complex as a significant theoretical construct, coupled with an increased emphasis on the mother–child relationship.

Mitchell referred to Limentani's paper "The limits of heterosexuality: the vagina man" ([1984] 1989) where he described how heterosexuality, at a psychological and social level, may occur in men who show no signs of having negotiated the castration complex. In some cases, Limentani found that there seemed to be no signs of the castration complex at all, resulting in the absence of an internalised prohibiting and positive father as a figure for identification. Limentani thought that the "vagina man's" solution was not a defence against homosexuality; instead, it was a solution for primitive anxiety by identification with the woman rather than a relationship based on object choice. The "vagina man" reverted to or stayed in the original merged mother–infant relationship, where the father is psychically absent.

Mitchell contended that if the clinical observation that there is no castration complex and no symbolic father in some heterosexuals is correct, we are faced with a number of questions: has the father as an internal object been destroyed in the mind? If this is the case, are we dealing with an apparently "normal" heterosexuality with a psychotic underlying structure? She argued that:

> although the heterosexuality may work well enough at the level of the couple, "fathering" (actual or symbolic) will be very difficult or even traumatic since psychically any child of the "vagina man" will be experienced not as the father's offspring but rather as a result of the mother's betrayal, and enormous sibling rivalry will be evoked between father and child.
>
> (Mitchell 1998: p. 3)

She suggested that the "vagina man's" mode of operating by identification, with consequent lack of boundaries and poor sense of self, and the underlying primal rage and jealousy, may be the prototype of the child abuser. Marks (Ch. 5 this volume) from a different perspective refers to a similar constellation of family breakdown following childbirth in couples who have remained attached to the pre-Oedipal mother, excluding or cancelling father out.

Fatherhood and child development

Psychoanalytic literature has, until recently, focused on the father's negative effects on development. Burgner (1985: p. 311) studied the significance of the absent father. She described the effect on both child and adults when the father is lost in the first years of life. In psychoanalytic treatment, these patients were revealed as impaired in their capacity to separate from their primary object. They remained ambivalently attached to the mother, who affected their sexual identity and their self-confidence in their adult roles as partners and parents. Wallerstein and Kelly's (1980) research reflected the continuing psychological importance of both parents, the longing for an absent father and an overall higher incidence of unhappiness and depression over a five-year follow-up period, a theme taken up by Youell in Ch. 9 (this volume).

The father's role in distorted and abusive family relationships has been extensively studied. Shengold vividly described the devastating effects on the victim:

> What happens to the child subjected to soul murder is so terrible, so overwhelming, and usually so recurrent that the child must not feel it and cannot register it, and resorts to massive isolation of feeling, which is maintained by brainwashing (a mixture of confusion, denial and identifying with the aggressor).
>
> (Shengold 1989: p. 25)

Trowell (1997) suggested that the impact of sexual abuse in the child constitutes an impingement registered as trauma, by which the unconscious mind is penetrated and contaminated. The child is usually forced to handle a split between the apparently normal and caring adult and the bizarre experience of their intrusion, which is felt as "madness". Anna Freud (1987) commented that the sexual abuse of the child by their own parents belongs to a category of its own. She argued that the abused child is not only exposed to an inappropriate sexual encounter but is also damaged by a type of stimulation for which s/he is developmentally unprepared.

More recently, authors have begun to look at the positive role and function of the father within the family (Abelin 1975; Ross 1979; Samuels, 1985; Cath *et al.* 1989; Marks and Lovestone 1995). There is overall agreement that the specific and positive role of the father in the child's psychological maturation has been overlooked. Several papers in this book, particularly those by Target and Fonagy (Ch. 3), Marks (Ch. 5) and Flynn (Ch. 13), address this topic in some detail.

How the father contributes to and affects children's development remains uncertain. Two important and interrelated questions are a focus of interest. First, are fathers really necessary? Second, are fathers different from mothers, and if so how? What is "a good enough father"? Is it to be described by the nurturing qualities or by other attributes?

Samuels (1996) takes the extreme view that although the maternal and paternal functions are different they can be carried out by the same person and are not necessarily gender related. The general view, however, is that of the parental couple as a fundamental template, representing different functions. The father's indirect role of offering emotional support and containment to the nursing mother or holding to the nursing couple has been recognised. Increasing attention is being paid to the father's direct role (Muir 1989) in providing an alternative attachment figure and a bridge with the external world. Glasser (1985) refers to the father as an alternative object which protects against the fears of merging with the mother.

In relation to the mother–infant dyad the father is "someone else", who thinks about and gets involved with the child. Intrapsychically he represents a significant figure outside the mother–baby dyad. He provides a separate and different mental space for the child. Chiland (1982) pointed out that the father exists as a significant and separate figure from the very beginning. She writes:

> The concept of a purely dyadic relationship between infant and mother is now as unacceptable as the concept of a stage of normal autism. The father is present, often in the flesh, and in any event in the mother's psyche. The impact of the father's mothering or of his absence on the child probably depends on the internal and external relationships between the parents and on those each has with the child.
>
> (Chiland 1982: p. 377)

The experience of the father as a "third person" begins to foster the child's awareness of his own identity. It is a process which starts in infancy, continues through nursery and school, and reaches a climax in adolescence. This is when the relation to the Oedipal parents has to be worked through again, culminating in a process of emotional separation. There is evidence that the relationship to the father has a significant role in helping the adolescent acquire his own sense of self. This entails defining oneself as different from each parent. The absence of the father in this crucial period may produce lasting detrimental effects (see Blundell, Ch. 11 this volume).

In conclusion it is hoped that this brief overview highlights the importance of the father in psychoanalytic theorising as an organiser of mental life through the Oedipus complex, as a fundamental intrapsychic construct ("the internal father") and as a significant figure in the child's development.

References

Abelin, E. (1971) The role of the father in the separation–individuation process. In J.B. McDevitt and C.F. Settlage (eds), *Separation-Individuation*, New York: International Universities Press.

Abelin, E. (1975) Some further observations and comments on the earliest role of the father. *International Journal of Psychoanalysis*, 56, 293–302.

Benedek, T. (1970) The psychobiology of pregnancy. In E.J. Anthony and T. Benedek (eds), *Parenthood*, Boston: Little, Brown, pp. 137–151.

Biller, H. (1974) Paternal deprivation, cognitive functioning and the feminised classroom. In A. Davids (ed.), *Child Personality and Psychopathology*, New York: Wiley, pp. 11–52.

Bion, W. ([1959] 1961) *Experiences in Groups and Other Papers*, New York: Basic Books.

Bion, W. ([1962] 1977) Learning from experience. In *Seven Servants*, New York: Jason Aronson, pp. 1–111.

Bion, W. ([1963] 1977) Elements in Psychoanalysis. In *Seven Servants*, New York: Jason Aronson, pp. 1–110.

Bion, W. (1967) A theory of thinking. In *Second Thoughts*, London: Maresfield Library, pp. 110–119.

Birksted-Breen, D. (1993) General Introduction. In *The Gender Conundrum*, London: Routledge, pp. 1–39.

Birksted-Breen, D. (1996) Phallus, penis and mental space. *International Journal of Psychoanalysis*, 77, 649–657.

Bleandonu, G. (1994) *Wilfred Bion. His Life and Works 1897–1979*, London: Free Association Books.

Britton, R. (1989a) The missing link: parental sexuality in the Oedipus complex. In R. Britton, M. Feldman and E. O'Shaugnessy (eds), *The Oedipus Complex Today: Clinical Implications*, London: Karnac, pp. 83–101.

Britton, R. (1989b) Projective identification: communication or evasion. Unpublished paper given at the British Psychoanalytical Society in February.

Britton, R. (1992) Keeping things in mind. In R. Anderson (ed.), *Clinical Lectures on Klein and Bion*, London: Routledge, pp. 102–113.

Burgner, M. (1985) The Oedipal experience: effects on development of an absent father. *International Journal of Psychoanalysis*, 66, 311–320.

Cath, S.H., Gurwitt, A. and Ross, J.M. (1982) *Father and Child*. Boston: Little, Brown.

Cath, S.H., Gurwitt, A. and Gunsberg, L. (1989) *Fathers and their Families*, Hillsdale, N.J.: The Analytic Press.

Chasseguet-Smirgel, J. (1985) *Creativity and Perversion*. London: Free Association Books.

Chiland, C. (1982) A new look at fathers. *Psychoanalytic Study of the Child*, 37, 367–379.

Feldman, M. (1989) The Oedipus complex: manifestations in the inner world and the therapeutic situation. In J. Steiner (ed.), *The Oedipus Complex Today: Clinical Implications*, London: Karnac Books, pp. 103–128.

Freud, A. (1987) A psychoanalyst's view of sexual abuse by the parents. In P. Mrazek and C. Kempe (eds) *Sexually Abused Children and their Families*, Oxford: Pergamon Press, pp. 33–34.

Freud, S. (1900) *The Interpretation of Dreams*, Standard Edition 4, 5.

Freud, S. (1901) *The Psychopathology of Everyday Life*, Standard Edition 6.

Freud, S. (1905) Three essays on the theory of sexuality, Standard Edition 7: 125–245.

Freud, S. (1908) On the sexual theories of children, Standard Edition 9: 207–226.

Freud, S. (1909) Analysis of a phobia in a five-year-old boy, Standard Edition 10: 1–149.

Freud, S. (1910a) Leonardo da Vinci and a memory of his childhood, Standard Edition 11: 59–137.

Freud, S. (1910b) A special type of choice of object made by men, Standard Edition 11: 165–175.

Freud, S. (1913) Totem and taboo, Standard Edition 13: 1–162.

Freud, S. (1923) The infantile genital organisation, Standard Edition 19: 141–145.

Freud, S. (1924) The dissolution of the Oedipus complex, Standard Edition 19: 173–179.

Freud, S. (1925) Some psychical consequences of the anatomic distinction between the sexes, Standard Edition 19: 243–258.

Freud, S. (1930) Civilisation and its discontents, Standard Edition 21: 57–145.

Freud, S. (1931) Female sexuality, Standard Edition 21: 233–243.

Freud, S. (1939) Moses and monotheism: three essays, Standard Edition 23: 3–137.

Freud, S. (1950) Extracts from the Fliess papers [1892–1899], Standard Edition 1: 175–280.

Gitelson, M. (1952) A re-evaluation of the role of the Oedipus complex. *International Journal of Psychoanalysis*, 66, 351–355.

Glasser, M. (1985) "The weak spot" – some observations on male sexuality. *International Journal of Psychoanalysis*, 66, 405–414.

Greenacre, P. (1971) *Emotional Growth*. New York: International Universities Press.

Greenson, R.R. (1968) Dis-identifying from mother: its special importance for the boy. *International Journal of Psychoanalysis*, 49, 370–374.

Herzog, J. (1982) On father hunger: the father's role in the modulation of aggressive drives and fantasy. In S.H. Cath, A. Gurwitt and J.M. Ross (eds), *Father and Child*, Boston: Little, Brown, pp. 163–174.

Jones, E. (1927) The early development of female sexuality. *International Journal of Psychoanalysis*, 8, 459–472.

Klein, M. ([1928] 1975) Early stages of the Oedipus conflict. In *Love, Guilt and Reparation and Other Works (1921–1945)*, London: Hogarth Press, pp. 186–198.

Klein, M. ([1932] 1975) *The Psychoanalysis of Children*, London: Hogarth Press.

Klein, M. ([1935] 1975) A contribution to the psychogenesis of manic-depressive states. In *Love, Guilt and Reparation and Other Works (1921–1945)*, London: Hogarth Press, pp. 282–269.

Klein, M. ([1940] 1975) Mourning and its relation to manic-depressive states. In *Love, Guilt and Reparation and Other Works (1921–1945)*, London: Hogarth Press, pp. 344–369.

Klein, M. ([1945] 1975) The Oedipus complex in the light of early anxieties. In *Love, Guilt and Reparation and Other Works (1921–1945)*, London: Hogarth Press, pp. 370–419.

Kraemer, S. (1993) The postnatal development of fathers: how do they cope with their new roles? Unpublished paper.

Lacan. J. ([1949] 1966) Le stade du miroir comme formateur de la fonction du je telle que'elle nous est revelee dans l'experience psychoanalytique. In *Ecrits*, Paris: du Seuil, pp. 93–100.

Lamb, M. (ed.) (1976) *The Role of the Father in Child Development*, New York: Wiley.

Lansky, M.R. (1992) Symptom, system, and personality in fathers who fail. In *Fathers who Fail: Shame and Psychopathology in the Family System*. Hillsdale, N.J.: The Analytic Press, pp. 3–13.

Layland, R. (1985) In search of a loving father. In A. Samuels (ed.), *The Father: Contemporary Jungian Perspectives*, London: Free Association Books, pp. 154–169.

Limentani, A. ([1984] 1989) The limits of heterosexuality: the vagina-man. In *Between Freud and Klein*, London: Free Association Books, pp. 191–203.

Limentani, A. (1991) Neglected fathers in the aetiology and treatment of sexual deviation. *Bulletin of the British Psychoanalytical Society*, 27, 1–8.

Loewald, H. (1951) Ego and reality. In *Paper on Psychoanalysis*, New Haven: Yale University Press, pp. 3–20.

Marks, M. and Lovestone, S. (1995) The role of the father in parental postnatal mental health. *British Journal of Medical Psychology*, 68, 157–168.

Meltzer, D. (1973) *Sexual States of Mind*, Strath Tay: Clunie Press.

Mitchell, J. (1982) Feminine sexuality: introduction. In J. Mitchell and J. Rose (eds), *Jacques Lacan & The Ecole Freudienne*, London: Macmillan, pp. 1–26.

Mitchell, J. (1998) Sexuality, psychoanalysis and social change. In S. Grosz (ed.), *The Institute of Psychoanalysis News and Events. Summer 1998*. London: The Institute of Psychoanalysis.

Money-Kyrle, R. ([1971] 1978) The aim of psychoanalysis. In D. Meltzer and E. O'Shaughnessy (eds), *The Collected Papers of Roger Money-Kyrle*, Strath Tay: Clunie Press, pp. 442–449.

Muir, R. (1989) Fatherhood from the perspective of object relations theory and relational systems theory. In S.H. Cath, A. Gurwitt and L. Gunsberg (eds), *Fathers and their Families*, Hillsdale, N.J.: The Analytic Press, pp. 47–61.

Neubauer, P.B. (1989) Fathers as single parents: object relations beyond mother. In S.H. Cath, A. Gurwitt and L. Gunsberg (eds), *Fathers and their Families*, Hillsdale, N.J.: The Analytic Press, pp. 63–75.

Phillips, A. (1988) *Winnicott*, London: Fontana Press.

Reder, P. (1989) Freud's family. *British Journal of Psychiatry*, 154, 93–98.

Resnik, S. (1989) El padre en el psicoanalisis. *Revista de psychoanalysis, Asociacion Psicoanalitica Argentina*, 4, pp. 499–517.

Ross, J.M. (1979) Fathering: a review of some psychoanalytic contributions on paternity. *International Journal of Psychoanalysis*, 60, 317–326.

Samuels, A. (1985) *The Father. Contemporary Jungian Perspectives*, London: Free Association Books.

Samuels, A. (1996) The good-enough father of whatever sex. In C. Clulow (ed.), on "Partners Becoming Parents" Talks from the Tavistock Marital Studies. London: Sheldon Press, pp. 101–118.

Segal, H. (1979) *Klein*, Glasgow: Fontana.

Shengold, L. (1989) *Soul Murder. The Effects of Childhood Abuse and Deprivation*, London: Yale University Press.

Steiner, J. (1996) Revenge and resentment in the "Oedipus situation". *International Journal of Psychoanalysis*, 77, 433–443.

Temperley, J (1992) Is the Oedipus complex bad news for women? *Free Associations*, 4(30), 265–275.

Trowell, J. (1997) The psychodynamics of incest. In E.V. Welldon and C. Van Velsen (eds), *A Practical Guide to Forensic Psychotherapy*, London: Jessica Kingsley Publishers, pp. 33–41.

Tyson, P. (1986) Male gender identity, early developmental roots. In R.M. Freidman and L. Lerner (eds), *Towards a New Psychology of Men: Psychoanalytic and Social Perspectives*, New York: Guilford Press.

Wallerstein, J.S. and Kelly, J.B. (1980) *Surviving the Break-up*, London: Grant McIntyre Ltd.

Winnicott, D.W. ([1948] 1982) Reparation in respect of mother's organised defence against depression. In *Through Paediatrics to Psychoanalysis*, London: Hogarth Press, pp. 91–96.

Winnicott, D.W. ([1951] 1982) Transitional objects and transitional phenomena. In M. Khan (ed.), *Through Paediatrics to Psychoanalysis*, London: Hogarth Press, pp. 229–242.

Winnicott, D.W. ([1958] 1990) The capacity to be alone. In *The Maturational Process and the Facilitating Environment*, London: Karnac Books and The Institute of Psychoanalysis, pp. 29–36.

Winnicott, D.W. ([1960] 1990) The theory of the parent–infant relationship. In *The Maturational Process and the Facilitating Environment*, London: Karnac Books and the Institute of Psychoanalysis, pp. 37–55.

Winnicott, D.W. ([1968] 1991) Contemporary concepts of adolescent development and their implication for Higher Education. In *Playing and Reality* (4th edn), London: Routledge, pp. 148–150.

Mainly theoretical

3

FATHERS IN MODERN PSYCHOANALYSIS AND IN SOCIETY

The role of the father and child development

Mary Target and Peter Fonagy

Introduction

Colette Chiland, the French child psychiatrist and psychoanalyst, wrote in her paper about fathers: 'Nothing can be said about "the father" in general. Something can be said about a particular father conjoined with a particular mother, and about an absent father only in relation to the qualities of the mother' (1982: p. 371). Notwithstanding this obvious truth, psychoanalysts, particularly over the past quarter of a century, have evolved increasingly complex models of the role of 'the father' in normal development and in so doing made significant assumptions of homogeneity of family structure, individual behaviour and interpersonal relationships. Of course there is a paradox, or at least a dialectic in these generalisations. The nuclear family of Western society is to a considerable degree structured by gender roles. By contrast, the focus of psychoanalytic interest is invariably in deviations from such social norms that might explain, and arguably underpin, individual differences which lie at the heart of psychoanalytic clinical interest.

The dialectic which the homogeneity assumptions of psychoanalysis entail has been part and parcel of psychoanalytic writing from its earliest days. Psychoanalysts attempt to provide general developmental theories on the basis of exceptions from or negations of these ideas presented by clinical experience. Nowhere is this dialectic so readily apparent as in the psychoanalytic literature on fathers, where generalisations about the role of the father are readily made but remain poorly integrated with the observations of individual fathers with individual children under their care. In this chapter we shall critically consider three psychoanalytic theoretical frameworks within which the role of fathers has typically been considered: (1) the Oedipal father, (2) the father who enables separation from the mother, and (3) the role of the father as originator of triadic psychic capacities – specifically symbolic function. In the final section of the chapter we shall consider the role of the mother in 'creating' the father and the implication of this dynamic for our thinking about fathers as helping to structure the child's internal world.

The father of the Oedipal myth

A very specific paternal figure occupies the psychoanalytic centre stage. Oedipus transgressed the universal taboo against incest, having killed his father and married his mother (Freud, 1900). Freud explicated the image of this father across numerous studies (e.g. Freud, 1913, 1930, 1939) as an emasculating, dangerous, vengeful, authoritarian figure created by the child's mind as much on the basis of phylogenetic memory as by the projection of instinctual urges propelling him to consummate a sexual union with the mother. The boy is thought to employ his 'theory of mind' (Premack and Woodruff, 1978), or mentalising capacities (Fonagy, 1991; Morton and Frith, 1995), to construct an image of the father's likely reaction were he to recognise his son's secret ambitions. In fact, the child is implicitly assumed to use simulation (Gordon, 1992) of the father's mental state, constructing a picture of how he might feel were he to be threatened by a young pretender. Formulating the Oedipus complex along the developmental line of a mentalising capacity places it firmly in the fourth or fifth year of the child's life (Perner, 1991; Fonagy and Target, 1996; Target and Fonagy, 1996).

All this is not to say that four-year-olds are not troubled by Oedipal feelings. As John Munder Ross (1979) put it: 'sons did then [the turn of the century] and do now hate their fathers, do wish to take their place, notwithstanding their love and filial duty' (p. 319). To what extent is this a universal, a comment about fathers in general? Lebovici (1982), for example, discussed a French neo-Marxist theory (Deleuze and Guattari, 1972) that the Oedipus complex was an institution created by capitalists who favour 'familialism' to their own advantage. The Oedipus complex acts as a repressive agency aimed at thwarting 'desire productions' which would be anti-Oedipal (Deleuze and Guattari, 1972). Lebovici's response to this argument is to distinguish the Oedipal myth from the triangulation of object relations. It is the latter, rather than the former, which appears to justify the Oedipal situation as lying at the heart of the mental life of men. The universal presence of a vengeful father is not part of his argument. The representation of this authoritarian figure must, to some degree, depend on the actual behaviour of the actual father figure.

Along similar lines, it has been pointed out by a number of commentators on Freud's writings on the Oedipus complex that Freud's explication of the legend is crucially selective (e.g. Ross, 1979). Laius, terrified by a prophecy, rejects his son, Oedipus. and is killed by a man unknown to him. Oedipus' unconscious anger is most likely fuelled, not just by the king's position as a depriving and constraining overlord, but also as a potentially nurturant figure, who had painfully rejected his attachment needs. Anger, of course, was recognised by Bowlby (1973) as a natural response of the child to a threat to the attachment relationship, when the expectation of safety close to the attachment figure is jeopardised. It serves a signalling function ('I feel abandoned') which normally strengthens the relationship between child and caregiver, since it generally provokes an intensification of the caretaking response.

Placing Oedipal theory into its social context, we are naturally reminded that the Victorian father was, by and large, an absent one and indeed that the modern father does little better (Fuchs, 1988; Hochschild, 1989; Galinsky *et al.*, 1994). Ban and Lewis (1974), in interviews with middle-class fathers, found that play time with their one-year-old children amounted to an average of 15 minutes per day. A Mori poll reported in *The Guardian* (10 April 1997) showed that 20 per cent of 8–15-year-old children could not recall sharing an activity with their father in the previous week and that 80 per cent want their father to spend more time with them. The same survey, not inspired by psychoanalytic assumptions, showed that while 63 per cent of these children were worried about burglars, significantly fewer were concerned about school problems. It might not perhaps be far-fetched to suggest that certain aspects of the Oedipus myth, particularly the depiction of the father as hostile and censorious, may originate not from the phylogenetic mental structuralisation of the attitudes of the primeval horde but rather from the actual patterns of contact in the Western family.

A reductionist stereotyping of the representation of the father is also evident in Freud's report on Little Hans (Freud, 1909). Freud's description of this case is regarded as paradigmatic whenever the Oedipus complex is seriously scrutinised (Lebovici, 1982). Yet the castration threat to Little Hans, which arguably precipitated his phobic reaction following the birth of his baby sister and the incident with the horse, was not the father's doing. Rather, it was Hans' mother who warned him, having caught him playing with his 'widdler', that the doctor would come 'to cut it off'. Of course, the doctor arrives to assist in the violent and bloody birth of his sister, confirming the expectations he already harbours. The original threat, however, came from the mother and it is hard to imagine that Hans' dramatic reactions were independent of the insensitivity which her original threat implied. Hans might have been as (or more) frightened of his castrating mother as of his father, who by all accounts appeared to show an unusual level of interest in and understanding of his son. Hans' father took careful notes of his son's development at Freud's request, for Freud wanted to find illustrations for his new psychosexual theories (Freud, 1905) and indicated his commitment further by undertaking therapeutic work with the boy (Freud, 1909). From an attachment theory perspective we might see Hans' mother's behaviour as more pathogenic, in creating an emotional environment for Hans where his expression of attachment needs was met by frightening behaviour by the primary attachment figure (Main and Hesse, 1990).

Freud was aware that the Oedipal story of the vengeful threat by the parent of the same gender fitted more readily for boys than for girls (Freud, 1931, 1925). For women, the image of the threatening figure had to be the mother, the father being the love object. In the absence of the cultural imago (the vengeful authoritarian father), Freud is forced to claim that the Oedipus complex of the little girl is more likely to persist and is only slowly abandoned. His logic led him to intuitively improbable statements, such as: 'I cannot evade the notion (though I hesitate to give it expression) that for women the level of what is ethically normal is different from what it is in men' (Freud, 1925: p. 257). If the measure of the resolution of the Oedipus complex is indeed the sublimation of libidinal cathexis, its incorporation into the ego where it becomes the nucleus of its heir, the super-ego, there can be no doubt that girls are more, rather than less, successful at overcoming these age-specific conflicts. There has been no shortage of psycho-analytic accounts of the asymmetry in Oedipal experiences between the sexes (e.g. Horney, 1924; Kestenberg, 1956). An alternative explanation of the convoluted manoeuvrings which little girls undergo in shifting from mother to father as the primary love object may well be in terms of the relative unavailability of the father as a real attachment figure to both sexes.

These illustrations could be multiplied to make the same general point: the predominantly negative view of the father in classical psychoanalysis could be less to do with a cross-cultural universal than with a specific configuration of parental responsibilities within our own culture. The picture of the father is then coloured by his traditional role within the nuclear family structure. Our culture, at least until very recently, has accepted the unresponsiveness and insensitivity of one of the two caregiving figures to the child's attachment needs, leading unsurprisingly to hostility towards this figure on the part of the child. The hostility, a 'healthy' response to frustrated attachment, colours the child's perception of the father and might cumulatively engender a cultural underpinning for the mythology of patricide.

The father of individuation: the 'unattachment' theory of fathers

A separate and distinct role for the father was suggested by Hans Loewald (1951), and later by Mahler (Mahler and Gosliner, 1955) and Greenacre (1957). These contributions all highlighted the role of the father in assisting the child to acquire a sense of identity in the first years of life. Rooting his comments in Freud's (1921) description of the early father as an ego ideal, Loewald pointed to the positive 'exquisitely masculine' identification with him that lends powerful support against 'the danger of the womb' (1951: p. 16). This positive relationship, as well as the defensive relationship entailed in the threat of castration, serves to facilitate the boy's differentiation and escape from engulfment by the mother. Mahler's contribution extended Loewald's formulation in that Loewald said nothing as to the impact of the father on self-development in girls. It is claimed that during the practising sub-phase of the separation–individuation process, the father plays a key role in the development of the child's exploratory and early phallic attitudes. His role was thought to be even more critical in the rapprochement sub-phase, in disentangling the ego from the regressive pullback to symbiosis. The father was presumed to be able to perform this task because, Mahler thought, his relationship to the child did not have a symbiotic origin. The third of these authors, Greenacre, saw the father's role both in terms of offering support to the mother and in making a unique contribution to the omnipotent qualities in the child's life. The father may, for example, support the toddler's push towards self-determination via encouraging muscular activity, a sense of body self and the exploration of space. Greenacre sees the father as powerful, mysterious and glamorous, and contrasts this with the quotidian image of the mother.

The role of triangulation, the addition of a father representation to the representation of infant and mother, in creating psychic distance has been expanded on and extensively applied in psychoanalytic writings on the father's role. Lebovici (1982), for example, suggested that within the dyadic fantasies of an omnipotent mother the projection of the child's anger is likely to serve to make the mother seem even more dangerous, while desire for closeness with her may evoke the threat of regressive fusion. This issue is also taken up by Greenspan (1982), who points to the specific vulnerability of children with absent or unavailable fathers who thus lack the assistance of a third in their struggle to emerge from the dyadic drama with 'an imagined phallic aggressive mother' (p. 135). The father is necessary to support the child's aggressive drives and to help him mourn the loss of the earlier phase-specific relationship to the mother. The importance of this function is highlighted in cases where the mother is over-invested in the child, who may be forced to carry the burden of the mother's own sexual and aggressive conflicts.

An important clinical report from the Anna Freud Centre by Marion Burgner (1985) added weight to this point of view. She reported observations of 13 children at the Hampstead Clinic who had lost their fathers through parental separation or divorce in the first five years of life. She reports a 'protraction of the original narcissistic interference both in their self-development and in their sexual identity; they are adhesively and ambivalently tied to the remaining primary object' (p. 319). Only when the mother could make a reasonably lasting relationship with a man other than the father did the child appear to be able to experience a triangular Oedipal relationship. In other contexts, material which appeared to be Oedipal actually contained major components from pre-Oedipal developmental phases, such as primitive fears of object loss and anxiety-driven wishes for closeness. These ideas may be summarised as suggesting that the father as a real person represents an alternative to the developmental impasse of narcissistic deflation vs. the defensive grandiosity of the mother–child dyad. Fathering as a process serves most importantly to foster autonomy and the enhancement of individuation and independent functioning.

In a rarely cited paper, Wisdom (1976) described a similar model from a Kleinian point of view. Melanie Klein (1945), of course, assumed that the child searched for aspects of the father in the mother's body, and that frustration towards the mother's breast caused both boys and girls to abandon the longing for it and stimulated in them the desire for oral satisfaction through the father's penis. Klein notes that frustration and satisfaction give shape to the relationship between the baby and the good and bad breast, a conflict which is directly transferred onto the ulterior relationship with the father's penis. Without citing Loewald, Mahler or any of the other authors working in this field, Wisdom pointed out that the nature of the infant's relationships with the mother and father is qualitatively different. Of particular relevance, Wisdom suggested, is the quality of 'detachment' in father–infant relationship. The father was seen to encourage the child to accept frustrations, to demonstrate a capacity not to be overwhelmed by distressing events, not to play cuddling games, to give sympathy but also the impression that things are bearable. He associated this with 'penis introjection' as opposed to 'breast introjection'. Importantly, he asserted that the attitude of detachment was essential in overcoming the basic ambivalences, splits and projections of the paranoid–schizoid position: 'Penile introjection is needed for reparation in the depressive position; therefore, failure here could lead to the development of depression and therefore, homosexuality could emerge as a defence against depression' (1976: p. 238).

Thus he saw femininity in males as arising not out of castration anxiety but because of 'a complementary over-development of breast introjects' (1976: p. 238). As we can see, in essence, this Kleinian formulation is analogous to that of Loewald and the other North American writers who identify the role of the father as helping the internalisation of a sense of separateness which ultimately facilitates resolution of the ambivalences the child encounters in relation to the mother.

Perhaps the clearest and most evocative description of the role of father in the individuation process was that of Eugenio Gaddini (1976), an Italian psychoanalyst writing from a British Independent (Middle) Group perspective. He writes: 'Descriptively, we may consider him [the father] as a second object, although he would be more properly described as the first object which comes to the child from the external world' (1976, p. 398). Following Winnicott (1957, 1960, 1962), Gaddini suggests that the mother as an object comes from within the child and is thus undifferentiated from the mental area which serves the self. The father is an extraneous object, and later an external one. Gaddini suggests that, at times, in dreams occurring in the course of analysis, patients report the presence of a strange man or some unknown figure that stands for the primordial perception of the second object, which must have been very disconcerting to the baby. Acquiring a second object, Gaddini claims, means losing the original relationship of imitative identity with the mother, and this threat can disturb the acquisition of the second object (the process of differentiation of the father from the primary maternal relationship). The acquisition of the second object is of crucial significance to the achievement of mature object relationships, and is similarly fundamental to the task of analysis.

There is considerable, albeit indirect, observational evidence to support the contention that the father's contribution principally facilitates independent and resilient functioning in the infant. A number of large-scale studies have demon-strated that the greater the involvement of the father in an infant's early care the more rapidly the infant develops (Pedersen *et al.*, 1980) and the more likely the infant is to withstand stress and to be socially responsive. Abelin (1976) provided observations from Margaret Mahler's laboratory which partially support the father's unique role in the separation–individuation process. He confirms the role of the father as a 'most fascinating kind of object' (p. 294) in the practising sub-phase. He also notes that girls tend to attach themselves to the father earlier than do boys, and that boys tend to be less affectionate and more exploratory with male adults. The father is perceived as more powerful and is appealed to in cases of conflict with mother. From such evidence, Abelin concludes that the assumption that the father is necessary for the satisfactory resolution of the ambivalence that characterises the rapprochement sub-phase may be considered confirmed.

However, Abelin goes on to describe observations of Michael, a child with an obviously intensely involved and caring father – perhaps Abelin himself. First, Michael's relationship with his father had a symbiotic quality, contrary to Mahler's expectations. Michael seeks and accepts soothing and comforting from his father from eight months, and shows preference for being comforted by him when sick and when hurt. Abelin concludes that: 'their relationship seems to develop side-by-side with the mother relationship from the earliest weeks on and to share many of its "symbiotic" qualities' (1976: p. 298). Thus, even Mahler's laboratory could not provide unequivocal evidence for the father's role as mediator of the process of separation. The father does not emerge into the child's life in pure form, as if from another world. The father's and mother's roles may not be identical in terms of the child's psychic organisation, but nor are their roles as clearly distinguishable as some psychoanalytic writers have assumed. Having two parents, in different roles, may indeed make an important contri-bution to the development of the self-representation, but this does not assign a specific role to the father.

Further evidence for the overlap between the role of the mother and father comes from the work of Kyle Pruett (1983, 1985, 1989, 1992). This is a longitudinal, in-depth study of 17 families where the primary caretaker was the father. The findings over eight years support the view that the 'nurturing instinct' is not confined to females. Children develop extremely well in these families, and the child, far from demonstrating deficits in ego functions or object relatedness, seems more active, curious and less prone to pathological separation or stranger anxiety than infants whose primary dyadic relationship was with their mother. Gender identities remain stable, Oedipal resolutions seem to have been relatively successful, and the flexibility of gender role performance reported previously has continued to manifest itself, though in a more age-appropriate complexity. At eight-year follow up (Pruett and Litzenberger, 1992) a certain 'up front' style of communication is illustrated: 'We all know each other well; we find each other interesting; we find this way of knowing each other useful, fun and it is not pursued at another's expense. I can speak directly about my needs' (p. 94). It is probably true that the differences between maternal and paternal handling of infants are substantially reduced when the father is the primary rather than secondary caretaker (Field, 1978). Nonetheless, the case for a biologically distinct and specific intrapsychic role for the father is substantially weakened by these findings.

By contrast, Chused (1986) has warned that the resolution of the Oedipus conflict in paternally raised women might involve the repression of early dyadic experience with the father leaving the child without any conscious internal representation of a benevolent other. This, in turn, might give rise to a constellation of narcissistic vulnerability, a masochistic perception of all relationships, and intense genital pleasure and attachment to men coupled with overwhelming fears of losing the sexual object. Such women might present with an idealisation of men, both for their phallic powers and for their ability to be warm and giving. The woman looks to men rather than women for nurturance and the penis in her fantasies becomes endowed with magical, protective powers. 'Possession of the penis promises complete gratification without pain, a return to the fantasised union with an all-giving object' (p. 436). One might of course ask whether this picture is unique to paternally raised women, or whether it is the consequence of profound *maternal rejection*, real or imagined. Primary paternal caregiving within our culture might have adverse psychological sequelae solely because of the painful maternal rejection it can imply.

Clinical observational studies of absent fathers have made a distinct contribution to understanding the father's role. Herzog (1980) reported on 12 cases of boys (18–28 months) whose night terrors were associated with the loss of the father due to divorce or separation. Herzog argued that during the practising sub-phase of separation–individuation the little boy's aggressivity serves to assist him to grow and move away from the mother. During rapprochement, the boy's return to his mother might be impaired if she is depressed or angry, or overeager to have the boy share her bed. The boy lacks a model to help him manage his aggressive impulses; the impulses then turn against the self, giving a persecutor's colouring to the child's night-time thoughts and feelings. Solnit, some years earlier (1972), advanced a similar theory based on the case report of a 16-month-old girl. Unfortunately, it is difficult to discern from Herzog's clinical data whether the children's problems indeed arose out of the absence of the father or from the mother's acute distress about his absence.

A similar argument concerning a different condition was advanced by Stoller (1985). In a compelling paper, which describes nine cases of transsexual males, Stoller (1979) argues that a strong and masculine father encourages the separation of the boy from his mother's body and mind and encourages him to develop masculine attributes. As a separate being, he can desire his mother as opposed to desire to be her. On less substantial evidence, Stoller makes the same case for transsexual females – a father who was too close too soon may impede feminine identification. The fathers in the male transsexual group are thought to be either absent or to be an 'unmovably inadequate presence' (p. 863). This, combined with the mother's overpowering need to merge her beautiful son into herself, prevents the child from entering the Oedipal phase with its potential to define masculinity and femininity. Stoller himself points out that: 'this sounds terribly simple', but adds 'it may just be' (p. 861). Is it simply the absence of paternal influence that causes this profound and dramatic problem? Or is it, as is more likely the case, *the specific quality of fathering and mothering* which creates difficulties in the process of gender identity formation? Stoller's work illustrates a general problem with the individuation-focused theories of fatherhood. How could the absence of the father's influence on the process of individuation generate such very different pathologies?

It seems that psychoanalytic clinicians need merely to hear the words 'absent father' to infer a range of child psychopathology from distorted Oedipal development (Neubauer, 1960), to homosexuality (Siegelman, 1974), exhibitionism and voyeurism (Rosen, 1979), and anti-social behaviour (Biller, 1981). The literature on homosexuality illustrates the problem underlying this argument. Beiber and colleagues (Bieber *et al.*, 1962) have claimed that the presence of a 'constructive, supportive, warmly related father precludes the possibility of a homosexual son' (p. 311). On the basis of personal histories of homosexual men, they suggested that absent, detached, emotionally distant, or hostile fathers are largely responsible for the development of homosexuality, by failing to break the adhesive bind of the 'prehomosexual' child with his overprotective, possessive, seductive mother. Isay (1987), while in part confirming the accuracy of this observation (namely, that homosexual patients tend to give accounts of their fathers as distant during childhood and deny any attachment to them), claims that the reports of such patients should not be taken at face value. Isay offers an alternative account; namely, that similarly to heterosexual patients who defend themselves against erotic attachments to their mother by excluding memories of closeness, homosexual patients' early homoerotic fantasies about their father are repressed, leaving them with distorted memories of a barren father–child relationship. By helping patients to recover their early experiences of erotic attachment to their fathers (a homosexual childhood romance), they become less resistant to analysis. Isay concludes that: 'psychodynamic explanations, based on pathogenic parenting which promotes failures in identification, are insufficient to account for the sexual object choice' (p. 290). While this may be an overly pessimistic conclusion concerning the psychosocial roots of homo-sexuality, the controversy underlines the riskiness of trying to apply generalisa-tions about the developmental role of the father to individual problems.

What is perhaps most disappointing about these theoretically driven psychoanalytic explorations of early father–child relationships is that in trying to fit the father into an appropriate generic gender-specific role, the specific father is lost. The individual, idiosyncratic aspects of the father–child relationship are overlooked. Adam Limentani (1991) expressed regret that 'the scarcity of details in regard to the father's personality and his role in some cases described in the literature hinders our capacity to conceptualise about the condition under examination' (pp. 575–576). Even at levels of microscopic behavioural analysis, patterns of father–infant interaction appear to be stable and different from patterns of mother–infant interaction as early as the first month of life (Yogman, 1982). Here, attachment theory offers a great deal more than a father stereotype. For example, we know that the child's attachment to the mother is only slightly correlated with his pattern of attachment to the father (Fox *et al.*, 1991). Moreover, the father's representation of his own attachment history has almost as much influence on the child's security of attachment as that of the mother (Steele *et al.*, 1996). During the first 18 months of life, the two parents establish independent, but influential, attachment relationships with their child. The father's contribution is both additive and unique. For example, in our longi-tudinal study, we found that while secure attachment in infancy to the mother predicted early development of emotional understanding, if attachment to the father was also secure, the child's development was even further enhanced (Fonagy *et al.*, submitted). Others have shown that security of attachment to the father in infancy predicts the child's behaviour at school, particularly his or her interactions with peers (Suess *et al.*, 1992). The attachment theory approach, as well as findings from research generated by the theory, highlights the importance of the specific dynamic interaction between the father, his own history, his representation of the child and behaviour towards the young infant. These variations may make specific contributions to particular lines of development, but our current psychoanalytic theories do not yet allow us to draw out such connections.

The father whom mother made: the development of the psychic apparatus as the origin of symbolic function

A closely related idea, most clearly advanced by French psychoanalysts, concerns the role of the father in the formation of the child's psychic structure. Here, too, the emphasis is on the father who separates the infant from the mother but, probably under the influence of Lacan's 'paternal metaphor' concept, the experience of the father is seen as vital for the development of symbolic thought. Lacan (1953) considered the third person, the father, as essential, but his contribution was not restricted to specific developmental phases. In Lacan's view, not the real father but his symbolic function represents the essential third element which has to break open the collusion between mother and child. The introduction of the 'Nom du Père/Non du Père' represents the combination of the name and the '*no*' of the father, which serves to prevent the child from remaining uniquely the object of the mother's desire. For Lacan, the 'name of the father' represents the lawfulness of the systems of relationships expressed by language. It structures the child's entry into the symbolic world of culture as an individual (Lacan, 1964). It introduces the child to the world of symbols and language and saves him from psychoses (Rosenfeld, 1992; Borens, 1993).

There are indeed solid developmental reasons for linking the paternal role with symbolic thought. The development of representational thinking stems from the separation of the object from the child (Sigel, 1970). In Western families it is often the father who works outside the home, and his coming and going requires the child to construct, elaborate and label the absent figure. Classic studies by Brooks-Gunn and Lewis (1979) showed that the development of a capacity to provide verbal labels for pictures of fathers antedated by a couple of months that of providing verbal labels for mothers. The entrances and exits of fathers thus promote symbolic development and abstraction. This hypothesis is compatible with Freud's assumptions concerning the development of symbolic thought driven by frustration and hallucinatory wish-fulfilment (Freud, 1900, 1911).

Interference with the paternal role is seen as a major source of psycho-pathology. Freud himself laid the groundwork for these ideas in his writings on fetishism (Freud, 1927, 1940). He put forward the idea that the fetishist, when faced with the intense fear of the rival father and the associated fear of castration, produced a split within his ego as an alternative solution to Oedipal conflict. In creating a split an aspect of reality (the anatomical differences between the sexes) was completely disavowed. Yet at the same time, awareness of these differences is, of course, also retained. Several important French contributions have built on this formulation in elaborating the paternal role. For example, Braunschweig and Fain (1981) applied the notion of a defensive split in the ego to explain a form of disavowal of the father and his role within the pre-Oedipal triangle. Chasseguet-Smirgel (1985) also suggests that in perversions denial of the significance of the father accompanies the idealisation of pre-genital modes of sexual relationships. In part of the conscious psychic life father is absent, split off, and the individual shifts between dyadic and triadic conceptions as he disavows or accepts the paternal role. In an earlier paper, Chasseguet-Smirgel (1975) suggested that the paternal function creates a powerful incentive for the male child to repair his injured infantile narcissism through an identification with the father as ego ideal (Freud, 1914). These ideas complement the suggestions we have considered above whereby early triangulation protects the child by helping him to develop a representational system which moves beyond dyadic fantasies of relating to an omnipotent mother, and can allow him to integrate both aggressive and libidinal wishes (Lebovici, 1982).

These authors, perhaps far more than Anglo-Saxon writers, have been able to show how the mother's unconscious (or conscious) attitudes towards the child's father may be critical in determining the child's ability to create an internalisation of a triangular structure. Of specific importance here is the recognition that the parents' relationships to each other, as well as the child's relationship to each parent, contribute to this crucial mental representation (Laplanche and Pontalis, 1973). For example, Fain (1981) showed that the mother's desire for her partner actively promoted the separation or disengagement (*desetayage*) between mother and infant and stimulated the child's interest in the third. Joyce McDougall (1989) put this idea particularly eloquently when she wrote: 'A father who is dead may be carried within the child's mind as a very alive figure depending on the mother's way of talking about the father', and 'a father who is physically present might nevertheless be lived as symbolically lost, absent or dead in the child's inner world' (p. 209). She believes that even within the first year of the child's life, the mother may or may not handle the infant in a manner which implies the presence of a third.

Essentially the same model was proposed by Atkins (1984), who suggested that the infant may form a relationship to his/her father through the mother's mediation independent of the amount of direct contact the child has with the father. The mother can 'potentiate' the father's presence and vitalise him in his absence. The triangular family constellation has an impact on the child from birth on, even before the complex external triangular relationships have developed or become differentiated in the child's mental experience. The mother fosters an interest in other persons – especially the father. The way in which she brings the child into contact with the father can catalyse or interfere with the child's experience of him. For example, she can facilitate or inhibit the maintenance of other-directedness in the child, in the father's presence. Later, she can openly or subtly encourage the child to engage the father in mutual responsiveness and reciprocal dialogue (Beebe *et al.*, 1997). Similarly, she may or may not prompt the father to engage with the child. She can hold the infant out towards the father, smiling when the child stares at the father, talks, reaches, and so forth. She can emotionally colour such interchanges by combining them with warmth, love and attentiveness or withdrawal and rejection. Atkins (1981, 1982) suggests that the affective context may be quite open or mediated through subtle changes in her body contact with the infant, both of which may be registered directly as primitive affecto-motor representations (Jacobson, 1964).

This idea was elaborated by both Lebovici and Braunschweig (Braunschweig and Fain, 1981; Lebovici, 1982). These authors have distinguished between the baby which is represented in the mother's mind as the child of a real father, and an imaginary child who is the vehicle for the mother's unconscious, incestuous fantasies. For the mother to be able to accept that the child is an independent living being, linked not only to her but also to the child's father, she has to loosen her incestuous attachments to her own parental objects. Fain (1981) proposed that failure of triangulation arises out of the mother's equation of the baby with the penis she desires (Freud, 1917). The mother's desires thus support the narcissistic fantasy of a special, unique relationship with her child, because of her failure of symbolisation where she cannot accept the child as a separate being, but rather sees the child as part of her body. The child does not 'represent' but is her fantasy of physical and psychological completeness, and thus the father is denied the position of the third and the child is denied symbolic elaboration. The mother's attitude undermines the potential for Oedipal conflict and the child's ego ideal remains attached to a pre-genital model (Chasseguet-Smirgel, 1975). Consistent with Lacanian terminology, where the phallus symbolises separation, the mother who cannot separate from her child and allow space for a triadic representation is somewhat confusingly labelled 'the phallic another' (Braunschweig and Fain, 1981). Complementing the phallic mother is a father who acquiesces to or even promotes the arrangement (Kirshner, 1992). Limentani (1991), in reviewing this literature, is very critical of the impoverished description of the man 'who allows himself to be disqualified' (footnote on p. 575). His own paper is a preliminary attempt at redressing this balance.

Within this frame of reference the father is seen as an organising focus for identification. The actual presence of the father is not essential. A number of writers have provided examples of fatherless sons who are able to construct triangular structures via father surrogates or in fantasy (Buckley, 1985; Freud and Burlingham, 1944; Neubauer, 1960). Irrespective of the physical presence of a third person, what is suggested by the French literature is a complementary relationship wherein the mother allows the infant to exist as a separate entity, and an image of a third person is introduced into the infant's mental life, either through the infant's recognition of the mother's concern with another or through the establishment of an independent relationship between this other person and the child. The physical availability of the father may be neither sufficient nor necessary for triangulation to evolve. What does seem critical is a situation within which the child can envisage a relationship between two other, emotionally significant figures. The father may nevertheless be represented as absent, but perhaps not because of physical or emotional unavailability, through an attempt by the child to establish a compromise between acceptance of the paternal function and its narcissistic–dyadic disavowal (Kirshner, 1992); to quote Kirshner: 'maintaining the place of a "third" – the father who was there, but not there – while warding off those frightening male images which make the oedipal position too dangerous' (p. 1136).

The implication of Kirshner's statement is that even when the triadic structure lacks clarity in the patient's mind, it nevertheless exists in some form or another. The absent father has a space – he is remembered as unavailable. We also know, from infant observation, that as early as four or five months infants engage in triadic as well as dyadic interchanges with their parents (Stern, 1995). Thus it may be unhelpful to talk of triadification simply as present or absent. Nevertheless, as the above review indicates, there are qualitative differences in triadification related to the actual paternal image to which the child relates. It seems that the more the father is represented as a real person in addition to an image filtered through the mother's desires, the more successful and helpful triadification is. What is the reason for this? In our view, existing theories of triadification fail to account for it.

The triad within the self versus the triad within the mind

The triadic constellation is a given; there is always a place for the father. This is ensured, we suggest, by the genetically determined hardwiring of the child's nervous system, as well as the culturally normal presence of a third, of whatever gender, in the child's early environment. Why should the inevitable filtration and distortion of the father representation have such destructive potential for the child's emotional development?

In our view, the answer lies in the mental *location* of the father representation. To elaborate this point, first we have to reconsider some of our ideas about the development of the self and link this to triadic representations. Elsewhere, we have argued that in the absence of an intrinsic capacity for experiencing oneself as an intentional being (Dennett, 1987), as driven by mental states such as desires and fantasies, the child is dependent on the other to discover and develop his subjectivity with him (Fonagy and Target, 1995, 1997; Target and Fonagy, 1996). The child is thought about by the mother (or primary caregiver) as motivated by beliefs and wishes, and he becomes aware of this expectation and hence, gradually, of these states within himself, leading to the evolution of a psychological (mentalising) self-organisation. Thus in a sense it would be true to say that the child 'finds himself' in the caregiver's mind – that the clarity and coherence of one's sense of oneself as a psychological being is originally a function of the accuracy and distinctness of the representation of one's feelings and intentions in the mind of one's mother (or main caregiver). The perception of the self in the mind of the other *becomes* the representation of the child's experience, the representation of the representational world. Consistent with Winnicott's (1967) observations, we assume that the child who fails to develop a representation of an intentional self is likely to incorporate in his image of himself the representation of the other, sometimes mental, sometimes physical. The picture of the self will then be false: distorted, as the child's experience of himself is overly influenced by his early perceptions of what others think and feel, and strangely out of touch with what he himself or others are currently experiencing. This may be why many maltreated children (and adults) show failures of object permanence, with primitive separation anxiety or feelings of merger with the object. They continue existentially to depend on the presence of the other both for auxiliary reflective function (to continue to seek and find their intentionality, the self, in the mind of the other) and, more subtly, as a vehicle for the externalisation of parts of the self-representation which are experienced as alien and incongruent with the self. This alien other has been internalised as part of the self-structure, but without the appropriate links and associations which would enable a coherent functioning of the self-representation. *The other is within the self rather than represented in the mind.*

The same processes are at work in the creation of early triadic representations, and they may fail if the earlier dyadic experiences have compromised the child's developing experience of himself. Particularly when this has happened with the mother, a sense of the father's self may also be internalised into the child's developing self, rather than represented in the mind. If the father's perception of the child's states of mind is blocked or inaccurate, because of either the mother's interference or his own insensitivity or distortions, the father will occupy space within the child's self-representation, along with the maternal object rather than beyond it. In these potentially pathological circumstances triadification still occurs, but it is qualitatively different – it is now within the self. The key difference lies in the weakness of representation of a relationship between self and object. This representation is not, of course, usually completely absent, but some emotionally crucial aspects of self–other relationships are inadequately represented. What we see clinically in triadification which occurs within the self is an unstable self-structure, an incoherent self-representation, poorly developed primitive representations of relationships and, most commonly, a tendency to externalise parts of this unstable self representation and force others, within close physical proximity, to bear the burden of enacting for the individual a variety of unacceptable aspects of the self, originally of the objects as perceived by the child.

Thus, the fate of the paternal representation parallels that of the representation of the mother. In benign circumstances, mother and father both become established as object representations within the child's mind, independent and separate from the child's self-representation. In pathological cases, one or other of the primary objects may not be represented sufficiently separately and may become part of the child's self-representation, which is inevitably distorted. The two sets of object representations are parallel but not equivalent. Within this framework, the father still has a special, although no longer a unique or gender-specific, function which can soften the impact of a pathogenic maternal influence. One potential special role of the father as second object is in *the prevention or lessening of introjection of the mother's image into the self.* The father, if perceived as outside and as reflective of the child's emotional state, can reflect to the child the child's experience of the relationship with his primary object (Fonagy and Target, 1995). Knowledge and representation of a relationship emerge with difficulty, as did knowledge and awareness of simple mental states earlier in the baby's development. The child is involved in a relationship with the mother, but at first this relationship could not be represented, it could only be experienced. The third person, the child's second object, can help to create a representation of the dyadic relationship that is consistent with the child's concurrent experience, so it may be internalised as a representation of the relationship experience, which feels real and true to the child. The developmental lines of the father and mother are complementary, so that the same applies to the representation of the child's relationship with father. In this context, the mother is the second object, who perceives the child's experience of the relationship with father, represents it in her own mind and offers it to the child. As the child is inclined to look to the mother in developing second-order representations of self states, it is helpful when (a) there is a relationship between child and father and (b) this is accurately represented in the mother's mind.

Under optimal circumstances, the child internalises both relationship representations via this route and gradually evolves second-order representations of how he relates in specific ways to both mother and father. In this situation, the triad is in the child's mind but outside the child's self. When triadification fails, a situation arises where either the mother or father in the position of second object fails to reflect accurately the nature of the relationship between the child and the first object. For example, the child's mother may distort the child's representation of the father to the point that the father can no longer be perceived by the child as corresponding to any actual figure. This will compromise triadification both through making the child more likely to represent the actual father within the self, and through undermining the child's opportunity to represent the relationship between him and his mother through perceiving this in the father's mind; this draws the maternal object representation closer or even into the self. In either case the failure of triadification is the failure to represent the relationship as a relationship, and thus a pre-existing tendency for the non-reflective objects to be drawn into the self-representation is increased. Of course, the relationship representation is still present in the child's mind but it is no longer represented as a relationship – it has become part of the child's self-structure. What was a self–other relationship is now a self–self 'relationship'. Attachment to the other turns into attachment to the self. Paranoid suspicion is converted into chronic uncertainty. A relationship characterised by the experience of frustration or anger is relived as insatiability or constant self-criticism. Hatred of the other becomes self-loathing. Importantly, these are no longer relationship experiences which are, at least in principle, modifiable through conscious reflection and a wish to change. They have become painful experiences integrated into the self-structure, felt to be beyond control or the possibility of change. What is created by the failure of triadification is what we might call a projective or enactment pressure on the child. The only way of coping with these intolerable self-experiences is externalisation, making the other become the unbearable part of the self. Unable to reflect upon the relationship, the child is forced to live it. A clinical example will be given below, which is intended not as evidence of the model offered (which, if possible at all, would require much more extensive extracts from the clinical material) but as an illustration of it.

Sam, a boy of seven, was referred for treatment because of depression, infantile behaviour (he had not yet given up the bottle and continued to share his mother's bed), serious underachievement at school, and effeminacy (which included an insistence that his hair should not be cut). Sam and his mother, Priscilla, lived with Fred, a kind-hearted and decent man, who while ineffectual in coping with Priscilla's severe personality pathology clearly had Sam's interests at heart. Sam's father, a close friend of Fred's, had emigrated overseas with his new family shortly before Sam's referral for treatment. The relationship between the mother and father had ended before Sam's birth as he found life with her 'an intolerable perpetual piece of terrible theatre'. Fred, as a friend of both parents, provided for both Sam and Priscilla. His relationship with her was unusual, in that Priscilla expected him to act the part of the father even though their relationship was not sexual. He fulfilled his role with affection, yet he had his own children, both younger than Sam, by a girlfriend whom he visited briefly at weekends.

Sam was his mother's pride and joy. She provided him with overt affection and physical comfort, but in a highly seductive way. Priscilla suffered from severe depression and had frequent rages with Sam and Fred. There were times when she became quite out of control, threw crockery and broke furniture and would walk out and disappear, leaving Fred to cope as best he could. Priscilla was also dramatically insensitive to Sam's anxiety. She decided she was fed up with Sam sharing her bed and wished to lock him into his bedroom, even if he were to cry all night. She refused to accept the connection between the onset of Sam's multiple problems and his father's departure.

Of particular interest in Sam's presentation was his babyishness. He dribbled, asked to be fed, and smelt everything. His declared intention was to become a six-month-old baby girl. It is noteworthy that Priscilla, whilst an unusually attractive 30-year-old, had a very childlike appearance and infantile diction. In wanting to be a baby girl, Sam seemed to reveal not an identification with an immature maternal object, but rather the incorporation of that object into the self. Fred was clearly frightened of Priscilla, and this anxious, hostile relationship

61

was also incorporated into his self-structure. In one session marred by anxious resistance, Sam eventually reported a dream where he had killed a baby monkey. He was terrified and actually ran out of the consulting room and hid behind the door. The baby monkey was part of his self-representation. Sam's mother frequently referred to Sam as 'my little monkey'.

The bad monkey seems originally to have been Sam's perception of Priscilla, seen at moments when he sought his own identity in her extreme reactions to him. The representation was inconsistent with Sam's perception of himself and felt alien and a target of murderous impulses.

He was terrified of the monkey, just as he saw Fred as terrified of Priscilla. Priscilla, whilst constantly blaming Fred for insufficient contribution to the parenting of Sam, refused to acknowledge the existence of a relationship between the two. She frequently denigrated Fred, who justified his tolerance of Priscilla's excesses by saying that he needed to stay to protect Sam from her malevolent influence. In fact Fred appeared to be absent from Sam's internal world, he made little reference to him and fantasised about his biological father instead. His external relationship with Fred showed Sam's experience of an unmet need for support. This relationship also remained unrepresented, but in the analysis his sense of helplessness and passivity were partially relieved when his anger about Fred's passivity was verbalised and reflected on. This, and other aspects of his internal relationships, was first externalised in the transference, and the interpretative work assisted Sam in separating out these object relationship representations from the way that he himself was represented, and from how he experienced and expressed himself.

References

Abelin, E. L. (1976). Some further observations and comments on the earliest role of the father. *International Journal of Psycho-Analysis*, 56, 293–301.

Atkins, R. (1982). Discovering Daddy: The mother's role. In S. Cath, A. Gurwitt, and J. Ross (eds), *Father and Child: Developmental and Clinical Perspectives* (pp. 139–151). Boston: Little Brown.

Atkins, R. N. (1981). Finding one's father: The mother's contribution to early father representations. *Journal of the American Academy of Psychoanalysis*, 9, 539–559.

Atkins, R. N. (1984). Transitive vitalization and its impact on father-representation. *Contemporary Psychoanalysis*, 20, 663–676.

Ban, P. and Lewis, M. (1974). Mothers and fathers, girls and boys: Attachment behavior in the one-year-old. *Merrill-Palmer Quarterly*, 20, 195–204.

Beebe, B., Lachmann, F., and Jaffe, J. (1997). Mother–infant interaction structures and presymbolic self and object representations. *Psychoanalytic Dialogues*, 7, 113–182.

Bieber, I. *et al.* (1962). Homosexuality: a Psychoanalytic Study. New York: Basic Books.

Biller, H. B. (1981). The father and sex role development. In M. E. Lamb (ed.), *The Role of the Father in Child Development* (2nd edition) (pp. 319–358). New York: Wiley.

Borens, R. (1993) Vater sein dagegen sehr. *Zeitschrift fur psychoanlyse: Theorie und Praxis,* 8, 19–31.

Bowlby, J. (1973). *Attachment and Loss,* Vol. 2: *Separation: Anxiety and Anger.* London: Hogarth Press and Institute of Psycho-Analysis.

Braunschweig, D. and Fain, M. (1981). Bloc-notes et lanternes magiques. *Revue Français Psychanalise,* 45, 405–426.

Brooks-Gunn, J. and Lewis, M. (1979). 'Why mama and papa?' The development of social labels. *Child Development,* 50, 1203–1206.

Buckley, P. (1985). Determinants of object choice in adulthood: A test case of object-relations theory. *Journal of the American Psychoanalytic Association,* 33, 841–860.

Burgner, M. (1985). The Oedipal experience: Effects on development of an absent father. *International Journal of Psycho-Analysis,* 66, 311–319.

Chasseguet-Smirgel, J. (1975). *The Ego Ideal.* London: Free Association Books.

Chasseguet-Smirgel, J. (1985). *Creativity and Perversion.* London: Free Association Books.

Chiland, C. (1982). A new look at fathers. *Psychoanalytic Study of the Child,* 37, 367–379.

Chused, J. F. (1986). Consequences of paternal nurturing. *Psychoanalytic Study of the Child,* 41, 419–438.

Deleuze, G. and Guattari, F. (1972). *L'Anti-Oedipe: Capitalisme et Schizophrenie.* Paris: Editions de Minuit.

Dennett, D. (1987). *The Intentional Stance.* Cambridge, Mass.: MIT Press.

Fain, M. (1981). Diachronie, structure, conflict oedipien. *Revue Français Psychanalise,* 45, 985–997.

Field, T. (1978). Interactions behavior of primary versus secondary caretaker fathers. *Developmental Psychology,* 14, 83–184.

Fonagy, P. (1991). Thinking about thinking: Some clinical and theoretical considerations in the treatment of a borderline patient. *International Journal of Psycho-Analysis,* 72, 639–656.

Fonagy, P., Steele, M., Steele, H., and Holder, J. (submitted). Children securely attached in infancy perform better in belief–desire reasoning task at age five. *Child Development.*

Fonagy, P. and Target, M. (1995). Towards understanding violence: The use of the body and the role of the father. *International Journal of Psycho-Analysis,* 76, 487–502.

Fonagy, P. and Target, M. (1996). Playing with reality: 1. Theory of mind and the normal development of psychic reality. *International Journal of Psycho-Analysis,* 77, 217–233.

Fonagy, P. and Target, M. (1997). Attachment and reflective function: Their role in self-organization. *Development and Psychopathology,* 9, 679–700.

Fox, N. A., Kimmerly, N. L., and Schafer, W. D. (1991) Attachment to mother/attachment to father: A meta-analysis. *Child Development,* 62, 210–225.

Freud, S. (1900). The interpretation of dreams. In J. Strachey (ed.), *The Standard Edition of the Complete Psychological Works of Sigmund Freud* (Vols 4, 5, pp. 1–715). London: Hogarth Press.

Freud, S. (1905). Three essays on the theory of sexuality. In J. Strachey (ed.), *The Standard Edition of the Complete Psychological Works of Sigmund Freud* (Vol. 7, pp. 123–230). London: Hogarth Press.

Freud, S. (1909). Analysis of a phobia in a five-year-old boy. In J. Strachey (ed.), *The Standard Edition of the Complete Psychological Works of Sigmund Freud* (Vol. 10, pp. 1–147). London: Hogarth Press.

Freud, S. (1911). Formulations on the two principles of mental functioning. In J. Strachey (ed.), *The Standard Edition of the Complete Psychological Works of Sigmund Freud* (Vol. 12, pp. 67–104). London: Hogarth Press.

Freud, S. (1913). *Totem and Taboo*. London: Hogarth Press.

Freud, S. (1914). On narcissism: An introduction. In J. Strachey (ed.), *The Standard Edition of the Complete Psychological Works of Sigmund Freud* (Vol. 14, pp. 67–104). London: Hogarth Press.

Freud, S. (1917). On transformations of instinct as exemplified in anal eroticism. In J. Strachey (ed.), *The Standard Edition of the Complete Psychological works of Sigmund Freud* (Vol. 17, pp. 127–133). London: Hogarth Press.

Freud, S. (1921). Group psychology and the analysis of the ego. In J. Strachey (ed.), *The Standard Edition of the Complete Psychological Works of Sigmund Freud* (Vol. 18, pp. 69–143). London: Hogarth Press.

Freud, S. (1925). Some psychical consequences of the anatomical distinction between the sexes. In J. Strachey (ed.), *The Standard Edition of the Complete Psychological Works of Sigmund Freud* (Vol. 19, pp. 248–258). London: Hogarth Press.

Freud, S. (1927). Fetishism. In J. Strachey (ed.), *The Standard Edition of the Complete Psychological Works of Sigmund Freud* (Vol. 21, pp. 152–157). London: Hogarth Press.

Freud, S. (1930). Civilization and its discontents. In J. Strachey (ed.), *The Standard Edition of the Complete Psychological Works of Sigmund Freud* (Vol. 21, pp. 57–146). London: Hogarth Press.

Freud, S. (1931). Female sexuality. In J. Strachey (ed.), *The Standard Edition of the Complete Psychological Works of Sigmund Freud* (Vol. 21, pp. 221–246). London: Hogarth Press.

Freud, S. (1939). Moses and Monotheism. In J. Strachey (ed.), *The Standard Edition of the Complete Psychological Works of Sigmund Freud* (Vol. 23, pp. 3–137). London: Hogarth Press.

Freud, S. (1940). Splitting of the ego in the process of defense. In J. Strachey (ed.), *The Standard Edition of the Complete Psychological Works of Sigmund Freud* (Vol. 23, pp. 275–278). London: Hogarth Press.

Freud, A. and Burlingham, D. (1944). *Infants Without Families*. New York: International Universities Press.

Fuchs, V. (1988). *Women's Quest for Economic Equality*. Cambridge, Mass.: Harvard University Press.

Gaddini, E. (1976). On father formation in child development. *International Journal of Psycho-analysis*, 57, 397–401. [Also in Gaddini, E. (1992). *A Psychoanalytic Theory of Infantile Experience*. London: Routledge, pp. 83–89.]

Galinsky, E., Howes, C., Kontos, S., and Shinn, T. (1994). *The Study of Children in Family Child Care and Relative Care: Highlights of Findings*. New York: Families and Work Institute.

Gordon, R. M. (1992). Simulation theory: Objections and misconceptions. *Mind and Language*, 7, 11–34.

Greenacre, P. (1957). The childhood of the artist. *Psychoanalytic Study of the Child*, 12, 47–72.

Greenspan, S. (1982). The second other. In S. Cath, A. Gurwitt, and J. Ross (eds), *Father and Child: Developmental and Clinical Perspectives* (pp. 123–139). Boston: Little Brown.

Herzog, J. M. (1980). Sleep disturbance and father hunger in 18- to 28-month old boys – The Erlkonig Syndrome. *Psychoanalytic Study of the Child*, 35, 219–233.

Hochschild, A. (1989). *The Second Shift: Working Parents and the Revolution at Home*. New York: Viking.

Horney, K. (1924). On the genesis of the castration complex in women. *International Journal of Psycho-Analysis*, 5, 50–65.

Isay, R. (1987). Fathers and their homosexually inclined sons in childhood. *Psychoanalytic Study of the Child*, 42, 275–293.

Jacobson, E. (1964). *The Self and the Object World*. New York: International Universities Press.

Kestenberg, J. (1956). Vicissitudes of female sexuality. *Journal of the American Psychoanalytic Association*, 4, 453–476.

Kirshner, L. A. (1992). The absence of the father. *Journal of the American Psychoanalytic Association*, 40, 1117–1138.

Klein, M. (1945). The Oedipus complex in the light of early anxieties, *The Writings of Melanie Klein* (pp. 370–419). London: Hogarth Press (1975).

Lacan, J. (1953). Funktion und Feld des Sprechens und der Sprache in der Psychoanalyse, *Ecrits* (pp. 237–322). Paris: Editions du Seuil, 1966.

Lacan, J. (1964). *The Four Fundamental Concepts of Psychoanalysis*. New York: Norton, 1978.

Laplanche, J. and Pontalis, J. B. (1973). *The Language of Psychoanalysis*. New York: Norton.

Lebovici, S. (1982). The origins and development of the Oedipus complex. *International Journal of Psycho-Analysis*, 63, 201–215.

Limentani, A. (1991). Neglected fathers in the aetiology and treatment of sexual deviations. *International Journal of Psycho-Analysis*, 72, 573–584.

Loewald, H. W. (1951). Ego and reality, *Papers on Psychoanalysis* (pp. 3–20). New Haven: Yale University Press, 1980.

McDougall, J. (1989). The dead father. *International Journal of Psycho-Analysis*, 70, 205–220.

Mahler, M. S. and Gosliner, B. J. (1955). On symbiotic child psychosis: Genetic, dynamic and restitutive aspects. *Psychoanalytic Study of the Child*, 10, 195–212.

Main, M. and Hesse, E. (1990). Parents' unresolved traumatic experiences are related to infant disorganized attachment status: Is frightened and/or frightening parental behaviour the linking mechanism? In M. Greenberg, D. Cicchetti, and E. M. Cummings (eds), *Attachment in the Preschool Years: Theory, Research and Intervention* (pp. 161–182). Chicago: University of Chicago Press.

Morton, J. and Frith, U. (1995). Causal modelling: A structural approach to developmental psychology. In D. Cicchetti and D. J. Cohen (eds), *Developmental Psychopathology*. Vol. 1: *Theory and Methods* (pp. 357–390). New York: John Wiley.

Neubauer, P. B. (1960). The one-parent child and his Oedipal development. *Psychoanalytic Study of the Child*, 15, 286–309.

Pedersen, F. A., Anderson, B., and Kain, R. (1980). Parent–infant and husband–wife interactions observed at five months. In F. A. Pedersen (ed.), *The Father–Infant Relationship* (pp. 65–91). New York: Praeger.

Perner, J. (1991). *Understanding the Representational Mind*. Cambridge, Mass.: MIT Press.

Premack, D. and Woodruff, G. (1978). Does the chimpanzee have a 'theory of mind'? *Behavioural and Brain Sciences*, 1, 515–526.

Pruett, K. D. (1983). Infants of primary nurturing fathers. *Psychoanalytic Study of the Child*, 38, 257–456.

Pruett, K. D. (1985). Oedipal configurations in father-raised children. *Psychoanalytic Study of the Child*, 40, 435–481.

Pruett, K. D. (1989). The nurturing male. In S. Cath, A. Gurwitt, and L. Gunsberg (eds.), *Fathers and their Families* (pp. 309–408). Hillsdale, NJ: The Analytic Press.

Pruett, K. D. and Litzenberger, B. A. (1992). Latency development in children of primary nurturing fathers – eight-year follow-up. *Psychoanalytic Study of the Child*, 47, 85–101.

Rosen, I. (1979). Exhibitionism, scopophilia and voyeurism. In I. Rosen (ed.), *Sexual Deviation* (2nd edition) (pp. 139–195). Oxford: Oxford University Press.

Rosenfeld, D. (1992). Psychic changes in the paternal image. *International Journal of Psycho-Analysis*, 73, 757–771.

Ross, J. M. (1979). Fathering: A review of some psychoanalytic contributions on paternity. *International Journal of Psycho-Analysis*, 60, 317–326.

Siegelman, M. (1974). Parental background of male homosexuals and heterosexuals. *Archives on Sexual Behaviour*, 13, 3–18.

Sigel, I. (1970). The distancing hypothesis: A causal hypothesis for the acquisition of representational thought. In M. Jones (ed.), *Miami Symposium on the Prediction of Behaviour, 1968: Effects of Early Experiences*. Coral Gables: University of Miami Press.

Solnit, A. J. (1972). Aggression. *Journal of the American Psychoanalytic Association*, 20, 435–450.

Steele, H., Steele, M., and Fonagy, P. (1996). Associations among attachment classifications of mothers, fathers, and their infants. *Child Development*, 67, 541–555.

Stern, D. N. (1995). *The Motherhood Constellation: A Unified View of Parent–Infant Psychotherapy*. New York: Basic Books.

Stoller, R. J. (1979). Fathers of transsexual children. *Journal of the American Psychoanalytic Association*, 27, 837–866.

Stoller, R. J. (1985). *Presentations of Gender*. New Haven and London: Yale University Press.

Suess, G. J., Grossmann, K., and Sroufe, L. A. (1992). Effects of infant attachment to mother and father on quality of adaptation in preschool: From dyadic to individual organisation of self. *International Journal of Behavioural Development*, 15, 43–65.

Target, M. and Fonagy, P. (1996). Playing with reality II: The development of psychic reality from a theoretical perspective. *International Journal of Psycho-Analysis*, 77, 459–479.

Winnicott, D. W. (1957). *The Child and the Outside World: Developing Relationships*. London: Tavistock.

Winnicott, D. W. (1960). The theory of the parent–infant relationship. *International Journal of Psycho-Analysis*, 41, 585–595.

Winnicott, D. W. (1962). The theory of the parent–infant relationship – further remarks. *International Journal of Psycho-Analysis*, 43, 238–245.

Winnicott, D. W. (1967). Mirror-role of the mother and family in child development. In P. Lomas (ed.), *The Predicament of the Family: A Psycho-Analytical Symposium* (pp. 26–33). London: Hogarth Press.

Wisdom, J. O. (1976). The role of the father in the mind of parents, in psychoanalytic theory and in the life of the infant. *International Review of Psycho-Analysis*, 3, 231–239.

Yogman, M. W. (1982). Observations on the father–infant relationship. In S. H. Cath, A. R. Gurwitt, and J. M. Ross (eds), *Father and Child: Developmental and Clinical Perspectives* (pp. 101–122). Boston: Little Brown.

4

FATHERS IN THE INTERNAL WORLD

From boy to man to father

M. Fakhry Davids

Introduction

The idea of an internal world is central to object relations theory. It is a world of unconscious phantasy, made up of the self and other internal objects – persons, things, ideas and values that matter to us. The concept has proved a valuable clinical and theoretical resource, spawning detailed understandings of severe psychopathology (e.g. Rosenfeld, 1965), shedding light on the interaction between the individual and larger social groups (e.g. Jaques, 1955), and on human creative and destructive processes in general (e.g. Segal, 1986). All these contributions are built on a conceptualisation of the internal world as a vibrant, living entity that mediates between the individual as an animal, subject to instinctual desires, on the one hand, and as a member of our shared social world, on the other. It is the world of inner phantasy relationships that provides a template for our interactions with the outside world, is itself shaped by these, and is the wellspring of our psychic well-being and of creativity itself.

The internal world is not simply a representation within our minds of all the external objects that have mattered to us. In addition to qualities originating in external objects, internal objects also contain projected aspects of the self. This capacity to blend features of real external objects with projections is a momentous psychic achievement as it allows aspects of mental life unacceptable to the self to exist in objects that are contained within the mind. Unwanted, unpalatable, contradictory, feared and hated impulses, thoughts and feelings can all now have an internal home, opening the way for the self to enter into a rich array of relationships with the objects in which they are lodged. It is this that gives the inner world its vibrant, dynamic quality.

How is such a rich and varied internal world built up? In normal development internal objects are created out of interactions with the outside world. In the beginning these are driven by necessity since the infant's physical survival depends on someone else's care, and transactions associated with that care lead, gradually, to the first object, the internal mother, being set up in the mind. Because survival without such care is impossible, it follows that we will all have an internal mother.[1] Once the internal mother is established the infant has a precedent for fashioning further objects out of its interactions with others, and to this extent we could say that the shadow of the mother can be found in every object relationship we make.

If the object relations account for the universal presence of the mother in our inner worlds is an elegant one, there is no such obvious explanation for why the father, too, seems to appear universally. Whilst the interactions that lead to the establishment of the internal mother must necessarily take place, it is difficult to see the same applying to interactions with real fathers or father substitutes that might eventually generate the internal father. We know, for example, that an internal father can arise even when the child has had no direct experience of a father figure within the family. Theoretically, we deal with this problem by postulating that the presence of a father in the mother's mind is sufficient to compensate for his physical absence (e.g. Campbell, 1995; Mitchell, 1974). But this is not entirely satisfactory: why should the child seek out the father rather than any other object in the mother's mind; and why should the *universal presence* of one object require a real external relationship, whilst the other does not? The considerations involved are of course complex, and I shall return to them in greater detail later, but for the moment we should note simply that the object relations account for the universality of mother and father in the internal world seems uneven. For this reason object relations theory is often seen as biased in favour of the mother.

One approach to this problem is that of Andrew Samuels (1989), who considers the imbalance in the respective positions of mother and father within object relations theory to be due to a theoretical bias at its heart. He sees this as an attempt to put right a corresponding bias in Freud's original theory in which the father was central. Samuels argues that both these biases are symptomatic of a general contemporary tendency to accentuate overly the distinction between the sexes. Men and women are pressurised to disown qualities deemed to belong to the opposite sex, and this lends each an inflated and exaggerated feel since they now lack the natural, compensatory balance that the disowned qualities might bring. For example, in his view the sexually abusing father, so feared in our contemporary world, is an exaggerated version of the ordinarily sexual father who is, in turn, a natural counterpart of the biological, caring mother. Samuels views both the masculine and feminine as integral parts of the psyche – within the Jungian tradition *animus* and *anima* are both basic archetypal constituents of the mind. He thus posits a *plural psyche* in which masculine and feminine, mother and father, are both equally essential figures within the mind.

Whilst I do not know how much this conception of gender roles contributes to contemporary analytical psychology, I think it does little to shed light on the apparent bias within object relations theory. Within that tradition there is already considerable clinical awareness of the importance of the father, though this has not always been made explicit (but see e.g. Britton, 1989; Birksted-Breen, 1996; Campbell, 1995); but this does not suggest fathers are equivalent to mothers. Samuels proposes that the father be accepted as equivalent to the mother *a priori*; I believe that to do so makes it impossible to understand fully the nature of the differences between mother and father, both in development and in the inner world.

I suggest that it is mistaken to acknowledge that the mother and father have different roles in the mind, but then to insist that they are equivalent, as suggested by the notion of archetypes. Within the object relations tradition we see the father as one of the two primary objects in the mind; primary because the mother and father are probably the first objects to be built up there. However, the mother *is* the first. This fact has consequences which produce substantial differences in their respective statuses in the mind, which are obscured by the assumption of equivalence. The specific form and function the mother and father take in the internal world are the outcome of complex forces that flow from the fact that the mother is first, and it is these I wish to examine in this chapter.

The Oedipal father

A couple sought a psychoanalytic consultation as they had recently become concerned about their five-year-old son, Alex. The youngest of four siblings, he was a well-rounded, intelligent child who seemed to be thriving in most respects, but over recent months had become uncharacteristically difficult. The main point of friction centred on his adamant insistence on watching videotapes of a television series for older children in which a group of teenagers acquire supernatural powers with which they do violent battle with evil figures that threaten the world.[2] At first the parents thought his preoccupation with this series would probably pass – the other children too had gone through similar phases, though later than Alex. However, they became concerned that it was affecting other aspects of his behaviour in a way that had not happened with the others. For instance, he monopolised the television set in a tyrannical way, and became abusive whenever they tried to limit him. Attempts to do so brought out even more defiance, and, rather than be chastened, he seemed able to turn attempts at limit setting on their head, arranging it so that he felt in control of his own punishment. For example, if he sensed that a confrontation would end with his parents sending him to his bedroom, he would get in a pre-emptive strike by threatening to retreat there for the rest of the day were he not to get his way. On such occasions it seemed clear to the parents that beneath the bravado of increasing defiance was a distressed child, but all attempts to reach him seemed only to box him in further. Furthermore, his preoccupation with playing out the violent battles of the programmes now began to dominate his play with friends in a driven way that made him oblivious to their wishes and preferences. Previously he had been able to compromise with them, now he simply became ever more insistent on having his own way.

The parents wondered whether their failure to ensure that Alex spend the entire night in his own bed – something they had been fastidious about with the other children – might have contributed to his current difficulties. I myself thought that work on getting him to spend the night in his own bed would provide a useful focus for limit setting, as it would allow him to confront directly his hatred and violence connected with separation, which I thought had become entangled with age-appropriate Oedipal themes. I agreed with the mother's intuitive sense that her husband should take the lead in whatever they tried, as I thought this would enable Oedipal issues to surface in his mind. We decided that the father should say that as Alex was now growing up, he and his wife had decided that the time had come for Alex to sleep in his own bed at night. They realised that this might be difficult for him, and would help him by returning him there when he came into their bed. He would also not be allowed to watch age-inappropriate television programmes until he was a few years older. The parents were to convey that they both agreed that this was in his best interest, and they were to tolerate his hatred of being taken in hand.

A month later the couple reported that Alex had initially objected violently to this new regime, leading to an increase in his defiance and violent talk. His hatred of his parents was brought to a head: why should he sleep alone in his bed when his parents slept together in "our bed"? He was angry and defiant, and pined for his videotapes. However, his general behaviour gradually improved, and the au pair commented that he seemed to be a different child, on the way to becoming the child he had been before. His preoccupation with violent play diminished, he slowly became fond again of a wider range of television and video programmes, and seemed to rediscover the many other activities he used to enjoy. It seemed that in his internal world things had been restored to their proper place, and this gave him the peace of mind to face age-appropriate internal tasks in an ordinary way.

My understanding of Alex's developmental dynamics was rooted in the classical model of the Oedipus complex, which holds that the boy experiences sexual strivings towards his mother, accompanied by aggressive impulses towards the father who is felt as a rival for the mother's sexual love. Normally these feelings are experienced in the unconscious (where they are worked through to a satisfactory resolution), so that only some derivatives of the Oedipus situation make their way into consciousness. Alex, however, was quite open about such Oedipal content: for instance, he made it plain that he adored his mother and planned to marry her. He seemed to mean this so seriously that it troubled her; he hated his father, thought he had a disgusting smell, and would not now accept any care from him.[3] I thought that the nightly visit had reinforced a phantasy in Alex's mind that he had triumphed over his father's claim to an exclusive relationship with his mother. He may even have been in projective identification with his father through having witnessed the primal scene. The phantasy of Oedipal triumph had prevented him facing his hatred at being excluded from the sexual relationship between his parents. Instead, that hatred was projected into the father whom he displaced in phantasy, thus creating a feared, evil, foul-smelling monster, whom he could fight only through identification with his teenage heroes, whose superhuman power would afford omnipotent protection.[4]

To remedy this situation, it was necessary to help Alex recognise his father's claim to an exclusive relationship with his mother. In the first instance, it was necessary for the parents not to collude with his evasion of this fact, and, secondly, to contain the hatred associated with his recognition of it. Once begun, we could rely on his ego, which had already successfully negotiated earlier developmental tasks, to steer a reasonable course through the vicissitudes of love, hatred and desire in relation to his two primary objects that form the essential core of the Oedipus complex. (This work would take place internally, slowly, and, as I have already said, largely unconsciously.)

The Oedipus complex was a central aspect of Freud's theorising, and remains a cornerstone of psychoanalytic developmental theory.[5] In its longing for a sexual union with one parent, the child faces head-on the purely psychological nature of its desire – desire as desire, rather than as attached to instincts of self-preservation – as well as the fact that the social world places restrictions on the gratification of desire.[6] The psychological work of the Oedipus complex involves inner struggle and pain, and includes mourning for the lost world of childhood innocence when we believed anything was possible provided we really loved and were loved by our parent. This results in structural change within the mind: whereas previously authority existed quite literally as the voice of a parent, operating more or less as a foreign body in the mind prescribing certain courses of action and prohibiting others, henceforth that authority operates from within. Now it is felt as part of the child's own mind, and for this reason Freud (1923) regarded the superego – the inner agency that prescribes, prohibits and provides models for identification – as the heir to the Oedipus complex.

By the time the Oedipus complex comes to the fore both mother and father are already well established as internal objects, and one of its functions is to sharpen the distinction between them based on their symbolic, rather than actual, need-gratifying, roles. The crucial distinction between them revolves around a nexus of power, authority and restriction on desire, all of which are attributed

71

to the father: as the agent of castration[7] he plays a key role in the eventual sublimation of Oedipal desire. Faced with different aspects of the reality of castration both boy and girl relinquish their primary attachment to the mother. To the girl the father is not the inferior castrated being that the mother is, hence he replaces her[8] as the object of desire, thus instituting the wish to have his penis and baby. To the boy he is the father with the power to castrate, hence his decree that the mother belongs to him must be obeyed, and he eventually becomes an object of identification. This path, in which the boy identifies with the father, and the girl desires him, leads eventually to the sublimation of Oedipal desires. Both attribute power and authority to the father, and this depends crucially on an equation of penis with phallus. How does this equation happen?

Freud's view was that during the Oedipus complex the child becomes aware of the genital difference between the parents and gives it symbolic significance. However, he does not explain why the penis should be seen as powerful. Ruth Mack Brunswick (1940) suggests that an implicit awareness of sexual intercourse involving an active organ entering a receptive one brings alive an earlier dynamic – that between a passive infant/child dependent on an active breast/mother. Seeing the mother as the passive partner in intercourse presents an opportunity for overturning the child's perception of itself as passively dependent on an all-powerful mother, thus overcoming the narcissistic wound implicit in that earlier picture of itself. It is this dynamic, fuelled by narcissistic revenge against the mother, that is grafted onto the penis, thus making for the penis–phallus equation.

In my view this explanation does not go far enough. It is built around awareness of the facts of intercourse, as though it were a self-evident fact that, because the penis enters the vagina and not the other way round, the penis must necessarily be perceived as active and the vagina passive. In the first instance, we note that this requires the child to have witnessed, or be able to picture accurately, the sex act between a man and a woman. A more important question, though, is why the child does not perceive the sexual act more accurately for what it is – that penis and vagina are both active and powerful in the intercourse that produces the baby? To ignore this is to accept, uncritically, a particular construction of the relationship between the sexes as naturally correct and thus itself not in need of being theorised, and because of this some feminist writers have criticised psychoanalysis for its phallocentric bias (see Mitchell, 1974 for a review).

One defence of the psychoanalytic position is that theory is descriptive, not prescriptive.[9] The theory of the Oedipus complex *reflects* the mechanism by which the pre-existing distinction between the genders along the authority/power and active/passive dimensions is used to produce the structural change within the mind that I referred to earlier. In a truly matriarchal order we would expect mother and father to be ascribed different roles, and it is the meanings attached to these that would be reflected in Oedipal configurations observed under such conditions.[10] But this assumes that the distinction between the parents along the power/authority nexus already exists within the mind prior to the Oedipus complex. If this is so, we need to focus on the question I posed earlier: what makes us single out the father as *the* representative of power and authority? This question lies, I think, at the interface between the mind and the context within which it develops and functions, and it is to this that I now turn.

The father's place in the world

There are two approaches to the question of how the father comes to exist as the fount of power/authority within the inner world, one having an internal focus, the other an external one.

Freud himself sought the answer at the interface between the mind and its inner context: that of our inherited predispositions. In *Totem and Taboo* (1912) he argues that in the dim prehistory of the human race there was a real power struggle between a dominant and possessive primal father and his sons, which resulted in the murder of the father by his sons. This was an event that forced the sons to act in their collective interest, and thus formed the basis of group psychology, which insists that individual instinctual desire be sublimated in the interest of the greater good. Guilt associated with the murder resulted in the dead father being installed in his sons' minds with greater power and authority than he had while alive. Freud proposed that within the unconscious there are primal memories of this distant event, and that this is part of our phylogenetic inheritance. This important idea allowed Freud to fill the gap left in his theory of the Oedipus complex, for he could now postulate that endowing the father with power and authority is an inherited part of our psychological make-up. Whilst the mother is the primary caretaker, when we encounter the second parent we are pre-programmed, so to speak, to recognise him as the powerful father.

A similar idea has been developed within the object relations framework. Based on Melanie Klein's early suggestion that there is an innate capacity for knowledge itself (an epistemophilic instinct), Bion postulates that innate preconceptions "mate" with experience of events in a particular category (a "realisation") in order to produce the concept proper (Bion, 1962a).[11] Money-Kyrle (1968) goes on to suggest that one of the functions of the mind is to face the "facts of life", an activity that results in the versions of those facts particular to each individual. One such fact of life is that we are all the product of intercourse involving two different parents – thus an innate preconception of the father as a primary object, different from the mother, exists in the mind. Onto such a perceived difference, it is then possible to see that the child might project psychic content deriving from its own personal experience of those objects; for example, the narcissistic wound Mack Brunswick refers to.

The second line of approach I want to explore lies at the other interface – that between mind and social context – and flows from the work of Jacques Lacan[12] (see Lemaire, 1977 for a fuller exposition). Here I want to describe Lacan's new conceptualisation of castration. Using a structuralist understanding of language (Hawkes, 1977) he insists that meaning exists essentially externally to the speaker, being located within a signifying chain. For example, it is impossible to think of the colour white without also thinking of the colour black – its binary opposite – and many other colours and concepts related to white. All of these interrelated concepts make up the signifying chain, whose importance for us is twofold. First, although meanings within the signifying chain are eventually internalised, in the first instance they have an existence external to the speaker/thinker; second, such linguistic devices are the only ones available to humans to render their experience comprehensible. Thus, we use something that is "other" as the only way of having access to what is "us" – our experience, feelings, thoughts, etc. (Lacan, 1970). This paradox lies at the heart of our being, but in the gap between the moment that we feel something within and we become aware of it, Lacan sees fundamental alienation: where there was something real and indubitably our own, a word borrowed from an external signifying chain is inserted, claiming to speak for that real experience. This is reminiscent of Bion's description of beta elements as the basic unknowable substrate of psychic experience. In this form they are useless to the mind, and need prior transformation into alpha elements which can become the building blocks for any mental activity – feeling, perception, thinking (Bion, 1962b, 1963). In the first instance, alpha function – the name that Bion gives to the process of transformation from beta to alpha elements – has to be performed for the infant by someone else, and it is this function that is eventually internalised, thus enabling the transformation process to take place in the mind itself. Both Lacan and Bion seem to agree that, at root, this vital psychic process is "other" in origin. However, while Bion emphasises the achievement involved in alpha function, Lacan stresses the price we pay for it: for every signifier we use, some prior aspect of our being is lost. This is inherent in the human condition and, for Lacan, constitutes the essence of castration. Even as it illuminates our experience, it is inevitable that the Symbolic order – the order of language – will exert this castrating effect on our being. And when we begin to use words and other signifiers to convey our experience at first to the mother, later to ourselves, it is without awareness of the true nature of the process of which we partake. We partake because we have no choice, and it is only much later that we begin to have a sense of how the words and pictures we use about ourselves impose restrictions of their own.

According to Lacan's expanded definition castration is thus a fact of *human* existence. However, he argues that it is carried out in the "Name of the Father"

(Lacan, 1988), and that the image of the castrating father of the Oedipus complex accurately symbolises this situation – i.e. that castration falls within the domain of the father, not the mother. To understand why this is so we need to stand back to consider some unalterable differences between the genders.

We exist in a gendered world in which male and female necessarily have different roles and functions that stem ultimately from the realities of human reproduction, where gender differences are most stark. Whilst the sex act requires two persons of different genders, each playing their respective role, for it to result in conception, the subsequent *need* of the developing foetus for each of its two parents differs markedly. A pregnancy requires only the mother's healthy body to lead to a successful outcome, and the role of the biological father is peripheral. At worst the biological father is superfluous, at best he is useful (for instance in supporting the expectant mother), but he is not indispensable in the way she is.

Biological inequality is compounded further in the psychological realm. Just as the biological survival of the foetus depends on only one parent, so post-natal physical and psychological *survival*[13] depends on one person in the outside world. This inequality, too, is imposed by nature: it is a consequence of the human young coming into the world ill-equipped for independent existence. The inequality in the *need* for two biological parents means that in both biological and psychological spheres the mother – psychoanalytically, the first object – *is* the essential parent, and the father necessarily has a secondary place. It is this bias in favour of the mother that is reflected in object relations theory.

If nature has been less than even-handed towards the father by favouring the mother, then it has fallen to Culture[14] to restore the balance. This it has done in complex ways that persuasively define the man as master of all he surveys. One consequence of this is that the mothering so vital to every infant's psychological survival has been firmly relegated to a secondary, somewhat denigrated place: it is part of woman's work, but in a man's world. The mechanism by which this persuasive cultural phantasy of men as the possessors of power operates depends crucially on equating the penis with the phallus. This equation exists externally, in the world of meaning – within the human signifying chain that all of us accede to – and thus predates our individual existence. It is a construction that is driven, I think, by envy of the mother's reproductive role, and is part of a broad socio-political-historical compromise whose purpose is to render more palatable an otherwise unbearable inequality. Just as the primacy of the mother to the foetus and infant is a fact that has an existence independent of any one individual, so the father's authority exists as a real fact in the external world (i.e. within the symbolic order). Whilst the infant may not at first be aware of this, it is nonetheless subject to its effects from the very beginning of life (in the form of castration-of-being, carried out in the name of the father). The Oedipus complex can therefore be regarded as that nodal point in development when, in the child's mind, this fact is fully recognised and placed within its proper context. It is the moment of truth when the child recognises that concepts, which are now very much part of itself (e.g. boy, girl, mother, father, brother, sister), really have a whole life within a Symbolic order independent of the imaginary realm of omnipotent phantasy in its own mind – in which we believe we can make words mean what we want them to mean – and that the meanings inscribed in the Symbolic order will prevail. It is that moment when we realise we cannot make a concept mean what we want it to mean: to be a son or daughter means having to give up incestuous desire for one's parents, irrespective of our own wishes in the matter. This is quite simply because the Law construes the categories of son and daughter that way, and by now we cannot opt out of such constructions.[15] Even resistance to the Law would itself speak of its existence in, and recognition by, the mind. And it is the father, as the symbolic representative of human culture, who takes responsibility for all such constraints placed on the child's desire. Psychologically, this reflects a benign split, in which all love is now associated with one primary object, thus safeguarding it from the violence associated with the narcissistic injury implied by castration.

The father of infancy

As I have already indicated, the foetus's physical survival prior to birth depends on one parent, and its physical and psychological survival after birth depends on having a relationship with one primary caretaker – usually the mother. This primary caretaker is a relatively stable person in the outside world charged with responsibility for tending to the infant's needs, and optimal development will depend on the quality of that relationship. Out of this experience the object we will come to refer to as the internal mother gradually takes shape in the infant's mind. We call it a mother because all the crucial functions normally associated with mothering are performed by such an object – these include being receptive and sensitive to the state of the infant (e.g. its distress), empathising with the infant in order to understand its non-verbal communication, and responding to its needs – for instance through feeding, cleaning and all the other acts involved in taking care of a young baby. This role can theoretically also be performed by someone other than the biological mother[16] (e.g. a foster mother or the father), and we would still refer to the internal object that results from such experiences as a mother. When issues connected with these functions are mobilised in analysis we think of the transference as maternal, irrespective of the gender of the analyst.

If the first relationship is that with the mother, is there a role for the father during this earliest period? At the outset the infant is unable to understand that the need-gratifying mother is the same person as the depriving mother. It uses the mechanism of splitting to keep these two objects apart in its mind (which leads to idealisation of the former, and an experience of persecution when in the presence of the latter). It can then use projective identification to rid the mind of either, in order to protect the good from annihilation by the bad. These projected aspects are usually lodged in the mother, but this can create further difficulties in view of the infant's dependence on her. In such situations the father, by virtue of being less involved emotionally, can relieve the situation through his access to a fresh perspective. Probably the commonest example of this is when an infant gets into an inconsolable state and, despite her best efforts, it is just impossible for the mother to soothe "her baby". We could infer that the infant feels surrounded, and in danger of being engulfed by, a bad object: the mother, the room and everything associated with the bad internal state come together as one overwhelming persecution. As a consequence of having projected its good object (to preserve and protect it from the persecutory situation) the infant needs external help to rediscover it, but the mother cannot help since she is part of the persecutory situation. At such times a fresh parent with a fresh mind who, in the infant's perception, is not part of the persecuting situation, can step into the breach to rescue the situation. This can restore a calmer state. An essential part of that fresh view is an implicit understanding that the mother has done all she could, and her own determination to help her baby is based on the successful projection of an omnipotent infantile conviction that only the mother can relieve infantile distress. Obviously, such a conviction does not take account of the whole situation as I have just outlined it. It is for this reason that the capacity to think in the face of intense emotion is sometimes associated with the paternal function (paternal since it is built around the break-up of mutual omnipotent phantasy between mother and infant). "Castrating" functions that interfere with omnipotent phantasy are bound to be performed, irrespective of whether there is an actual father in the family, and this means that the effect of the father is indeed felt in infancy. When there is an actual father who can act in this way, we can think of him as performing a symbolic paternal function. I shall return to this theme.

Linked to this symbolic function, the father also has a more general role during infancy as a repository for split off aspects of the infant's experience with the mother. From a practical point of view, caring for an infant is hard work, and an extra pair of hands can provide vital support for the mother. However, initially the infant has a limited sense of this external reality and can do little more than distinguish its good experience from bad. Good experience is usually associated with need-fulfilment – when it is in the presence of the mother in tune with its needs, which usually means a mother in the act of attending to them. The infant feels in the presence of an idealised object – one capable of fulfilling all its needs, and magically banishing the state of neediness itself. On the other hand, when it is assailed from within by needy impulses it loses contact with this idealised object, and lapses into a persecuted state. As I have already indicated, this brings a fear of annihilation, and in the absence of any means of control over this situation, the infant uses the primitive mechanism of splitting, in which the source of that overwhelming anxiety is isolated from the rest of its experience, and evacuated by means of projective identification, resulting in a frightening, bad object. One of the earliest functions of someone in the external world clearly distinguishable from the mother is that it allows the infant to project into that object the split-off aspect of its experience of the mother, thus protecting its good experience/object.

A five-month-old baby, her mother and older brother arrived by air in a foreign city to visit good friends. Everyone commented on how well the two children had travelled, and how curious they were about all around them. On the first evening with their friends, both the baby and her older brother seemed settled until at one point their dark-skinned host caught her attention. She stared at him for a few moments with a mixture of interest and apprehension, then suddenly burst into tears and turned to the safety of her mother's arms. This was the other side of the baby who appeared to take all the upheaval of the day in her stride; the male host served as a useful repository for the threatening experience that she could not assimilate. Beneath her rather manic curiosity of the day lay a terrifying experience – leaving home and her father earlier that day, encountering one stranger after the other in a completely new world, a plane journey, etc. – that had been split off. Thus an object in the external world perceptibly different from the mother can bring into the open a frightening experience that otherwise would remain split off, perhaps storing up problems for the night.

Given that the infant has at its disposal only the primitive mechanisms of splitting and projective identification, it is as a repository for projective identification that the father in the conventional family serves an important psychological function for the baby. It is precisely because the father is physically so different from the mother – in terms of appearance, tone of voice, etc. – that it is possible for the infant to seize on this difference in order to give a physical, external form to split off experiences relating to the mother. Externally, the father can come to embody all the hated aspects of the mother, and vice versa, where each is actually a split-off aspect of the other. This has the function of protecting good inner experience, and temporarily warding off the anxiety of annihilation, but the result is that what appears to be two different objects are really two sides of the same one. This use of the figure of the father inter-feres with ordinary paternal functioning; for instance, the role of the father in bringing a fresh perspective is, paradoxically, unavailable at the very moment when it is needed most (i.e. when there is a problem with the mother). Let me give two clinical examples that illustrate this: first, a woman who splits off and projects into the father the good experience; second, a man who splits off the bad.

Mrs A had a disturbed early relationship with her mother, characterised by repeated separations, and struggled to hold on to a good analyst during separations in the analysis. Typically, the absent analyst would be felt as the presence in her mind of an awful, persecutory experience. After some years of analysis she woke one Saturday night from a frightening dream in which a thief had broken into their home. In the dream, as in reality, her husband was away on business, and she was terrified that she was in real danger. Eventually, she forced herself to get out of bed, reassured herself that the house was safe and the burglar alarm still on, and then tried to go back to sleep, but this took some time. She found herself mulling over my interpretations that during the weekend break she experienced longings for a mother-me of such intensity as to be unbearable. She evacuated this experience into me, thus had no access to it within her mind, but on a Monday she always feared that she was coming to a shut-out, frightening, demanding and critical analyst. She realised that in her dream she had access to the weekend feeling during the weekend itself – she could see the burglar as the shut-out infant her – and felt that the analysis must be making progress. By now she was in a half-asleep state, and found her mouth making sucking movements, and as she became aware of this she realised fleetingly that she had the sensation of a penis in her mouth. Ordinarily she would have been frightened by such an occurrence, but, as she realised the following morning, the sensation had the effect of soothing her to sleep. I interpreted that the penis stood for the analytic breast: it is an infant's concrete representation of the experience of being comforted by the presence in her mind of a good, understanding breast. However, this patient's relationship with her mother was a very troubled one, in which traumatic premature separation was equated with her mother hating her, and the soothing function of the breast was thus split off and projected into the father with whom she had a better relationship.

By contrast, my next example is of a patient who had a more idealised relationship with his mother.

Mr B was an intelligent and gifted man with a history of violent suicide attempts. He liked his mother, a cultured woman, and was attracted to her physical features and character traits in women, but he felt her to be physically fragile and emotionally vulnerable. From previous psychotherapy he understood that he had a grievance against her for having a second sibling within fifteen months of his own birth – he had felt dropped by his newly pregnant mother.

Following a two-week break, for many weeks he would either miss sessions altogether, or arrive very late, as he found it almost impossible to get out of bed in the morning. It became clear that his bed gave him the sensation of being held warm and safe – the experience of the mother of early infancy – from which he felt prematurely ejected into the world of analysis and work. We worked on this theme for some time, and one morning when he made himself get up to face the session rather than reset the alarm for another hour in bed, he reported that he had felt quite sick in the bathroom. He thought this must be something he inherited from his father.

Like Mr B, his father was a precociously successful businessman. His best memories were of his father, on the spur of the moment on a summer's afternoon, leaving the business in the hands of his workers in order to take the children out to have some fun. Recalling this gave him a warm feeling, since it showed something so typical of his father: that he used his authority in a way that was sensitive to the needs of the children, laying down the law where appropriate, knowing just when the rules could be relaxed to take advantage of an opportunity to relax together. However, there was one incongruous fact about him. After getting out of bed in the mornings he made straight for the bathroom, where he could be heard having a coughing fit so violent that it often woke the household. They would fear he was going to be sick, but eventually he would light a cigarette while on the toilet, defecate, and after a few minutes he would seem more settled, have his shower and proceed to ready himself for the day. This is what made him think his father had the same dread of the world as he.

I understood the following: the infant in my patient was in identification with a pregnant mother with morning sickness, and this concealed a complex object relationship that slowly came to light in the analysis. It included an unprocessed experience in which separation was equated with the parental intercourse[17] that produced the new baby. This stirred raw hatred in him, but since his mind was not sufficiently developed to contain such perceptions and emotions, the hatred grew in intensity, resulting in a primitive murderousness[18] (given form, for instance, in the suicide attempts). This was sensed as very dangerous: internally it threatened him with annihilation – confirmed in dreams at the time – and it could not be projected into his mother since he sensed her vulnerability. His solution was to dislodge this entire infantile experience into his father, who now contained the sick infant and all the unprocessed emotions locked up there. The obvious evidence of his father's ability to use his judgement – in the way he exercised his power and authority – eased the patient's fear that his father had been damaged by the projection, and might retaliate.

It is clear that both Mrs A and Mr B have a father, clearly recognisable as such,[19] in their inner worlds; but both use the father as a repository for split-off aspects of psychic experience that belong to their relationship with the mother. This limits the extent to which the real qualities of the father can be a source of fresh learning from experience – for instance, it might provide an opportunity for less fraught interactions when things are tense with the mother. Under more favourable circumstances one might expect a more or less good-enough experience with each parent, so that the child might prefer now one, now the other, depending on its need or preference at any particular moment. This would facilitate the development of proper reality testing, so that the real characteristics of each parent come into play according to the demands of the situation the child faces, and this allows the child to differentiate the parents from each other on the basis of such qualities. By the time the child reaches the Oedipus complex proper, this results in two parents in the mind towards whom it has ambivalent feelings, both love and hate, rather than the more skewed situations presented by Mrs A and Mr B.

If these are examples of things going wrong in the early relationship with the mother that are then displaced into the relationship with the father, what would be the configuration of things going right?

The father and mental space

I have emphasised that the mother is the first object to emerge in the internal world. When the father emerges in his own right it is therefore as the second object; thus the question of his relationship with the first becomes an issue in a way that does not arise with the mother. This clinical observation has led to the current view that Oedipal issues present themselves to the child much earlier than Freud had originally thought, albeit in a very different form (see Steiner, 1989). For this reason Britton (1989, 1998) suggests that in phantasy, separation is always experienced as the mother retreating to the other room – the parental bedroom – with the second object, the father. What the infant imagines taking place there depends, of course, on its own internal state – in particular on what it seeks to project. Let me give a normal and a pathological example of this.

A 13-month-old baby whose mother had recently returned to work was observed at the end of the day, after he had been collected from his grandmother's. The early morning separations were difficult, and when his mother returned in the evening he would cold-shoulder her and initially refuse to be fed and comforted. But after some time he would allow his mother back in, and once he had been generally tended by his parents – feed, bath, etc. – he appeared to like nothing better than lying on a settee, apparently taking pleasure in his parents' conversation with each other as they went about their evening chores. This was his preferred activity at that time of night and it had an unmistakably settling effect on him. This baby seemed able to tolerate the awareness of his two parents having a relationship with each other and it is this that will form the basis of an internal space, which underpins the capacity to be alone, and is the wellspring of imagination and creativity. One might speculate that his mother's capacity to tolerate his rage (in the form of cold-shouldering) contained that response to the separation, and allowed him to tolerate and take pleasure from an intercourse between his parents happening in his presence.

This is in contrast to the situation in the inner world of Ms C, an intelligent, successful and much-admired businesswoman. In an analysis marked by a lack of spontaneous communication from her inner world, she reported the following dream:

The details were vague, but I was on my way to analysis, which was, I think, here in Hampstead, but the consulting room was in a different place. When I came in you were sitting at a desk, writing a letter. You told me that you

81

had decided to stop my analysis, and that you were just writing to the other analyst to let him know. It was not entirely clear how it worked, but in the dream it seemed that I see two analysts for my analysis – I come to you and then immediately after I go to another. The other analyst was further up the hill, I think, because there were many trees nearby which suggested it was near the heath. But he had a milk float on which he saw me, not for a session in the usual way, but, it seemed, to give me a lift from place to place.

The dream suggests that the patient experiences analytic care as involving two parents. However, they are not as sharply differentiated from each other as would be a more conventional mother and father. Not only are they of the same gender, but they also appear as functionally interchangeable: when one brings potentially disturbing news of an analytic feed drying up, the other immediately offers the reassurance that he has plenty of milk available "on the back". The second "parent" is also not genuinely supportive: rather than a lift in order to hold and comfort a distressed her, and then help her confront the difficulty that has arisen with the first "parent", the second, who is higher up than the first, "gives her a lift" from place to place. This suggests a manic mood, reminding us of the finding that fathers tend to stimulate and excite their infants more than mothers do (Neubauer, 1989, cited by Widzer, 1993). I think, therefore, that although the patient was brought up in a conventional nuclear family, she has nevertheless internalised a "faulty" set of parents. What went wrong?

The patient's analysis had been a long and difficult one, characterised by an as-if quality (Malcolm, 1992) in which overt compliance concealed a lack of genuine emotional contact, mirroring the lack of openness to her inner world which I have already referred to. In the sessions preceding this one I had been able to track how almost any moment of genuine contact would immediately be followed by something intensely hostile within her, the consequence of which would be further compliance – she would follow my drift, apparently co-operating, but in a way that would be completely false (e.g. totally intellectual). Recently, when I drew attention to this, she would eventually say that she was always able to guess what her mother wanted from her, and then be the dutiful daughter. The previous week she dreamt

she was with her partner on the steps of a local hospital, clearly pregnant, with a helpful doctor in the background, but then realised that a horrible brown fluid was coming out from her, running down her legs.

Her associations were that she was having a miscarriage. It was possible to interpret this situation as the fate inside her of any interpretation that reaches her – a cruel, bloody process gets going which results in the understanding of it in her mind being utterly mangled and then pushed out.

For Ms C the elementary process of receiving something real from an analyst is profoundly difficult. This is an expression of a highly disturbed internal mother–infant relationship in which the infant cannot tolerate the awareness of being fed by a mother. Such awareness immediately mobilises envy – not of the feed but of the mother's capacities to produce something that is in tune with her infant's need. The dream I have just described is part of this constellation. Usually, however, the patient solves the problem of envy by becoming projectively identified with the mother: she is the mother, and the mother is the infant whose needs she will dutifully attend to. This obliterates the generational difference between them, and leaves two equivalent partners, making her able to ignore her dependence.

This view places the mother–infant relationship at the core of this patient's difficulties. But what then is the role of the father? When the mother withdraws from her to join the father, she projects into that space the version of the infant–mother couple that I have just described, so that she has a phantasy of the parental intercourse involving two equivalent figures. But I do not think she is entirely successful in maintaining this. In the analysis itself, for instance, she is acutely sensitive to my making an interpretation (which involves perceiving my functioning as an analyst), and then does much work to restore her equilibrium in the way I have described (through compliance). She has a second line of defence, illuminated by the details of the first dream: the father is recruited into the role of being an alternative, idealised mother who has all the milk she could possibly desire, and who conducts the analysis in a way that lifts her above any feeding difficulties. I think of this figure as a father as he is clearly male in her dream, and the lift may stand for the father's ability to have an erection, which she herself appropriates. One could speculate that she has an unconscious phantasy of appropriating the father's penis, with which she would enter the mother in intercourse (Segal, 1973). This phantasy obliterated awareness of her own exclusion by the parental intercourse (and its equivalent in the transference), and dramatises between three persons the underlying problem of envy observed repeatedly in the analysis: what she cannot stand is the intercourse in her mother's mind that produces an understanding of her child's mental state which, of course, accentuates her infantile dependency.

From infant to boy to man to father

This conceptualisation of the father in the inner world sees the mother and the father as two distinct objects in the mind, each with its own domain. Developmentally, interactions with an external mother precede those with any other object, thus the mother is the first object to emerge in the inner world. The father is the second.

Viewed in a broader context, any attempt to understand the respective roles of mother and father has to take into account three immutable facts:

1 that the woman has the essential procreative role;
2 that the physical and psychological survival of the human infant *requires* the care of *one* other person; and
3 that the transformation of a biological baby into a fully functioning member of human society (i.e. socialisation) involves more than mere physical and psychological survival.

We can think of a human bio-cultural "order" – encompassing all those forces that must act in concert in order to ensure the long-term survival of human society (which, of course, requires the survival of its individual members as humans rather than mere biological organisms) – as shaping a response to these facts that accommodates the need for *both* parents to share the psychological task of rearing their young. This avoids excessive envy of the female's reproductive primacy, which would be quite unbearable, and incompatible with the survival of human society. The end-products of this accommodation involve a split in responsibility: the mother's domain is those aspects pertaining to survival of the individual, and thus includes nurturance of the infant and child; the father's extends over the elements that will eventually enable us to take our place in society *as humans*. We could say that these sets of functions are carried out in the name of the mother and father respectively, and the internal objects mother and father emerge in the inner world as a consequence of their being carried out, irrespective of whether the person doing so is the actual mother or father.

At the most elementary level, the mother's domain covers such issues as the recognition of need and the capacity/will to respond to it, and extends into a range of dependency issues such as envy, possession of the object, narcissism and, eventually, concern for the object. (The interactions involved are complex, but include being attended to, understood, receiving a feed and other care from the object, giving pleasure to the object, and gradually becoming aware of the nature of this nurturing interaction.) Broadly, we can think of this as starting with the experience of need and its gratification, and extending into the realm of omni-potent phantasy, in which mental activity (e.g. hallucinatory wish fulfilment) is used to by-pass the awareness of restrictions on, and limitations to, gratification imposed by reality. The father is responsible for the survival in the individual of those elements that will allow him to take his place as a human, and since all group living depends, at root, on impulse control, the father's domain can be thought of as extending over mental activity based on the recognition that all good things come to an end – i.e. there are boundaries imposed on need gratification by external reality. At its most elementary level this covers such issues as deprivation, separation from the good object, the laying down of boundaries, and "gate-keeping" in general, all of which stir up hatred. Put another way, it is the father who is defined as coming between the nursing mother–infant couple locked in mutual omnipotent, wish-fulfilling phantasy. When the mother herself acts to do so, she does so in the name of the father. Providing the hatred stirred up by such acts can be tolerated it gradually becomes possible to delay gratification, impulses can be controlled, and frustration tolerated sufficiently to allow the apparatus for thinking to develop (Bion, 1962a), and it is this trajectory that sets us on the path to becoming human.

It is therefore inconceivable that anyone might develop beyond infancy without experiencing interactions belonging to *both* categories, thus it is inevitable that both mother and father will emerge as objects in the internal world. But do such interactions have to be with two different external objects? I think not: whilst it is obviously *necessary* to have at least one caregiver, which would create the internal mother, it would be perfectly conceivable that (usually) she could provide the experiences in the domain of the father that would lead to an internal father being established in the infant's mind. As long as a father exists in the mind of that external caregiver (i.e. at its most elementary level), she exposes the infant to restrictions on its desire and, no matter how ambivalently, the infant will have the experience on which the development of an internal father depends. It is this that creates the lack of equivalence between mother and father that I referred to at the beginning of this chapter: not having an external mother is incompatible with survival; not having an external father leads not to the absence of a father in the inner world but, save in the most exceptional cases, to emotional difficulties. For example, in even the worst cases of paranoia associated with pathology in the earliest mother–child relationship, it is usually possible to find an internal father, an object other than the mother, often confused with a very harsh, critical and punitive superego. It is not that the father does not exist in the mind, but he assumes a particular pathological form. The exceptions I have just referred to would be single mothers with a good relationship with an internal father, provided that the fact of being a single mother is itself not associated with problematic relationships with the internal father.

The object that is to become, in the mind of the adult, recognisable as the father has a complex developmental trajectory, and the presence of an external father affords a real relationship, separate from that with the mother, that helps the infant and child along this path. During early infancy, the father serves as a repository for the infant's experience of the "bad", depriving mother, and this allows the infant to consolidate its relationship with the good object, which is essential for psychic growth. In this there is, unbeknownst to the infant, an uncanny coincidence between its use of the father and his designated symbolic role focused on the frustration of instinctual need in the service of reality. The father is the hated depriving object, and this requires the father to have a capacity to be hated. The father has to accept that the central nurturing relationship involves the mother, and that he is excluded from the mother–infant couple. Internally this revives his exclusion from the parental couple in his own childhood, and the extent to which he can tolerate this will govern his capacity to manage the fathering role. When this position is reversed, and the father has become the "good" object and the mother the "bad" (as in the example of Mrs A on pp. 78–79), there has been a turning away from the mother, and the requirement is then for the father to be able to overcome his envious triumph over the mother in order to help the infant find his or her psychologically good object in the nurturing mother once more.

With the infant's increasing access to depressive position functioning, the need for splitting and projective identification lessens, and there is correspondingly less need for the infant to use the father as a repository for "bad" experience. This allows for greater awareness of the real qualities of both parents, differentiation between them on the basis of their capacity to respond to his or her needs, wishes and preferences, and this leads to a more complex, differentiated relationship with each. It is also one of the first ways of getting to know a more differentiated external reality and the pleasures available there. To put together the previously demonised father with the reality of who he actually is opens up the possibility of greater class integration in the infant's mind – e.g. it is not the fact that he is the father which matters, but his capacity to respond to the infant's needs, and that all humans might have such qualities. Obviously the parent's own psychopathology (e.g. ambivalence that the father might have towards either role) might interfere with such development. Important developments flow from this; for instance, an infant who previously preferred the mother might begin to realise that the father is actually more tender. In order to facilitate such development it is necessary for the father to give up the certainty involved in the relatively frozen role of "macho" bad guy, and be reasonably at ease with different aspects of his feelings and responses evoked by his infant and child. The depressive position is not attained once and for all; rather, states of greater integration are interspersed with the more paranoid–schizoid state, which dominates when anxiety is greater. This turning away again on the part of the infant may inflict a narcissistic wound on the father, which needs to be borne. From an emotional point of view, the end product of the transition to depressive position functioning is that both parents are cathected in an ambivalent way, but with the subtle difference that one has the role, on the whole, of being the nurturing parent whilst the other tends to be the one laying down limits. As a result, the internal father associated with normal depressive position functioning is a more complex one, incorporating more of the real qualities of the actual father or father figure.

The relative calm of the depressive position opens the way for an explosion in the infant's involvement with the outside world (Stern, 1985), which, when things go well, gives rise to a sense of well-being in the world. This is based on an innocent, omnipotent belief that the world is one's oyster, a feeling punctuated by a return to paranoid–schizoid functioning if faced by anxiety. The Oedipus complex can be viewed as such a regression in the face of the infant's anxiety associated with sexual strivings towards the parent of the opposite sex. It is during the Oedipus complex that the reality of the symbolic roles of mother and father respectively, and the child's position in relation to them, is confronted head on. Omnipotence is challenged by an awareness of the reality of castration; the father is perceived as its agent, and the Oedipus complex is an attempt to come to terms with this. The father is cathected ambivalently, and in the course of the Oedipus complex a range of intense feelings are experienced towards him, ranging from extreme love to extreme hatred. In consequence the reality of his symbolic castrating role is accepted as fact, and this is either identified with by the boy, or submitted to by the girl. The father now becomes the authority figure *in the mind* responsible for breaking up imaginary, wish-fulfilling phantasy in the interest of submission to human law. For the child, once the Oedipus complex wanes, it is freed from the intensity of the intra-family drama to make a series of complex relationships with substitutes in the external world as a way of managing intense feelings that are now very close to the surface. This turning of interest to the outside world is itself an acceptance of the law of the father that the mother belongs to him. An external father figure in the family, at relative peace with his own Oedipal issues, allows the child to get closer to experiencing derivatives of this drama in a personalised way (as in the example of Alex), and this facilitates its resolution. However, an external father is not essential since it is a process driven internally by the unavailability of one's object for the purposes of fulfilling omnipotent Oedipal sexual phantasy. The child who does not have a father will therefore find father figures in the outside world for this purpose, providing of course that the father in the mother's mind insists on breaking up imaginary gratification based on such phantasy. During the long latency period that follows the child moves away from the central drama in the family in order to find objects of identification acceptable to the ego, and to develop an elaborate world of inner phantasy relationships around them.

A further period of intense anxiety occurs during puberty when the maturing body renders phantasy less safe than it was during latency, since it is now physically possible to act upon both sexual and aggressive phantasy (Laufer and Laufer, 1984). The castrating father that evoked murderous feelings is now felt to be in real danger, and the women towards whom the boy had violent sexual fantasies, in identification with an aggressively castrating father, are also now felt to be in real danger, and this creates a crisis for the ego which it usually takes many years to resolve. The path of this resolution is complex, but includes progressive experimentation with taking on roles, not yet completely owned because of the intense anxieties attached to them, in order to translate into practice the phantasy solutions rehearsed during latency. The peer group becomes important since it allows projective identification to flourish: one group member will take on the overtly sexual, seductive role in relation to girls whilst completely dislodging fear and anxiety into his peers, and vice versa, and this allows for testing sexual and aggressive phantasies against reality. Others may temporarily become anti-social delinquents, etc. But, from an internal point of view, the issues that are being reworked, now with greater reality and hence anxiety, are the same ones that were resolved in phantasy during the Oedipus complex. The internal father of adolescence is no different from the internal father post-Oedipus complex, but now the pressing issue, brought to the fore by the maturing body, is real identification with him. This is the final step in the transition to fatherhood.

Becoming a father entails identifying with the internal symbolic father in real and concrete ways. The developmental path is a complex one, consisting of many different components: the early father of splitting, the more real, whole person of the father encountered in depressive position functioning, the castrating authority figure of the Oedipus complex, and the real sexual/aggressive father encountered in the adolescent's body. The way in which each of these issues is confronted has an influence on the colour and shape of the internal father, but what distinguishes him from other objects is his symbolic role of insisting on the path that leads away from omnipotent phantasy and towards submitting naked impulse to externally dictated control. This is essential for group living. Because the father is the second object to emerge in the inner world, the relationship with the mother always forms the hidden backdrop to the infant–father relationship (in a way that does not happen with the infant–mother relationship).

Psychoanalytic treatment within the object relations tradition is sometimes criticised for not paying enough attention to the father. I hope that it is obvious from my discussion to see why it is not possible to conduct an analysis without being on the side of the father's solution to the problem of desire: analysis itself is based on knowing one's desire rather than gratifying it, which is firmly within the domain of the father. Given this bias within the structure of analysis, even an analysis that explicitly addresses only the maternal transference should set right the balance between the internal parents. Let me end with a clinical example.

Mr D, a man in his early forties, sought psychoanalytic psychotherapy after repeated attempts to find help through alcohol dependency and other treatments. Always something of a loner, he became an alcoholic during his late teens and early twenties, which provided a way of dealing with the many anxieties he faced after leaving home and college. He aspired to be a journalist but in the end "lacked the stomach" for all that cut-throat competition and, instead, took an administrative job in the profession. Because of his drinking he had never really had a proper relationship with a woman, though he was interested, and on the odd occasion when he did end up in bed with a woman he was impotent. At first he presumed this was due to the drink. However, though he had managed to quit drinking altogether nearly ten years ago, impotence remained a problem. He had sought a number of physical and behavioural treatments, without any success, before he was eventually referred to group therapy, from whence he came to me.

The patient had an older, tomboy sister who was his father's favourite whilst he was his mother's, a position he disliked but could not confront, other than by moving to college in a different city. However, he kept regular contact with his mother, particularly since the death of his father shortly before he gave up alcohol. In childhood his mother had confided in him that she was very unhappy with his father because he was so dominant and assertive, and more or less raised him as a no-trouble-to-anyone sissy. He never joined in the rough and tumble in the playground, and in the course of his treatment it became clear that in phantasy he was his mother's real partner. This concealed tremendous hatred towards her for a number of failures – for instance, not taking seriously his repeated complaints that he was bullied by a teacher, or that he could not cope with one of his school subjects. The phantasy of being his mother's partner reinstated an idealised mother–infant couple in which his hatred of her was projected into his father, making for an excessively violent and aggressive figure with whom he could not identify, and to whom he could not turn for help.

I interpreted his impotence as flowing from an idea that his sexual penis contained violent impulses that would damage a woman, and there were many opportunities for showing him the source of his violence in the ongoing battles with his mother. The content of his sessions centred almost exclusively on his relationship with his mother, which we worked with in the transference, and after some four years of treatment he eventually formed a relationship with a woman, with whom he ceased to be impotent. He at first pooh-poohed inter-pretations that his impotence had a meaning, but came to take them more seriously when he could see that it was linked to the state of his relationship with her. When he repressed anger and hatred towards her he became impotent, and this usually improved when he did the emotional work to understand what was going on in his mind, and to discuss matters with her rather than withdraw into a "loner" state. After a further year of therapy they decided to move to her country of origin, and the treatment ended.

This brief account of treatment illustrates that though its content may focus almost exclusively on the relationship with the internal mother (via the maternal transference) it is the activity of analysis itself that serves as a model of a father with whom it is possible for the patient to identify. It is a paternal model, since its central aspects involve maintaining boundaries and accurately understand-ing the patient's predicament rather than gratifying his infantile wishes directly (e.g. with a cosy sympathy). Both of these are within the symbolic realm of the father. Although it was the symbolic father that was present, he was actually, in his body, able to identify with that potent father – effects of the presence of the symbolic father were absolutely real.

Notes

1 The route by which this first object is installed in the mind is thus an anaclitic one, with the process of mourning (Freud, 1917) as one of its key components.

2 The "Power Rangers" are successively transformed from the human into larger and more powerful forms — each of which is matched by a similar transmutation by the forces of evil — so that they end up doing battle on ever-larger stages.

3 Which made for some difficulty as the parents needed to share the parenting tasks.

4 For the purposes of brevity I am omitting clinical detail that illuminates how the separation theme blended with the Oedipal issues I am highlighting here.

5 Even if it may not be so central in our understanding of psychopathology, or a focus in clinical work, today.

6 Through the incest taboo, as far as Oedipal desire is concerned.

7 The terms "castrated" and "non-castrated" refer to the perception of the child, not actual reality; although the fact that we all bought into such ideas as children will in turn influence the shape of our consensual reality.

8 Who is held responsible for her castrated state.

9 Juliet Mitchell (1974) herself argues that psychoanalytic theories that set out to correct observed imbalances limit their ability to illuminate the psychological power by which such imbalances — no matter how distasteful — are inscribed in the mind.

10 There is an interesting discussion in Mitchell (1974) as to whether a truly matriarchal order (in the terms discussed here) exists anywhere: apparently anthropologists have yet to find one.

11 For example: an innate preconception of a breast needs the experience of a feed to produce the concept of the breast in the infant's mind.

12 Lacan's writings are often impenetrable, some think self-consciously so, given that he wants to make the point that it is impossible to get at the truth except through grappling with the many tricks that language plays on us (see Frosh, 1994). In line with this, it is impossible for me to tell how much of the necessarily schematic approach outlined here is Lacan's meaning, and how much is my own understanding in response to reading him.

13 As opposed to optimal development.

14 The capital "C" denotes a reference to human culture itself, not a specific variant of it. From the point of view of *psychic* development, Culture is as much an external given as Nature. The mind has to accommodate both, and the structure of the inner world is marked by decisive responses to each.

15 I am using "son" and "daughter" as examples, there are of course many further permutations of meaning implicit in such psychological work.

16 I am concentrating here on conceptual issues, and leave aside empirical questions such as whether there is a link between the pre- and post-birth bond between mother and baby (see Piontelli, 1992).

17 Formulations such as these are in the observer's terms; from the infant's point of view the experience is unformulated since it cannot be processed (Bion, 1962a).

18 Given the level of the patient's disturbance, when I did address this it was in its

projected form, in an analyst-oriented interpretation (Steiner, 1993): the mother/ analyst who abandons him is the murderer.

19 As a whole- or part-object.

References

Bion, W.R. (1962a). A theory of thinking. *International Journal of Psycho-Analysis* 43, 306–310.

Bion, W.R. (1962b). *Learning from Experience*. London: Heinemann.

Bion, W.R. (1963). *Elements of Psycho-analysis*. London: William Heinemann Medical Books.

Birksted-Breen, D. (1996). Phallus, penis and mental space. *International Journal of Psycho-Analysis* 77, 649–657.

Britton, R. (1989). The missing link: parental sexuality in the Oedipus complex. In R. Britton, M. Feldman and E. O'Shaughnessy (eds) *The Oedipus Complex Today*. London: Karnac Books, pp. 83–102.

Britton, R. (1998). *Belief and Imagination: Explorations in Psychoanalysis*. London and New York: Routledge.

Brunswick, R.M. (1940). The pre-oedipal phase of the libido development. *The Psychoanalytic Quarterly* 9, 293.

Campbell, D. (1995). The role of the father in the pre-suicidal state. *International Journal of Psycho-Analysis* 76, 315–323.

Freud, S. (1912). *Totem and Taboo*. In Standard Edition 13. London: Hogarth Press and Institute of Psycho-Analysis, pp. 1–161.

Freud, S. (1917). *Mourning and Melancholia*. In Standard Edition 14. London: Hogarth Press and Institute of Psycho-Analysis, pp. 239–258.

Freud, S. (1923). *The Ego and the Id*. In Standard Edition 19. London: Hogarth Press and The Institute of Psycho-Analysis.

Frosh, S. (1994). *Sexual Difference: Masculinity and Psychoanalysis*. London and New York: Routledge.

Hawkes, T. (1977). *Structuralism and Semiotics*. London: Methuen.

Jaques, E. (1955). Social systems as a defence against persecutory and depressive anxiety. In M.H. Klein, P. Heimann and R. Money-Kyrle (eds) *New Directions in Psycho-Analysis*. London: Tavistock Publications.

Lacan, J. (1970). Of structure as an inmixing of an Otherness prerequisite to any Subject whatever. In R.D. Macksey (ed.) *The Structuralist Controversy: The Languages of Criticism and the Sciences of Man*. Baltimore and London: The Johns Hopkins University Press.

Lacan, J. (1988). *The Seminar of Jacques Lacan*. Book II: *The Ego in Freud's Theory and in the Technique of Psychoanalysis 1954–1955*. Cambridge: Cambridge University Press.

Laufer, E. and Laufer, M. (1984). *Adolescence and Developmental Breakdown*. New Haven, Conn.: Yale University Press.

Lemaire, A. (1977). *Jacques Lacan*. London, Henley and Boston: Routledge and Kegan Paul.

Malcolm, R.R. (1992). As if: the phenomenon of not learning. In R. Anderson (ed.) *Clinical Lectures on Klein and Bion*. London and New York: Routledge.

Mitchell, J. (1974). *Psychoanalysis and Feminism*. London: Allen Lane.

Money-Kyrle, R. (1968). Cognitive development. *International Journal of Psycho-Analysis* 49, 691–698.

Piontelli, A. (1992). *From Foetus to Child: An Observational and Psychoanalytic Study*. London and New York: Tavistock/Routledge.

Rosenfeld, H.A. (1965). *Psychotic States: A Psychoanalytical Approach*. London: Hogarth Press. Reprinted by Maresfield Reprints, 1982.

Samuels, A. (1989). *The Plural Psyche: Personality, Morality and the Father*. London and New York: Tavistock/Routledge.

Segal, H. (1973). *Introduction to the Work of Melanie Klein*. London: Hogarth Press and Institute of Psycho-Analysis.

Segal, H. (1986). *The Work of Hanna Segal: A Kleinian Approach to Clinical Practice*. London: Free Associations/Maresfield Library.

Steiner, J. (ed.) (1989). *The Oedipus Complex Today*. London: Karnac Books.

Steiner, J. (1993). *Psychic Retreats: Pathological Organisations in Psychotic, Neurotic and Borderline Patients*. London and New York: Routledge.

Stern, D.N. (1985). *The Interpersonal World of the Infant: A View from Psychoanalysis and Developmental Psychology*. New York: Basic Books.

Widzer, M.E. (1993). Book Review: *Fathers and their Families* (edited by S.H. Cath, A. Gurwitt and L. Ginsberg). *Journal of the American Psychoanalytic Association* 41, 288–290.

5

LETTING FATHERS IN

Maureen Marks

Introduction

Winnicott reminded us that there is no baby without a mother (Winnicott, 1958). He also said that usually "it depends on what mother does about it whether father does or does not get to know his baby" (Winnicott, 1957, p. 81). I would add: and how much and in what way the baby does or does not get to know its father. In this chapter I discuss some of the difficulties women may have in promoting their baby's relationship with the father and those that men may have in taking on the role of an involved father. In order to think about these difficulties it becomes apparent that we need to know what fathers are for. I suggest that the presence of a sexual father and mother couple, in each of the couple's minds, determines both the extent to which a woman will welcome her sexual partner into the relationship she has with their infant, and whether or not he will be able to become involved. This configuration, in each of the partners' minds, will affect whether or not their child can have in its mind a linked mother and father. It also lays the ground for the development in the child of a certain creative kind of mind and the capacity as an adult and parent to welcome a sexual and potent father.

There is considerable variety, both historically and culturally, in fathers' involvement with their children. In recent years in the Western world the role of fathers in the family has been changing significantly. In the modern, Western, nuclear family, mothers and fathers spend much more time together than they did in the past and their roles are much less differentiated. Women no longer need to rely entirely on their husbands for material support or for obtaining power and status. Likewise, men now have social permission to be actively involved in parenting, and increasingly want to be given greater access to their children. Fathers are encouraged to attend antenatal classes, to be present at the delivery, help with childcare. However, along with this lessening of parental role definition, increasing numbers of women are bringing up children on their own, either because of marital breakdown and consequent marital separation, usually initiated by the woman, or because women are deciding to have children without partners in the first place. In the latter, the relationship between the child's parents may be limited to the sexual contact which created the child or there may be no direct contact with him at all – the father's contribution being merely to provide sperm.

In contrast, in a non-Western country like Japan, women usually stop work when they get married, divorce is still relatively uncommon, and parenthood outside marriage is very rare. For Japanese couples the role of mother and father is very clear-cut. It is customary for pregnant women to return to their family homes to have their babies seven or eight months after conception. After delivery, mother and infant are looked after by the woman's mother, and return to the marital home and husband/father when the baby is a couple of months old. This tradition, *satogaeribunben*, is still not uncommon, although now grandmothers may go to their daughters' homes instead. The husband's place in the family is very much one of being on the outside or absent. For example, mother and infant sleep together, usually in the same futon, always in the same room, until the child is at least three and often five years old. The husband sleeps in a different room during this time. He spends little time with his family, working very long hours and returning home late each evening.

One major difference between these two cultures is the extent to which the social situation *demands* that a father and a linked parental couple are included in the new family configuration, and hence the extent to which each of the couple and the infant are exposed to this situation. In the Western nuclear family we expect that fathers should be involved, in Japan they are excluded. This means that the social pressure on each of the marital couple to tolerate father's inclusion is currently greater in the West than it is in Japan. In Japan, mother and infant are not required to negotiate the difficulties encountered in including father. Nor is father – he does not expect to be included and stays away. Couples stay together even though, or because, they do not see much of each other and may no longer have a sexual relationship. These are two examples of ways in which fathers are excluded: in the West, couples separate, in the East they stay together but lead separate lives. However, the upshot is the same – the child remains in a close relationship with the mother from which the father is excluded.

What makes the existence of fathers tolerable, which both these cultures, in their different ways, exemplify, and what are the consequences for children when fathers are excluded? I will illustrate the psychodynamics involved by describing a particular psychic configuration in which the arrival of their baby is experienced by the procreative couple as potentially catastrophic. This configuration involves difficulties in each of the couple tolerating the existence of a father and of a creative couple. I will discuss, first, how an individual's experience of his or her own father and the parental couple is a precursor to this difficulty in adult life. In turn, the experience of father is influenced by not only the actual father and actual parental couple but also by the mother and father in the individual's mother's mind, and this itself will be a consequence of the mother's own experience of the father and parental couple in her mother's mind and so on, back through the generations. It is considered that these inter-generational psychic configurations have important consequences for each generation's capacity for generativity, both physically and cognitively.

Fathers and childbirth

There comes a time in the intimate relationship between a man and woman, which I will refer to for convenience as a marital relationship to imply some degree of formal commitment and/or permanence, when the couple decide to have a child. Each of them has entered into their existing relationship with a way of relating that has enabled them to stay together and to reach this point of creating a baby. To establish this much, consciously or more probably uncon-sciously, they have met certain needs in each other and some kind of equilibrium has been achieved. I want to consider the problems in being parents which stem from the move from this equilibrium, especially when it has been predominantly a pre-Oedipal, two-person relationship, to one which involves three persons, with the arrival of a child.

The process I want to discuss starts before the baby is born, but the period when this triangular aspect of parenting is perhaps most difficult and experienced with greatest intensity is probably in the first month or so after the infant's birth. The pattern of relating which is established at this time is likely to continue, so that by the time Oedipal conflicts are encountered they are likely to be negotiated in a manner similar to that used to negotiate early postnatal difficulties; likewise, the problems of puberty and those when the child has become an adult and confronts its own difficulties with parenting. It is likely, too, that the same difficulties will resurface, albeit with some diminishment of intensity, depending on how much the couple have learned from experience, with the birth of subsequent children.

Essentially, the task for the mother, father and infant involves tolerating the link between two people they desire and which excludes them. This situation cannot be harmonious. This is because the links are not identical. First, bio-logically, each link is unique. The infant began life inside mother and continues to feed from her after birth. Likewise, the sexual link, based on difference, between mother and father has a physical reality and this link between difference usually created the infant in the first place. The infant does not have the equipment to have sexually successful contact with its parents and thus create itself. Second, what each person wants is inherently different. Laplanche and Pontalis (1973) point out that the child's experience of the Oedipal triangle does not involve only the child's desires but also the unconscious desires of both parents, seduction, and the relations between the parents . . . it is the different types of relation between the three points of the triangle which – at least as much as any parental image – are destined to be internalised and to survive in the structure of the personality.

(Laplanche and Pontalis, 1973, p. 286)

Note, too, that it is the father and infant who are at risk of exclusion. Mother *is* the queen bee. She could, if she wishes, concentrate on the baby, leaving no room for the father; or she could, if she wishes, concentrate on the father and leave no room for the baby. The point is that each individual's task is different. The mother's is allowing the father to have a relationship with the infant whilst managing two intense relationships herself (Balint, 1993); the father's is tolerating his exclusion from mother's with infant and at the same time continuing in the one he has with his wife, as well as developing a new one with his infant.

Third, the parents' capacity to negotiate this configuration will be influenced by their own early unconscious experience of their own parents' unconscious communications. I emphasise here the unconscious nature of these early interactions because the most profound communications between parents and their very young infants are essentially pre-verbal, primitive, and unelaborated. That is, the parents are not so much identified with their own parents at this time since they have introjected their un-thought about and hence un-understood fears and attitudes, and these therefore tend to be acted out without conscious awareness. The parents' parents can therefore be uncannily present at this time and influence the next generation's capacity to adjust to their new family situation (cf. Balint, 1993; Feldman, 1989).

Mother's mediation of father

The mother, father and parental couple in the new mother's mind have particular impact and will influence the way her infant experiences father. There is no father without the child's mother, and the father–infant relationship has to be understood in the context of the mother's relationships with the father and with the child and how she thinks about and conducts these relationships. The mother's relationship with the child's father will partly be influenced by her expectations, conscious and unconscious, about the role of the father. In turn, these expectations will have been influenced by how she experienced her own father, as mediated by her own mother, and so on, back through the generations. This is important because the infant's experience of the father, whatever his actuality, is modified by how the mother presents the father to their infant. It would seem, then, that an idea of father is an idea of a relationship that starts, not with the father and his infant but with a father and mother and a mother and infant, and behind this generations of mother–father–infant relationships (cf. "the child's super-ego is in fact constructed on the model not of its parents but its parents' super-ego" – Freud, 1933, p. 67). How and whether a woman can make room for the father is likely to be influenced by this configuration.

What are fathers for?

I want to discuss certain psychodynamic factors which may make the recognition and inclusion of fathers difficult. What does having a father provide? Is there something unique about the experience of a father that is important to our psychological structure? It is in understanding these issues that we can begin to understand how women's unconscious attitudes about fathers and fathering may mediate not only the extent to which fathers can be involved with their children but also the extent to which the children can themselves develop into creative adults who are able to allow a father existence.

A second object

Fathers provide children and their mothers with an object, other than the mother, and this helps the mother and infant to dis–identify from their symbiotic merged relationship. That is, the father is a child's primary experience of someone other than the mother (Mahler *et al.*, 1975), an antidote to too much mothering (Raphael–Leff, 1991), and the child has an important place in the mind of someone else other than the mother. It is a process which starts before the child is born. When the mother thinks of the child inside her, if she and her partner are together having the child, she thinks of a child who also exists in someone else's mind. This means that even before the child is born it has an existence which is separate from her. Later, it means that the child experiences an object which has a separate existence. This has consequences for both the mother and child. It means that the mother can risk forgetting her child, even risk hating her child – she can hand him over (in her mind) to the father. The knowledge that someone else is thinking of and involved with the child frees the mother from her infant. It also frees the infant from the mother. It means that the child will have space to experience himself, can risk hating the mother, can even risk killing her in his mind, because there is someone else there to keep him alive.

Many of the very depressed mothers admitted to the psychiatric mother and baby unit have great difficulty in giving their babies room to experience themselves or anyone else. They carry them around, are reluctant to hand over their care, and tend to their slightest sound. They can't stop thinking about them. They are taken over by them. The idea that the baby may sometimes want and need room to experience himself (hunger, aloneness) gives them some relief and they can sometimes then begin to share the care of the child; as they become less bound up with the infant they begin to feel less depressed.

Mother and infant need someone else to intervene to prevent them from remaining stuck in a merged, claustrophobic, potentially murderous relationship. Without this, the child's psychic individuation may become impeded, with consequences for its cognitive and emotional development. Child development research in the States has found that infants identify pictures of their fathers and began to generalise "father" to refer to a picture of any male at an earlier age than for mothers (see Gunsberg, 1982). This capacity for symbolic representation depends on the development of an ability to discriminate an other from the self and then to represent mentally, in its absence, that other. The earlier symbolising of fathers is thought to be due to the combined effect of fathers being absent more than mothers and of mothers facilitating the symbolising process by referring to the father in his absence. From a different stance, this process could be described as the mother containing the infant's anxieties about absence and the mental space this leaves so that it becomes possible for the child to think about the father as existing but absent, rather than evacuate the unthought about experience of absence (Bion, 1962). The father here is someone important to the child and the mother, but who is more distant or more often absent than the mother, a combination of which may be necessary before a readiness in the child to symbolise becomes a capacity to do so.

Thus, having a father means that there is someone other than the mother emotionally involved with the infant, and this has a number of important consequences for the mother and infant. He provides the mother and infant with some relief from each other, gives weight to the infant's separate reality and may also influence the development of the infant's capacity to symbolise.

A male second object

But does this have to be the father, or could it be anyone who is close to and involved with mother and child – for example, an extended family member or friend? Does it even need to be male? It is widely held that a child needs close experience of both sexes filling clearly defined sex roles to acquire the idea of what is male/masculine and what is not male (i.e. female/feminine). This view usually starts with some concept of what is purely "male" (for example, aggression and activity) and purely "female" (for example, indulgence and passivity). Paternal attitudes and behaviour and their effects on the child's development are said to differ from maternal ones in that they structure the child's inborn predispositions to activity and motility – for example, the father's mode of interacting with and handling the child is more active and aggressive (Money and Ehrhardt, 1972; Kestenberg *et al.*, 1982).

Developmental psychologists who have studied father–infant interactions have shown that the father–infant relationship is not equivalent to the mother–infant one. To start with, fathers spend less time with their infants. When they *are* with them, the interactions appear to be more active and exciting than mother–infant ones. For example, Brazelton *et al.* (1979) studied child–father and child–mother interactions at intervals during the first six months in face-to-face play situations. The fathers' interactions were described as "heightened and playful" compared to the mothers' which were more "smoothly modulated and contained". Lamb (1981) reports that fathers are more inclined to engage in physically stimulating and unpredictable play than mothers. Lamb also makes an interesting distinction between infant *attachment* behaviours (e.g. crying or asking to be held) and *affiliative* ones (e.g. smiling and vocalising), which he suggests are less focused on specific attachment figures. He reports that infants are attached to both parents but that they prefer their mothers when distressed. In contrast, on measures of affiliative behaviour they tend to show a preference for fathers during the first two years of life.

These accounts indicate how the father's more active and affiliative *behaviour* – masculine(?) behaviour – with the child might influence attitudes and sex-role identification; but there is nothing unique to the father in this – it could be any man who is intimately involved in the family. Second, in all these accounts, implied but not made explicit, is that the impact of the father on the infant is one involving relationships (inside–outside, merged–separate, present–absent, male–female). And once you consider internal objects and the relationships between them, it becomes evident that one feature which distinguishes the infant's father from any other adult is that the father has an intimate and sexual relationship with the infant's mother, a relationship of which the child's very existence is usually a consequence. How might the father's location in this sexual/procreative context be important to the mother and infant?

Fathers and maternal postnatal psychiatric breakdown

An understanding of certain psychodynamic factors sometimes found in mothers who suffer a psychiatric breakdown after childbirth helps to illuminate the function of a father who is linked sexually to the infant's mother.

One parental situation which seems to lead to particular difficulty in negotiating the new family structure is when mothers (and fathers) had had very close relationships with their own mothers and these were relationships from which fathers had been excluded. Usually, the new couple's relationship replicates the one they'd had with mother – they are a unit, as one, twins. However, as the woman's pregnancy progresses and she becomes increasingly absorbed in her relationship with the foetus, the man becomes more and more excluded and different. Not only is she in her own world with the infant, but the very fact of the pregnancy makes their prenatal denial of the difference between them no longer tenable. (Some men cope with this by identifying with the pregnant woman. They, too, are pregnant and may even get physical symptoms. I remember observing this in one couple. It was their first baby and he was very involved with the pregnancy, attending all the antenatal classes and so on. After delivery he became very busy at work, leaving early in the morning and returning late at night. His wife, left on her own for long hours with her child, became quite depressed.)

Once the child is born there are competing relationships. How is the woman to cope with being taken up with her baby and yet at the same time acknowledge the baby's father? Will she be able to allow her partner his involvement with the infant? Current patterns of relationship will be derived at least in part from past experience, particularly early experience with key figures, and with the arrival of the idea of a baby, then a foetus, then a separate baby, the influence of the new parents' own experience of parenting becomes particularly dominant.

Let me turn now to couples for whom having a child results in severe psychiatric breakdown in one of them (usually the mother). The research findings show that one of the consistent factors associated with postpartum psychotic breakdown in women is that of the marital relationship. For example, different studies have found that women who are dissatisfied with their partners (Marks *et al.*, 1992a), or whose partners are uncommunicative (Marks *et al.*, 1992b), or who have no partner (Kendell *et al.*, 1987), are also more likely to break down after childbirth. Women admitted to a psychiatric mother and baby unit are more likely to have partners who are similarly suffering symptoms of psychological distress than either partners of post-partum women without any psychiatric history or partners of non-parturient women admitted to psychiatric hospital (Lovestone and Kumar, 1993). Their partners are also more likely to have had a psychiatric illness in the past than men in the other two groups. Further, they are more likely to report difficulties in their early relationship with their own father (but not mother).

The picture which is beginning to emerge from research such as this suggests a *couple* for whom the experience of childbirth is particularly difficult, and that the difficulty may be in part related to a damaged representation of the role of the father and the parental couple in the minds of *both* parents. The common early experience appears to have been one in which the tie to the mother was very close and the father excluded or denigrated. For these couples, both mother and father experience considerable difficulty in negotiating the change in family structure that a new baby brings.

A case study

Elizabeth is a tiny, pale, child-like woman, in her early thirties, who became severely depressed about two weeks after the birth of her baby and spent the first year of her baby's life in mother and baby units away from her husband. The couple had difficulties in conceiving, and she had two attempts at in vitro fertilisation, finally becoming pregnant after trying for a baby for eight years. During her pregnancy she suffered very severe vomiting which lasted for four months. She says that she was ecstatic for the first two weeks after her baby was born but then started to become depressed and began to vomit again. At one year post-partum she was still depressed and vomiting, especially after visits home to her husband.

Elizabeth came from an apparently ordinary middle-class family consisting of a mother, father and an older brother. The father's mother also lived with them. Elizabeth's father hated his mother and her mother hated having her in the house. The mother said that she (the father's mother) was there when they returned from their honeymoon. Elizabeth described her childhood experience of her father as "not playing any part" in the children's upbringing. "We never got on with him, but it's never mentioned." She said that he worked long hours, that he drank too much, that he would always come home in a bad mood, irritable, because of the drink. When he arrived home – "He's here!" – her brother would go to his room. She would stay and sit with her mother. Together, they would "humour him for 5 minutes after he'd eaten his tea, then he'd go to sleep and not wake until 10 p.m. Then it didn't matter as it was time for me [Elizabeth] to go to bed." Apparently, this routine was always followed because "otherwise, no matter what, he'd end up rowing about something. Mum would say don't give him an opportunity, don't give him a reason. Mum would go to any lengths to avoid having a row. The number of times she would bite her tongue." So, the picture Elizabeth presents is that of an angry, potentially violent father, who played no part in the family.

I can't say what Elizabeth's father was like. But I get the impression that her mother may also have contributed to Elizabeth's impression of him and may also have discouraged her from having contact with him. For example, Elizabeth said that her father "never did anything, did no harm, but he's not a very warm person". She said that on Sunday evening he'd be all right, because he'd had his drink at lunchtime. However, she also told me that Sunday evenings was the time chosen by her mother to give her school tuition.

Elizabeth presents a picture of a man who has not left his mother but hates her, a wife/mother who can't enter into a relationship with her daughter and husband together, and who can't bear to allow her daughter to have her own relationship with the father – a father who is experienced as at one and the same time threatening, intruding ("He's here!"), weak, to be humoured and disavowed (not playing any part). The household is one in which there is intense, pervasive, but unexpressed hatred, and in the centre of this hatred the calm pool of mother and daughter sitting together. When the father wakes, his daughter goes to sleep: the husband and wife's potentially violent relationship is thereby also disavowed.

When Elizabeth first left home to go to college she gave up after one term and went back home to her mother. She said she had been too lonely. Eventually, at 21 years, she managed to move to a different town, with a girlfriend who had arranged the move for her. Mother didn't want her to do this – she didn't like the girlfriend. Within three months of moving out from home Elizabeth had met her husband. She described it as a gradual attachment – "He's not a movie star – he grew on me." They married after a year and apart from the difficulties about conception things went well until the pregnancy began. Now she describes with sadness the deteriorating relationship with her husband, saying she's becoming aware that she is doing the same as her mother did. She describes her husband as "highly strung" and says that he doesn't like getting angry because he thinks it's the end of the world. Elizabeth's relationship with her husband seems to replicate the one she had had with her mother. Like her mother, and unlike her father, he can't bear getting angry. She has now become the one who is angry, but has to vomit this out.

The couple's capacity to tolerate parenthood

McDougall (1989), discussing patients who somatise, has remarked on a psychic configuration in which the paternal imago appears damaged or even totally absent from the patient's inner psychic world, usually because the sex and presence of the father seem to have played only a little role in the mother's life. When the mother cannot bear to relinquish a fusional relationship with the infant, the infant establishes a feeling of separate identity only with considerable difficulty. McDougall highlights the importance of the father in providing the mother with sexual and narcissistic satisfaction, because otherwise the infant will feel required to fulfil this desired but impossible task. Under these circumstances the image of the internal mother becomes extremely dangerous because

> When there is no fantasy of the father's penis playing a libidinally and narcissistically enhancing role in the mother's life, the mental representation of the mother's sex . . . becomes that of a limitless void . . . constantly enticing yet at the same time terrifying.
>
> (McDougall, 1989, p. 45)

According to McDougall, an inevitable consequence of this state of affairs is that the mother is experienced as forbidding the child to think. Certain highly charged thoughts which the mother cannot bear become totally forbidden. Again and again, Elizabeth expressed her anger that the difficulties with her father have never been acknowledged. She says "It's like it never happened. That he's been a good dad. It's not discussed. It's never mentioned. Things are always presented on the basis that everything's wonderful." In Elizabeth's case thinking is experienced as hateful, violent, possibly catastrophic – it could be the end of the world – it is intolerable and has to be vomited out.

Evidence from infant development research and clinical work with adults suggests that parents' own early experience of the conjunction of father with mother has implications not just for psycho-sexual development but for the development of certain cognitive and social capacities as well, and it is all these features together which in turn influence the extent to which the new mother and new father can survive the triangular family configuration and allow a father existence.

For example, Brazelton, who extensively studied parent–infant interactions in the first year of life, concluded that the triadic nature of the infant's contact with parents is an important feature of development: it provides a situation in which stable expectable responses are different for each parent and this allows a particular type of learning to take place; namely, one which involves managing relations between more than one other, who in turn are influenced by each other, in relation to the self (Brazelton *et al.*, 1979).

Abelin (1975), an American associate of Margaret Mahler, described the process whereby the infant apprehends and internalises the relationship between his parents as a prototypical experience which is both traumatic and organising. In his infant-observation work he noted that the infant's rivalry with parents can be seen as early as the second half year. He also suggests that before that the father is dimly perceived as a rival, but the perception may immediately be pushed aside by the child. (Unconsciously perceived; un-understood?) He argues that the child's experience of himself as a self develops from this situation. Previous to this the child could experience himself only in relation to someone. In the triangular situation, the child notices the father and mother relating to each other. The child feels left out. With nobody to relate to his experience of himself becomes suspended. He can only do so by imagining himself in his rival's place: "There must be an I like him wanting her." Abelin suggests that it is in this situation that the child first sees himself. "Unconscious imitation of the symbiotic object becomes a wish for the object and simultaneously a discovery of the self" (p. 294). The mutual relationships between these three mental images herald the beginning of reciprocity and constitute the foundation of the thinking processes. That is, there is a structural symmetry between cognitive development and psychosocial and sexual development. He adds that often fatherless boys have a pre-Oedipal, all or nothing quality to their relationships and that certain ego functions are also impaired (Neurbauer, 1960; Burgner, 1985). I would add likewise fatherless girls, and that both boys *and* girls will in turn find it difficult to make room for the fathers of their own children.

Britton (1989) similarly discussed the importance to the child of what he terms the "primal family triangle". The child experiences two links connecting it separately with each parent and is also confronted with a third link which excludes it. Britton argues that if the link between the parents can be tolerated (and this involves allowing the conjunction of love and hate) then it becomes a prototype for a relationship in which the child is a witness and not a participant. Relationships can be observed, and conversely the child can then envisage being observed. Like Abelin, Britton suggests that "this provides us with a capacity to see ourselves in interaction with others, for entertaining another point of view while retaining our own, for reflecting on ourselves whilst being ourselves".

Feldman (1989) also believed that there is a relationship between the quality of thinking and the nature of the parental couple represented in the person's mind. He suggests that the development of the capacity to allow thoughts and ideas to interact in a creative way rests on the child having an internal model of parental intercourse that is on balance a creative activity. If the model of the parental couple is one that is dangerous and destructive then thinking will be perverse or inhibited (Elizabeth's "It's never mentioned."). Feldman suggests that the child's internal model of the parental couple will be based in part on the infant's accurate perceptions and intuitions about his parents' relationship, on the child's own phantasies and projections, and on projections from his parents of their internal model of the parental couple. Both Britton and Feldman suggest, from clinical work with analytic patients, that when the internal model of the parental couple is absent or impaired, the capacity to think creatively – to allow ideas and thoughts to interact and to draw ideas to their conclusion – also becomes impaired. Second, both Britton and Feldman report that for such patients the idea of parental conjugation is hateful, dangerous and associated with imminent catastrophe and disintegration.

Conclusion

There being a (sexual) father and mother, at least in the mother's mind, lays the ground for the development of a certain creative kind of mind (cognitive and social) in her offspring. What might be the impact on this process of the various new family configurations which have arisen in the Western world in recent years, particularly those in which fathers are absent or impaired? As yet this is still unclear, but, as Mitchell (1998) has pointed out, there must be consequences. She cites the examples of the "vagina man" (Limentani, 1989) and "womanliness as a masquerade" (Rivière, 1929) where apparent heterosexual activity is actually a disguised return to a fused mother–infant relationship in which the father is psychically absent. She adds that such relationships may work well as long as "fathering" (actual or symbolic) is not required. If the couple do have offspring these will be experienced not as the father's but rather as the result of the mother's betrayal.

It would appear that the early experience of a father and mother, their conjunction and difference, contributes to the development of a psychological configuration which experiences the bringing together of difference as life-enhancing and makes possible the creation of new physical and psychic life. The difficulty for women is one of tolerating the tension that this inevitably creates. It is so much easier to withdraw into the seductively cosy world of sameness and safety. The difficulty for men is to bear the fact that they cannot be mothers, never have a baby inside them, that they are on the outside sometimes, and not fly off into the world of work or new relationships. If both partners can tolerate the conjunction of their differences and allow for the possibility that something new and worth while might emerge, not only their own lives but also those of their children will be enhanced.

For couples who have not been allowed to experience a father the arrival of their child can be psychically dangerous. If the new parent identifies with the baby then each is forced to acknowledge the baby in fusion with the mother, the father excluded, and, at the same time, the father and mother in their fusion, the baby excluded. The feelings of exclusion and loss, hatred and envy of the fused pair, being a third person looking on, which each parent has gone to such lengths to deny, are unavoidable but intolerable. The only solution for some is an ablation of the father, or mental breakdown.

References

Abelin, E.L. (1975) Some further observations and comments on the earliest role of the father. *International Journal of Psycho-Analysis*, 56, 293–302.

Balint, E. (1993) *Before I was I*. Free Association Books, London.

Bion, W.R. (1962) *Learning From Experience*. William Heineman, London.

Britton, R. (1989) The missing link: parental sexuality in the Oedipus complex. In: R. Britton, M. Feldman, and E. O'Shaughnessy (eds) *The Oedipus Complex Today*. Karnac Books, London, pp. 83–102.

Brazelton, T.B., Yogman, M.W., Als, H. and Tronick, E. (1979) The infant as a focus for family reciprocity. In: M. Lewis and L.A. Rosenblum (eds) *The Child and Its Family*. Plenum, New York.

Burgner, M. (1985) The oedipal experience: effects on development of an absent father. *International Journal of Psycho-Analysis*, 66, 311–320.

Feldman, M. (1989) The Oedipus complex: manifestations in the inner world and the therapeutic situation. In: R. Britton, M. Feldman, and E. O'Shaughnessy (eds) *The Oedipus Complex Today*. Karnac Books, London, pp. 103–128.

Freud, S. (1933) New Introductory Lectures on Psychoanalysis. *Vol. 22 Standard Edition*, Hogarth Press, London, 1964.

Gunsberg, L. (1982) Selected critical review of psychological investigations of the early father–infant relationship. In: S.H. Cath, A.R. Gurwitt, and J.M. Ross (eds) *Father and Child: Developmental and Clinical Perspectives*. Little Brown and Co., Boston, pp. 65–82.

Kendell, R.E., Chalmers, J.L. and Platz, C. (1987) Epidemiology of puerperal illness. *British Journal of Psychiatry*, 150, 662–673.

Kestenberg, J.S., Marcus, H., Sossin, K.M. and Stevenson, R. (1982) The development of paternal attitudes. In: S.H. Cath, A.R. Gurwitt, and J.M. Ross (eds) *Father and Child: Developmental and Clinical Perspectives*. Little Brown and Co., Boston, pp. 204–217.

Lamb, M.E. (1981) The development of father–infant relationships. In: M.E. Lamb (ed.) *The Role of the Father in Child Development*. John Wiley and Sons, New York, pp. 459–488.

Laplanche, J. and Pontalis, J.B. (1973) *The Language of Psychoanalysis*. Hogarth Press, London.

Limentani, A. (1989) To the limits of male heterosexuality, the vagina man. In: *Between Freud and Klein*. Free Association Books, London.

Lovestone, S. and Kumar, R. (1993) Postnatal psychiatric illness: the impact on spouses. *British Journal of Psychiatry*, 163, 210–216.

McDougall, J. (1989) *Theatres of the Body*. Free Association Books, London.

Mahler, M.S., Pine, F. and Bergman, A. (1975) *The Psychological Birth of an Infant*. Basic Books, New York.

Marks, M.N., Wieck, A., Checkley, S.A. and Kumar, R. (1992a) Contribution of psychological and social factors to psychotic and non-psychotic relapse after childbirth in women with previous histories of affective disorder. *Journal of Affective Disorders*, 29, 253–264.

Marks, M.N., Wieck, A., Seymour, A., Checkley, S.A. and Kumar, R. (1992b) Women whose mental illnesses recur after childbirth and partners' levels of Expressed Emotion during late pregnancy. *British Journal of Psychiatry*, 161, 211–216.

Mitchell, J. (1998) Sexuality psychoanalysis and social changes. *News* (Summer). Institute of Psychoanalysis, London.

Money, J.M. and Ehrhardt, A.A. (1972) *Man and Woman, Boy and Girl: The Differentiation and Dimorphism of Gender Identity from Conception to Maturity*. Johns Hopkins University Press, Baltimore.

Neubauer, P.B. (1960) The one-parent child and his oedipal development. *Psychoanalytic Study of the Child*, 15, 286–309.

Raphael-Leff, J. (1991) *Psychological Processes of Childbearing*. Chapman and Hall, London.

Rivière, J. (1929) Womanliness as a masquerade. In: A. Hughes (ed.) *The Inner World of Joan Riviere*. Karnac Books, London.

Winnicott, D.W. (1957) *The Child and The Family*. Tavistock Publications, London.

Winnicott, D.W. (1958) Primary maternal preoccupation. In: *Collected Papers: Through Paediatrics to Psychoanalysis*. Tavistock Publications, London, pp. 300–305.

106

6

FOREVER FATHER'S DAUGHTER

The Athene–Antigone complex

Ronald Britton

Introduction

In this chapter I want to describe a particular kind of relationship of women to their fathers that is disadvantageous to their development, inasmuch as it is at the expense of their relationship to their mothers and hence to their eventual relationship with themselves as mature women. I think that it derives from difficulties in their infantile maternal relationship and a compensatory idealisation of their relationship with the father.

This may seem life saving, and indeed it may be so in some cases during the early stages of development, but if it is perpetuated it becomes itself an obstacle to their fulfilment as women. The particular relationship I have in mind I call the Athene–Antigone complex.

I suggest that we can regard Athene, motherless, triumphant progeny of 'a great father', and Antigone, motherless supporter of 'a great father in decline', as personifications of psychic attitudes that women may adopt as their self-definition: forever father's daughter. In either position their sense of self-importance is derived from being father's daughter and from regarding this as the most significant of all possible relationships. In the position of Athene the importance is derived from being the incarnation of her father's ideas; as Antigone it comes from being her father's indispensable handmaid and guardian. Some women occupy these positions permanently, thus making them the basis of an enduring character formation. Others do so only at particular times or in particular parts of their lives. In both of these positions the quintessential self-definition is that of being 'father's daughter'. The woman does not define herself as her mother's daughter, nor does she as a sister, nor as a wife, and certainly not as a mother – even though she might have any or all of these relationships. In this belief system it is the father who is presumed to be of importance, and his daughter derives her significance by being the reincarnation of his power, like Athene, or the guarantor of his posterity, like Antigone.

The goddess Athene was born 'fully armed' out of her father Zeus' head, to become his 'champion' and the personification of his wisdom.[1] Antigone was motherless in a different sense; as child of the incestuous union of Oedipus with his mother Jocasta, her own mother was in fact her paternal grandmother, and her destiny was to become guide and support to the ageing, blind Oedipus, like a child mothering a father. The name Antigone in Greek can be read as meaning 'in place of a mother' (Graves 1992).

Margaret Thatcher was a notable twentieth-century example in politics of a woman who appeared to regard herself as an Athene. This mythic identification has occurred to others, notably Leo Abse in his 'politician's psycho-biography' of the former Prime Minister (1989). As he pointed out 'no acknowledgement of indebtedness is ever made to her mother'. He quotes her as saying 'I just owe everything to my father' (ibid. p. 23), and he wrote 'the contemptible mother is blotted out; even as Athena – goddess of war – sprang fully armed from the head of Zeus, so Thatcher claims a parthenogenic birth' (ibid.).

Anna Freud is an obvious example of 'an Antigone'. Indeed, Freud himself referred to his daughter Anna as Antigone, as increasingly he relied on her to communicate for him and to organise his professional life in those years when his cancer of the mouth affected his speech and his advancing age restricted his mobility. Wordsworth similarly regarded his daughter Dorothea as his 'Antigone': she became his eyes and his amanuensis in the years when his sight deteriorated. Anna Freud never married, which troubled her father, whereas in Dorothea's case Wordsworth only belatedly and reluctantly gave his blessing for her marriage. Both men saw themselves as mother's 'chosen' son and made some conscious identification of themselves with Oedipus (Britton 1998).

Literature provides us with many examples of women with an Athene or Antigone complex. In Ibsen's *Hedda Gabler* we can see General Gabler's daughter, the proud possessor of his pistols, as an 'Athene', and it is not difficult to see Jane Eyre as the blinded Mr Rochester's 'Antigone' in the novel of that name. If one is to do the obvious and peruse Shakespeare for examples, the romantic comedy *The Tempest* offers us Prospero and Miranda as the wishful models of omniscient father and motherless, dutiful daughter safely marooned on the island of the father's magical powers. In contrast to the romance of fatherhood in *The Tempest*, Shakespeare gives us the tragic model of fathers and daughters. In *King Lear* his play offers us the breakdown of the world King Lear meant to be constructed out of father–daughter bondage. In that play there are two aspiring 'Athene's' (Regan and Goneril) and one obvious 'Antigone' (Cordelia). It is, however, the refusal of *any* of the motherless daughters to play Antigone to the satisfaction of their father that seems to provoke Lear into madness.

The way the two mythic figures can be linked is concretely represented by the medal given to Anna Freud by the International Psychoanalytic Association in 1971 at the Vienna Congress. This was specially crafted to commemorate the occasion of her return to the city she had shared with her father. It consisted of a silver ring with a Roman coin in the centre bearing the head of Athene and had inscribed on the rim 'Auf meine treue Anna–Antigone gestützt. Sigmund Freud' (Rangell 1984: p. 39).

Apollo, brother of Athene, regarded his sister as the only woman fit for office by virtue of being her father's clone unsullied by intrauterine residence. He also regarded all mankind as essentially the progeny of the father: the mother's role being simply that of incubator. A similar disparagement of womanhood and of the female body to that of Apollo is at the core of both the Athene and Antigone positions. In the former there is a triumphant denial, by phallic identification, of being an ordinary woman, and in the latter, a more subtle female denigration via masochistic, self-disparagement. With their phallic idealisation and their devaluation of femininity, they exemplify the theory of the 'female castration' or 'masculinity complex'. In my opinion Freud was accurate in his description of this complex as something that can be found in the analyses of some women, but he was misguided in regarding it a part of normal female development. I go further and suggest that his two analyses of his daughter Anna played a significant part in his adoption of his new theory of normal female sexual development and his unusual insistence on it.

That Freud analysed his daughter seems shocking to any reader familiar with modern analysis, but we need to bear in mind that it was not so at the time. The transference theories we inherited from that first generation changed analytic practice profoundly, but as with most radical discoveries it is not the generation that discovers them that realises their full practical implications but their successors. Nevertheless, I feel apprehensive writing about Freud's misguided attempt to both help and train his daughter – especially as I am emphasising its unfortunate consequences for the subsequent history of psychoanalysis. It is absolutely necessary that we return to re-examine these now historical events armed with documentary knowledge and current psychoanalytic concepts. However, it is not a comfortable thing to do, particularly as we live in a culture of disparagement which is hungry for any information that might be used to discredit rather than inform.

Criticisms of Freud's new views on female sexuality from within the psychoanalytic profession followed quickly on the heels of his papers. As Joan Rivière pointed out, in her stern criticism of her former analyst's new theory, it displaced all his other ideas about women (1934: pp. 126–129). It also displaced his earlier theories of the 'Oedipus complex' and puts aside his notion of the centrality of the primal scene that had led him to suggest that this might be based on an innate phylogenetic phantasy. It even led him to write 'it is only in male children that there occurs the fateful conjunction of love for the one parent and hatred of the other as a rival' (Freud 1931: p. 229). It was as if he had forgotten his very first words on the phenomenon, written in a letter to Fleiss before it had even gained the name 'Oedipus complex': 'This death wish is directed in sons against their father and in daughters against their mother' (Freud 1897: p. 255).

Thanks to the excellent biography of Anna Freud (Young-Bruehl 1988), and the careful exploration by Blass (1993) of Anna's first analytic paper, 'Beating Fantasies and Daydreams', we have access to her analysis in an unusual way. Anna Freud herself was the analytic patient whom she presented as the subject of the paper she gave to the Viennese Psychoanalytic Society in 1922. Her father had already produced a paper on the same subject ('A Child is Being Beaten') in 1919, and it is clear that Anna's analysis with him, which began in 1918, was at least one of its sources. At the onset of this first analysis Anna wrote a poem with the lines:

In my own service, I would sing my soul
David would I be, and King Saul as well.
(Young-Bruehl 1988: p. 82)

It is clear that she imagined playing David to her father's King Saul from her daydreams; what this poem suggests is that she imagines in the process becoming a new version of King Saul herself. This Athenesque fantasy at the beginning of her first analysis, at a time when Freud was monarch of all he surveyed in the psychoanalytic kingdom, seems expectantly triumphant. However, following the tragic blow of the death of his favourite daughter Sophie and the ensuing death of her son, his beloved grandchild; the development of his own cancer; the defection of his analytic favourite Ferenczi; and the sudden death of his ablest supporter Abraham, Freud's state of mind was very different. Anna's position then became Antigonesque; she was the support of the ageing seer and the guardian of the grave.

The beating fantasies described in Anna Freud's paper are the masturbatory fantasies of a girl in which a boy is beaten by a man. Her paper discusses the relationship between these infantile masochistic fantasies and the later development of the girl's daydreams or 'nice stories'. These 'nice stories', however, are masochistic romances involving (for example) a knight who holds a boy prisoner in his castle and threatens torture which is never carried out, instead a reconciliation occuring. Anna Freud took the view that these daydreams were *sublimations* of the original masturbatory fantasies as they did not include sexual gratification and were resolved by forgiveness and reconciliation. She regarded the masturbation as the source of shame and guilt; unlike her, Freud regarded the guilt as derived from *the content* of the masturbatory fantasies. Neither of them notes this difference of opinion nor comments on their different views of the daydreams which Anna regarded as sublimation and a route to creativity, whereas in her father's account they are seen as disguised beating fantasies and a source of sexual gratification (Blass 1993: pp. 70–1). This difference of opinion on the reason for the guilt of masturbation and of the psychic value of daydreams seems to me like a forerunner of later sharply controversial differences between Anna Freud and Melanie Klein.

It seems clear from her beating fantasies and the 'nice stories' (daydreams), that in her wishful thinking Anna Freud saw herself as a boy in relation to a man. There is no mention of the 'girl's' mother at all in her paper. The paper Anna Freud wrote on herself was her membership paper, and Freud presided at the presentation in the Vienna Society. 'I will feel like Junius Brutus the elder when he had to judge his own son. Perhaps she is going to make a decisive step', he wrote to his friend Max Eitingon. As Elisabeth Young-Bruehl comments: 'Junius Brutus's son – so the legend has it – was executed after his father had ruled against him' (Young-Bruehl 1988: p. 108). So in this casual epistolary comment Freud makes Anna his son and puts her in the position she occupied as the young man of her daydreams, imprisoned by a knight fearing torture and condemnation only to be triumphantly reconciled.

Mahoney (1997: p. 49) implies that there was in the analysis an enactment of the 'beating phantasies' which were the subject of both of their papers. Increasingly attention has focused on the two analyses and the possible effects on Anna. In this chapter I am more concerned with the effect which analysing his daughter had on Freud's analytic theories of female sexuality. The female castration or masculinity complex, described by Janine Chasseguet-Smirgel as phallic monism (1976), was obviously a pronounced feature of Anna Freud's analysis. I suggest that this led to Freud making phallic monism the basis of a revised account of normal female sexual development. His theory rapidly became controversial within psychoanalysis and it has remained so ever since. It also made psychoanalysis seem unacceptable to feminists of both sexes, as Freud predicted it would. It seemed not only counterintuitive, but counter to the thrust of his own previous thinking about the Oedipus complex in the normal development of both sexes. My belief is that he espoused his new theory of female sexuality as a reaction to his analysis of his own daughter's psychopathology. Analysts, unless careful, are apt with particularly powerful or significant patients to take the patient's view of their idiosyncratic development as normative and not atypical, and to modify theory to conform with this.

At the time Anna Freud began her first analysis with her father in 1918 he was in the final great creative period of his psychoanalytic theorising. 'Mourning and Melancholia' lay behind him; 'The Ego and the Id' was soon to come, with his new dual theory of the instincts, his revision of his theory of anxiety and of the individual's ambivalent relationship to reality. By the time he took Anna into a second analysis in 1924 Freud was no longer the main source of new analytic theory. The new developments were originating from the most creative amongst his followers, and Vienna was no longer the single, psychoanalytic centre-point of psychoanalysis but part of an axis that included Berlin, Budapest and London. The first critique of Freud's theory was by Karen Horney in 1924 and it remains one of the most trenchant. She accepted Freud's description of the 'masculinity complex' in some women, but made clear she saw it as a deviation from normal development. Horney saw 'primary penis envy' in the girl as ubiquitous and inevitable as part of children's envious feelings about the parental couple and their mutual sexuality. 'Secondary penis envy', or the 'masculinity complex', she saw as a defensive organisation against Oedipal attachment to the father as the primary love object. Joan Rivière was to follow this critique with a complete dismissal of Freud's theory of female sexuality in her otherwise very favourable review of his 'New Introductory Lectures on Psychoanalysis' (Rivière 1934). In more recent times, in a notable re-examination and rejection of the theory, Janine Chasseguet-Smirgel contests Freud's claim that the young child of either sex is unaware of the vagina. She contrasts the picture of mother as a woman who lacks everything with the maternal imago of the mother as the woman who has everything (Chasseguet-Smirgel 1976). This latter figure came to the fore in the theories of Melanie Klein, based on her analysis of children that began in the early 1920s. It was attacked by Anna Freud, first from Vienna and then, following her father's death, with renewed force in London.

Melanie Klein's work with young children had, as Freud hoped child analysis would, confirmed a great many of the theories of childhood sexuality that had been based on adult analysis. However, they also added a great deal more theory and changed others. She made the primal scene – that is, the child's view of parental sexuality as witnessed and as imagined – as the opening act of the Oedipal drama. It was to be followed by homosexual and heterosexual fantasised entanglements between parent and child of either sex, hopefully not enacted but only imagined in masturbatory fantasies. The classical Oedipus complex was to be the climax, with a depressive anti-climax in a final act of restitution of the primal couple in which the child once more was to be the onlooker (Britton 1992). For Klein the usual situation of the girl was envy of her mother's possession inside her of the father's penis, together with the babies that in the girl's fantasies waited there. The double blow for the girl was to see her father satisfy her mother with his penis, which she did not possess, whilst aware that she did not have breasts and babies like her mother; nor, unlike her brother, did she have anything that mother did not have. In this scheme of things the wish underlying the girl's masculinity complex would be to take her father's penis away *from* her mother for herself. For the girl to see her mother as penis-less ('castrated') would therefore be to see her as damaged and robbed by the girl's wishes, leading to depressive anxiety and guilt. The masculinity complex in its triumphant Athenesque form would in this scenario be a manic denial of the mother's significance and a contemptuous dismissal of mothers as defective creatures. In the Antigone position the mother's significance is again denied and all concern is for the stricken father who, now that he no longer possesses his former magical phallic powers, is solely dependent on his daughter for his remaining life and for his memorial in death. Using the terminology which Anna Freud coined herself, the position of Athene can be seen as 'identification with the aggressor' and that of Antigone as 'altruistic surrender'. In Anna Freud's chapter on 'altruistic surrender' in *The Ego and the Mechanisms of Defence* (1936: p. 128), she describes herself in disguise as 'the governess'. The case of 'the governess' admirably illustrates what I am calling the Antigone position. Another analytic paper in which the case study is of the author herself in disguise (Hughes 1997), offers an excellent description of an aspiring Athene: Joan Rivière's 'Womanliness as a Masquerade' (Rivière 1929).

The Athene–Antigone complex in practice

If we regard Freud's female masculinity complex not as normal development but as a particular pathological organisation (Steiner 1987) we can examine our analytic experience with those women who manifest it in one way or another. I will base my description on a number of cases I have encountered in analysis and supervision. For reasons of confidentiality I will not single out any case and will emphasis those features that were common in otherwise disparate people.

My analytic experience suggests that a goodly number of women move into an Athene or Antigone position temporarily as part of the cyclical movements that occur within the onward movement of an analysis. A smaller number reside at one or other poles of this position for a large part of the time, and an even smaller number totally organise their lives, their belief systems and their relationships in conformity with it.

Freud (1931: p. 284) described three possibilities:

1 'The first leads to her turning her back on sexuality altogether.'
2 In the second, he wrote, 'she clings in obstinate self-assertion to her threatened masculinity: the hope of getting a penis sometimes is cherished to an incredibly late age and becomes the aim of her life, whilst the phantasy of really being a man, in spite of everything, often dominates long periods of her life'.
3 He describes the third as a 'very circuitous path' at the end of which she arrives at the 'normal feminine attitude' of 'the Oedipus complex in its feminine form'.

The first of these resembles what I have called 'Antigone's position' – a life without sex and in servitude to a man. The second could be called the 'Athene position'. The third and hopeful line, the 'very circuitous path' to a 'normal

113

feminine attitude', is the one we would like to see followed in the course of an analysis. On the way, such an analysis gives us an opportunity to gain further knowledge of these pathological organisations and to speculate on their origins.

My own experience is that whilst the patient is in Athene's position she forms an idealised transference of a particular kind. The analyst, if he is a man, is regarded as the source of wisdom and his thinking is given an erotic significance. The exchanges between analyst and patient are also given special significance, and thus the link between them is idealised. This link is also in fantasy a penis and the transactions of analysis are taken to be symbolic intercourse. This magical penis–link is felt to be a shared possession as long as the patient believes that there is *mutual* idealisation. It is essentially a form of manic defence, in which the claim of being omnipotent or omniscient is not made by the patient; nor is that of personally possessing the father's idealised penis. Athene is content to be the Sorcerer's Apprentice, Zeus' daughter, his 'right-hand man', God's only prophet, the goddess of wisdom. The claim to be omniscient, to be God, to possess the omnipotent penis, would lead to rapid disillusion or a drastic severance with reality. The attributive projection of this fantasied omnipotent penis/mind into the father, however, enables it to be preserved by nothing more drastic than hero worship and an illusion of mutual idealisation.

The collapse of this illusion does not lead to a sense of loss initially but to the fantasy of having been literally or symbolically 'castrated'. If the phallus is symbolically equated with the intellect the consequent feeling of castration is experienced as losing all mental potency, of being stupid. In the Athene–Antigone complex this state of castration is rapidly projected into the transference father who is then seen as infirm, impotent and in need of his daughter's ministrations. This can then be actualised in a life devoted to 'nun-like' service; in this the penis is not thought of as non-existent or unattainable but simply unclaimed, sacrificed in an act of sexual renunciation. It is then preserved as a voluntarily relinquished possibility or unclaimed possession. It is like the child of a nobleman renouncing his inherited title whilst preserving the sense of aristocratic entitlement. A life of devotion with the father but without sex can then be idealised. The analytic version of this is an 'altruistic surrender' to the analyst's perceived need to be provided with a grateful patient who does not need analytic potency to make her happy or well but whose satisfaction lies in the success of her ministration to the analyst's self-belief. His analytic blindness is compensated for by his devoted patient's self-analysis; the insights derived from this being laid at his feet. She is as George Eliot describes Dorothea in *Middlemarch*, someone who would have accepted as her husband the aged Milton after his blindness.

In all these scenarios the mother is missing. It has been suggested by a number of authors that the masculinity complex stems from early problems in the maternal relationship. This has proved to be so in all the cases of this kind that I have analysed or supervised. The appearance of a maternal transference and the recollection and working through of that troubled relationship has been a crucial part of the analysis as it moved towards a more ordinary Oedipus complex. In the Athene–Antigone complex the mother is missing in two ways: as the source of maternal love and understanding, and as a rival for the father's affections. And yet even with the father it is not really the relationship of parent and child that is idealised but that of husband and surrogate wife; not the lost infantile relationship that is hungered for but the relationship of the primal parental couple that can never be had.

Experience of analysing a number of patients has convinced me that for some people of either sex the infant–mother relationship, which most people long to re-experience, is imagined to be inferior to the relationship of the primal couple. This seems to be for reasons to do with the early infantile experience, and also with the childhood mother's idealised internal relationship with her own childhood father and now her husband. The usual idealisation of infancy, with its accompanying dream of a return to the bliss of beginning, is missing, being replaced by an idealisation of the imagined parental relationship. In men this often leads to a sense of inferiority that one could say was a male castration complex. It is characterised by hero worship of intellectually or physically powerful men, coupled with daydreams of sexual encounters with women perceived as 'sex objects' and not as maternal or understanding women. It may be associated with promiscuity in some, and in others a parallel fantasy life pursued in daydreams or pornography.

In women this idealisation of the primal scene may result in a similar addiction to daydreams, or escapist fiction, that offers fantasised identification in a version of the imagined 'romantic' primal scene. An enormous market of books and films exists to cater for this appetite. The daydreams may become, as Freud suggested, the basis of hysteria. In such cases I have claimed there is an acquisitive projective identification, so that the author of the daydream is forever playing the part of the woman in the idealised union (Britton 1999). In some women, however, the idealisation settles exclusively on the father and his penis; the mother with her breast and womb are regarded as insignificant. It is in these cases that the 'female castration or masculinity complex' comes into existence. In this the important attribute is the penis in its literal or symbolic form.

In the Athene position the woman is protected from experiencing jealousy, covetousness, desire for revenge or any feelings of inferiority by the manic fantasy of sharing with the father his phallus and its magical powers. She therefore lacks nothing worth having since the mother's attributes are regarded as worthless. Generosity of attitude towards those less fortunate is easily available, as is the sort of virtuous wisdom that comes from feeling above the selfish or vengeful feelings that lead others to commit acts of crime or folly. When she is in the Antigone position she does not feel so favoured since she no longer has a share in the father's potency; she is only the keeper of the flame of past glory, and principal attendant on his present weakness. When the conviction of possessing this privileged position weakens there is exposure to the considerable jealousy of siblings, who are believed to be the alternative occupants of the imagined position. It is only when belief in the validity of the imagined exclusive relationship with the father is relinquished that feelings of envy and inferiority fully emerge. Initially this is in the form of penis envy. The transference father, by virtue of possessing his magical penis, is believed to be immune from the sufferings the patient now experiences. The ideal penis, it is believed, protects its possessor from feelings of helplessness, inferiority, privation, and, most of all, from envy itself.

The relinquishment of this belief, though it dissipates the sense of grievance which arises from the notion that something totally desirable has been withheld, ushers in a general sense of disillusionment, bitterness, and envy of those more fortunate in their love life and in their childhood experience. If this can be worked through in analysis and in life, a more tolerable but far from ideal state follows. The bitterness and envy is assuaged by the realisation that no one possesses the ideal attributes once assumed to exist, and that no one is immune to jealousy and envy. Sympathy for oneself and others softens the sharp edge of disappointment and discontent. If the belief is retained that others might possess the still-idealised position once claimed for the self, the injury is aggravated and wounded pride is added to the pain of loss. It is this state that has been described as the 'female castration complex', which has been regarded by some analysts as the condition of women in general. I believe that is not the case. It is, I believe, a particular syndrome that is prominent in some women; it has its counterpart in men. We could simply call it a 'castration complex' that results from phallic idealisation and the belief that one has been deprived of possessing this in its ideal form and its symbolic intellectual attributes omnipotence and omniscience. In conjunction with this the vital significance of the mother in the internal life of the individual is denied and her counterpart in the outside world devalued.

The *importance* of the father and his place in the internal world of us all is emphasised elsewhere in this book. In this chapter what I have described are the adverse effects of regarding him as *all-important*. The 'father complex' reached its zenith in psychoanalytic theorising about the same time as the 'female castration complex' was promulgated. I think the effect of this was as distorting in the development of psychoanalytic theory as it is in the development of the individual. Then the pendulum swung and some analytic theorising made the mother *all-important*: this in turn led to the undervaluation of those aspects of psychic function associated with the internal father, such as objectivity. For psychic balance we need two internal parents; whatever the case for single parenthood in the outside world I think there is no case for it in the internal world.

In normal development the perception by the child of the parents' coming together independently of him unites his psychic world. The primal family triangle provides the child with two links connecting him separately with each parent and confronts him with the link between the parents which excludes him. If the link between the parents perceived in love and hate can be tolerated in the child's mind, it provides him with a prototype for an object relationship of a third kind in which he is a witness and not a participant. A *third position* then comes into existence from which object relationships can be observed. Given this, we can also envisage being observed. This provides us with a capacity for seeing ourselves in interaction with others and for entertaining another point of view whilst retaining our own: for observing ourselves whilst being ourselves. In a paper entitled 'The Missing Link: Parental Sexuality in the Oedipus Situation', I called the mental freedom provided by this process *triangular space* (Britton 1989). In this triangle the father is in one situation the observer of the child's relationship with the mother, in another the love object whose relationship with the child is observed by the mother, or in a third is perceived as the mother's partner by the child as witness.

In this internal triangular situation the father's penis, as Dana Birksted–Breen (1996) pointed out, is a creative link between the parents; in contrast with this the phallus can become a narcissistic object of idealisation and power. I suggest that it is in the latter situation, when the father's phallus becomes the staff of office and not the link with the mother, that it is associated with the 'castration or masculinity complex'.

Note

1 There are various accounts of Athene's birth; this is her priest's version. Zeus was afraid that Metis, pregnant with his daughter, would subsequently bear a son who would depose him. So he swallowed Metis and developed a raging headache which was relieved when Hermes made a breach in his skull 'from which Athene sprang fully armed with a mighty shout' (Graves 1992: p. 46).

References

Abse, L.(1989) *Margaret, Daughter of Beatrice. A Politician's Psycho-biography of Margaret Thatcher*, London, Jonathan Cape.

Birksted-Breen, D. (1996) 'Phallus, penis and mental space', *International Journal of Psycho-Analysis*, 77, 649–657.

Blass, R.B. (1993) 'Insights into the struggle of creativity – a rereading of Anna Freud's "Beating fantasies and day-dreams"', *Psychoanalytic Study of the Child*, 48, 67–97.

Britton, R. (1989) 'The missing link: parental sexuality in the Oedipus situation', in R. Britton, M. Feldman and E. O'Shaughnessy (eds) *The Oedipus Complex Today*, London, Karnac Books, pp. 83–102.

Britton, R. (1992) 'The Oedipus and the depressive position', in R. Anderson (ed.) *Clinical Lectures on Klein and Bion*, London, Routledge, pp. 34–45.

Britton, R. (1998) *Belief and Imagination*, London, Routledge.

Britton, R. (1999) 'Getting in on the Act: the Hysterical Solution'. *International Journal of Psychoanalysis*, 80, 1–14.

Chasseguet-Smirgel, J. (1976) 'Freud and female sexuality – the consideration of some blind spots in the exploration of the "Dark Continent"', *International Journal of Psycho-Analysis*, 57, 276–286.

Freud, A. (1936) The Ego and the Mechanisms of Defence, in *Writings Vol. 2: 1965–71* (Reprinted 1993 London, Karnac Books).

Freud, S. (1897) Draft N, Letter 64, 31 May 1897, *Extracts from the Fleiss Papers*, Standard Edition 1, 255–257.

Freud, S. (1919) "A Child is being Beaten": A contribution to the study of the origin of sexual perversions', Standard Edition 17, 175–205.

Freud, S. (1931) 'Female sexuality', Standard Edition 21, 223–246.

Graves, R. (1992) *The Greek Myths* (combined edition), London, Penguin Books.

Horney, K. (1924) 'On the genesis of the castration complex in women', *International Journal of Psycho-Analysis,* 5, 50–65.

Hughes, A. (1997) 'Personal experiences – professional interests. Joan Riviere and femininity', *International Journal of Psycho-Analysis*, 78(5), 899–912.

Mahoney, P.J. (1997) 'A child is being beaten: A clinical, historical and textual study', in E.S. Person (ed.) *On Freud's 'A Child is Being Beaten'*, New Haven, Conn., Yale University Press.

Rangell, L. (1984) 'The Anna Freud Experience', *Psychoanalytic Study of the Child*, 39, 29–43.

Rivière, J. (1929) Womanliness as a masquerade. In A. Hughes (ed.), *The inner world of Joan Rivière*, London, Karnac Books.

Rivière, J. (1934) 'Review of Sigmund Freud, *New Introductory Lectures on Psycho-Analysis*', in A.A. Hughes (ed.) *The inner world of Joan Rivière*, London, Karnac Books, pp. 117–132.

Steiner, J. (1987) 'The interplay between pathological organisations and the paranoid-schizoid and depressive positions', *International Journal of Psycho-Analysis*, 68, 69–80.

Young-Bruehl, E. (1988) *Anna Freud*, London, Macmillan.

7

GRANDFATHERS

Abraham Brafman

A man in his fifties has been in analysis for some time and, at some point, tells of the birth of his grandchild in a matter of fact way, making it clear that his emotions are more focused on the details of his affair with a young female colleague. Various interpretations spring to mind – for example, living out a fantasy of being at the age when he had children himself, displacement of his feelings for his daughter, etc. Another man in his mid-forties recounts the birth of his grandchild and does not hide his pride in having this happening to celebrate: disguised competitive impulses with his son or son-in-law, repressed incestuous fantasies toward his daughter might be possible interpretations. A man in his fifties shows intense anger and frustration that his only son has decided to undergo a vasectomy to ensure he conceives no children, which deprives our patient of becoming a grandfather – guilt for failing to ensure continuity of the family, envy of his son (as our patient might have wished, himself, not to have children)? When another man shows happiness and concern over his child, but totally ignores the newly born grandchild, is he holding on to a fantasy of this still being *his* child, rather than somebody else's spouse and now a parent? And the fifty-year-old who professes contentment at being a bachelor? And the father who voices his distress at the fact that his son's emigration will mean that he may never see any eventual grandchild? Or the other father who indicates a similar sentiment after discovering that his child is homosexual? Or a middle-aged man who has been through two marriages and boasts of having managed not to put another child in the world? Are these men only displaying feelings linked to their own parents and their own childhood experiences?

The examples could be multiplied, but the various possible (oversimplified) interpretations were listed in order to show that our usual repertoire of inter-pretations of triangular relationships can be sufficient to help us cope with the majority of actual or potential grandfathers that might come to our consulting

119

rooms. But the question ought to arise: are these people, and are we, living in the same environment that existed in late nineteenth century and throughout the twentieth? Clearly, this is not the case, but does it make any difference in the context of our clinical work?

The psyche of our individual patient may well struggle with the same conflicts that we and our predecessors had to contend with and this will justify our resorting to the same formulations we were taught, but at least when articulating our interventions we must take into account the patient's environment and actual life experiences. I would argue that to ignore our present life conditions may still be compatible with reasonably competent work, but I believe we may lose sight of factors that deserve closer attention.

The century following Freud's original formulations of human emotional development has been marked by very dramatic changes in the structure of all levels of society. The original core family, where husband and wife belonged to a shared cultural background and could count on an extended family for support and role modelling, was a unit to which the concepts of the Oedipal conflicts applied easily and convincingly. Migrations over the century have produced a complex mixture of biological, social and emotional changes that have affected every minor detail of family building and child rearing. The "sexual liberation" movement of the 1960s introduced values in the Western world that still defy clear conceptualization. From the suffragettes to the present "women's lib" movement, woman's role in our society is undergoing a process of change, with implications we are still struggling to comprehend. We have had two world wars and an endless stream of other conflagrations which have led to the death of young and old and brought new values to the notions of self-determination and independence. Perhaps even more significant than all these factors has been the growth of multinationals and ever-bigger local and national institutions, which have produced an appalling neglect of the needs of individuals, who have become pawns in the fight for increased productivity and profits. Generations that stay together, sharing linguistic and cultural values, transmitting modes of living that distinguish that particular family from their neighbours and friends who belong to the same community – these are found only in a few places in our modern world. The old family unit has become an exception, no longer the rule. The extended family is now mostly a matter of sentiment and fantasy, rather than part of daily living.

The challenge we face is that when we focus on an individual and his internal, unconscious world, we can still use with considerable intellectual comfort the same original concepts of Freud, Klein, Winnicott, etc. But if we take into account that individual's conscious life experience, we have problems to solve. An up-to-date example would be the child brought up by a homosexual couple: how does this influence the notion of an inborn awareness of triangular relationships? And how do we see the development of gender identity and the positive and negative Oedipal impulses in these children? What to make of a grandfather's comments when referring to the grandchild born to his daughter through artificial insemination because she lives in a homosexual marriage?

There has been an enormous change in the relationship between generations, and the main difference lies in the change in ideas about *continuity*. The biblical notion of man's duty to ensure the propagation of the species stems from the wish to preserve continuity, to transmit to succeeding generations those values held by the elders of the culture. Together with our increased life expectancy, we now have a much-altered perspective of time and distance. If women can now have children in their forties, people in the Western world have learnt that they can no longer easily find a job after they reach the late thirties. Flying across oceans, telephoning or e-mailing distant relations is now commonplace. And yet vast numbers of children have never met their grandparents, and many grandparents have had to accept that when their children move to another continent, country or even city, they may never see any eventual grandchild.

The significance of being a grandfather depends on the person's position in life and his experiences throughout his life. A man who could only have a child after innumerable technical interventions will value his child and eventual grandchild in a particularly poignant manner. A man who survived a potentially lethal condition will cherish his child and grandchild quite differently from other men who haven't had to face similar life-threatening circumstances. But we also find men who "produce children" to please their wives and who take no interest in that child or the eventual grandchild – and, somehow, these are men who are not likely ever to seek our help.

From childhood, the image of "grandpa" conjures up ideas of "really old", which carries the implication of "the first one to die". In spite of this, as the years move on, we find ourselves developing highly personal yardsticks that determine how old we feel. Some people feel life is still in front of them at the same chronological age at which another person feels they have missed their chance of getting anywhere.

The concept of time

Each person has his own sense of time. Many people establish a conscious, explicit landmark, which acquires a significance all its own – "thirty" is often seen as the age beyond which freedom and some degree of unselfconsciousness must be left behind; not long ago, this was also the point at which people (particularly women) were expected to have married a partner, if not also to have had children. Other people set themselves deadlines on the basis of family events – for example, the death of a parent, particularly those who died young; children of older parents tend to feel "there is still plenty of time ahead" for years longer than most of their peers.

The concept of age

Erikson (1950) has written the definitive text on "age" as seen by an observer. We use attributes to characterize age and we speak of mature and sensible to define "older", much as we may use impulsive and fickle as ways of saying "child-like". But (from a subjective perspective) each individual has his own image of "how old" he is, though on the whole nobody consciously associates his feelings and behaviour to the count of years he has lived. A grandfather in his fifties, who tells us of love affairs with younger women, will certainly be seen as denying his age, but we do not apply the same interpretation to another man of the same age who has remained a bachelor. The analyst has his own private view of age, as does his patient, and it can be difficult to decide whether an interpretation of the age-appropriateness or otherwise of a particular behaviour is dictated by objective or subjective factors. The point at which a man becomes a grandfather illustrates this issue very clearly: some men have looked forward to this event and feel gratified and fulfilled, much as others react to it as no more than another development in the life of the family around them.

An endless spiral

The flow of generations might be seen as a spiral along which we progress, forever adapting to each further point we reach. We look forward and watch our descendants coming along, much as we look back and are struck by the ever-increasing fuzziness of the images of those who preceded us.

> My grandfather told me that in the Bible it is written that love lasts for three generations. I thought this sounded puzzling, as I imagined love was beyond such measured evaluations. When my son was born I was shocked to find my grandfather musing, apologetically, that he felt this child too far away, beyond the reach of his love and comprehension. I was upset and I thought he was trying to exculpate his feelings, hiding behind arguments supposedly sanctioned by the holy book. Some decades later, I discovered that some of my grandchildren found it very difficult to disguise their lack of interest in stories about my parents.

Catching myself believing that my grandfather (and the Bible?) was right, after all, I felt quite relieved when I found that other grandchildren were most inquisitive about my/our ancestors. What makes for this difference? The literature on survivors of the Holocaust has created the image of people being so overwhelmed by their memories of pain and their guilt for surviving that they try to keep this secret from children and grandchildren, but many of our descendants do not want to be burdened with the knowledge of those painful experiences. In such a subtle and complex interaction it may be impossible to establish which is cause and which is effect. This is another example of how misleading it can be to put forward an all-embracing statement, since people who want to recount their past may be just as common as others who want to forget it – much as children may or may not show interest in the past.

The different perspectives representing each stage in this developmental process are vividly illustrated in two stories:

In a community where old people were taken to a distant mountain to await death, besides adequate clothes, they were given only an elaborate and delicate bowl for their meals. One day, when the father was taking the grandfather to the mountain, the grandfather began to cry very bitterly. The father tried to console him with words about the past and the future, but the old man interrupted him: "No, it's not for me that I'm crying – I'm thinking how painful it is that one day you will also have to make this journey!"

Rappaport quotes a similar story from the brothers Grimm:

Once upon a time there was a very old man, whose eyes had become dim, whose ears were deaf and whose knees were trembling. When he was sitting at the table and could hardly hold his spoon, he spilled the soup on the tablecloth and some of it also dribbled from his mouth. His son and daughter-in-law were disgusted and, therefore, the old grandfather finally had to sit behind the stove in the corner and they gave him his food in a small earthen bowl and not enough food. Sadly, he looked at the table and his eyes were wet. One day, his trembling hands could not hold the bowl and it fell on the floor and broke. The young woman scolded him but he said nothing and only sighed. She bought him a little wooden bowl for a few pennies, from which he then had to eat. While they were sitting, the four-year-old grandson collected little wooden boards on the floor. "What are you doing there?", asked the father. "I am making a little trough", the child replied, "from which father and mother are going to eat, when I shall be big."

(Rappaport 1958)

This second story vividly depicts a most important point in the relationship between the three generations: first and foremost, for the growing child, the grandfather constitutes a live and ongoing demonstration of how the father treats his own father. If the grandfather hopes to be seen as an individual in his own right, the grandson discovers who and what he is on the basis of observing how the father treats him. I will return to this point, as I consider it of fundamental importance.

Continuity

Like many other people in their generation my grandparents had migrated to a new country, bringing their children with them. By the time my peers were born, our parents had already moved a long way from the values of the previous generation. They used the new language and, much more significantly, became gradually distanced from the religious and cultural beliefs and practices of the previous generation. Such dramatic changes would be rare in families living for many generations in the same place, but in the last century such moves were commonplace in response to war, racial conflicts or employment conditions. This resulted in a very clear distinction between the images of parents and grandparents. Many of my peers could not converse freely with their grandparents because they lacked a common language. Most of us grew up with the idea that grandparents represented values which were dramatically different from all that our parents stood for. Our grandparents had to accommodate to the idea that however gratified they were with the birth of grandchildren, their contact with them was very limited, and that with the passage of time these grandchildren would probably move further and further away from them.

It is only when seeing Eastern or very religious patients that I find what many of us still believe is "normal": parents who treat their own parents and grandparents as the source of authority, living as if each generation is no more than a part of a continuum. In these families, if one of its members claims individual rights, he is seen as infringing a sacred principle of life. The vast majority of my patients come from backgrounds where it would be impossible to delineate features we associate with the concept of "continuity": their family histories are so diverse that it is very rare to find two people with the same experiences. Predictably, grandparents speak of joys or anxieties related to their grandchildren's lives, but the sense of distance is almost visible; they struggle to preserve the feeling of closeness and continuity with their children, but this is virtually absent when they focus on the next generation.

Young and Stogdon (2000) have recently called attention to the increasing proportion of grandparents who look after their grandchildren, due to a variety of problems that result in the parents being unable to care for their children. They quote the United States Census for 1999 as showing that 4.7 million grandparents lived with their grandchildren. "Climbing divorce rates, teenage pregnancies and drug use are cited as the main reasons for grandparents being in a supportive role" (p. 3). They believe that

> What we are seeing is a revival in the importance of the extended family. This is going on alongside a vital change in its structure. When studies of families in Bethnal Green, in the East End of London, were first being done in the 1950s, the extended family had a very large lateral extension. Some people had dozens, even hundreds, of relatives living locally – married brothers and

sisters and their nephews and nieces and all the in-laws. . . . As fertility has continued to fall and families have become smaller, the lateral has given way to the vertical.

(Young and Stogdon 2000, p. 4)

This new "vertical pattern" is a response to a breakdown in parental care, but it can only be activated when there is some significant relationship, even if limited, between parents and grandparents. The impression I have from clinical experience is that only in a limited number of families does this link remain close enough, both emotionally and geographically. In the majority of cases, when parenting breaks down, the child can seldom count on the presence of grandparents. If Young and Stogdon are right, we may be moving to a new pattern of relationship between generations, but for the moment I fear we see mostly a severe breakdown in these, so that we find grandparents isolated, living with their remaining friends or neighbours, while parents and children are somewhere distant, trying to build links with whatever community they happen to find themselves in.

Becoming a grandfather

It will have become clear that I am trying to describe grandfathers in general, not only those seen in therapy. As a rule, we only see professionally those people for whom something has gone wrong; many men become grandfathers and manage to carry on with their lives without our help. The arrival of the third generation constitutes a major event for all grandparents, though there are fundamental differences in the reaction of grandmothers and grandfathers. One grandmother summarized her feelings very aptly: "You become a mother again, both to your daughter and to your grandchild." Experience has shown that mothers fare infinitely better during puerperium when able to count on their mother's support. The Cassel Hospital (Ham Common, Surrey, England) ran a unit for women who had suffered a puerperal breakdown, and it was repeatedly found that recovery was quicker and more effective for those women whose mothers were available to help them. There is, nevertheless, a subtle area for conflict here, since a daughter may resent her mother "competing" for her new child. Predictably, some women will require help over longer periods than others and the grandmother will need considerable empathy and sensitivity to gauge the degree and the length of her supporting presence.

The situation is different for the man. Those cultures where men could enact their participation in the delivery through "*couvade*" offered them a model of sharing the woman's labour which was transmitted through generations, but in our society it is still rare for men to take an active part in the wife's labour. This puts the man in the position of outsider, and perhaps it is not surprising that all our theories of early infant development put exclusive emphasis on the role of the mother, even though in those families where the father was an active participant in the actual delivery he tends to continue this close involvement in the subsequent phases of the baby's development. But, in general terms, the birth of the baby is seen as an event in the woman's life and therefore, not surprisingly, the arrival of a grandchild will again be seen as belonging "to the women".

A man's reaction to becoming a grandfather seems to depend on his age. The older he feels, the more he is able to welcome the event and this seems to be linked to the notion that the job of preserving the continuity of the family has been achieved. Younger men seem to feel they "are not quite ready for it" and do not know quite what to make of the situation, tending then to react to their child's feelings at the event; that is, the grandchild itself does not initially figure in the equation. At best, the baby is seen as "a child", not quite "a grandchild". Religious Jews have a different perspective, since when it is a grandson that is born this is cause for great celebration, in view of the symbolic value this child plays in the father's and grandfather's relationship to God.

Seeing the baby as a person is a more complex challenge for grandfathers. Initially, their feelings relate to their own child, though those who took part in their wives' labour can empathize far more easily with the birth situation and the baby itself. I think it takes quite some time before the grandfather will recognize the individuality of the baby and extend his feelings to the parents to encompass the presence of the baby as a person in his/her own right. An area of potentially serious conflicts exists here, when the mother feels her baby is not being valued sufficiently. I knew of a grandfather who was naïve and insensitive enough to comment that the recently born grandchild was not so beautiful as the mother, his own child . . .

Being a grandfather

As time goes on, the position of the grandfather depends almost totally on his relationship with his child and child-in-law. Both Jones (1918) and Rappaport (1958) in their analyses of the role of the grandfather in a person's life lay the same emphasis on the individual's relationship to his father/parents as the primary factor in determining or colouring his relationship to the older generation. As mentioned earlier the grandchild will look to his parents to check how *they* treat the grandparents. The bond between child and parent is one of those few factors which appear "instinctive, inborn" beyond doubt, as it contains love, dependence, attachment from the very beginning, but the relationship with the grandparents will develop as part of a process influenced by multiple and subtle factors. On the whole, the mother and grandmother tend to be close enough to ensure the grandchild's easier relationship to the grandmother, but the grandfather will often arouse feelings of jealousy and fears of competition from the child's father. Perhaps my view is coloured by being male, but I do have the impression that grandmothers "have it easier" and that grandfathers have to tread more cautiously and work harder to obtain and preserve a position in the new family context.

As the child grows older, the grandfather's position is greatly influenced by the social and geographical situation of the family. When the three generations live near each other and have a good relationship between them, the grandfather has an easier "task" *vis-à-vis* his grandchildren, but he still has to struggle to win his position in the grandchildren's lives. When parents value the grandfather, he will be seen as the "older" father figure – somebody who occupies an important role in the family. But he will only be recognized as a person in his own right (i.e., as the man he believes he is) after much hard work with the grandchildren. This demands that he *wants* to be close to the grandchildren, and this is not a universal stance. Many grandfathers are content with the occasional contact with their grandchildren, if at all, being much closer to their own children. These are the grandfathers who probably gave rise to the image of Father Christmas – the source of those presents that the parents might not be easily able to afford – but to be seen only once a year.

Focusing on individual grandfathers in therapy and discussing how they see their grandchildren, it is not difficult to formulate explanations for whatever feelings they voice: links with their own childhood and their parents and grandparents, for example. My own impression is that there are also other important and relevant factors that must be investigated, even if they are far more difficult to explain. Those grandparents I saw in the consulting room were always far more concerned with their children than with the grandchildren – and when they focused on these, invariably their feelings involved how they felt about how the parents treated the grandchildren. At such points an interpretation of "trying to prove (he) is a better father than his son", or that he is "carrying out a rescuing fantasy", fails to do justice to the social, moral and emotional complexity of the situation. When the grandchildren are older, moving into adolescence or in their teens, they tend to be seen more clearly as individuals in their own right (i.e., loved when rewarding, and disappointing and annoying when creating trouble). During their earlier years, however, grandfathers will usually keep at a distance and only seldom play an active role in the child's life – and, again, it can be almost impossible to discern how much this distance is created by the grandfather's conscious and unconscious feelings or how much it is an appropriate response to the feelings and attitudes of the grandchild's parents.

As soon as the parents cease to be self-sufficient in their parenting role, we move into the area that Young and Stogdon (2000) discussed in their article. Grandfather, when well-off, may become a provider of money, much as some others will take over a variety of functions, supporting some or all members of the young family. When social and/or geographical conditions do not allow grandparents to move into the picture, each family will follow a different route.

127

Being a grandfather can be very difficult if a man does not have work or other areas of activity and sources of gratification outside his family. If the parents' family is well functioning, the grandfather will tend to be a visitor, unless circumstances have led to the families living together or very near each other. But if parents manage to bring up their children successfully without the help of the older generation, a grandfather may find his presence being welcome, but only until a certain point. I remember a grandfather celebrating how he could stay with his grandchildren as long as they were giving him pleasure, but he was free to leave as soon as they began to be troublesome. But the reverse of this picture is when the grandfather overstays his welcome and the parents react to this in such a way that the grandchildren pick up that it is time to become troublesome and cause grandparents to leave. Another grandparent summarized this situation as "seeing children and grandchildren is fine, but only as a visitor" (i.e., the art of knowing when to leave). But this is no problem at all if the grandparents have alternative places, people and activities to turn to, which, sadly, is often not the case.

With advancing age, grandparents can find themselves quite isolated from their family. Those fortunate enough to have lived long in a supporting community can manage to weather this specific kind of isolation, but those who have moved around and have no ties with neighbours and no meaningful contact with friends can find themselves at the mercy of social agencies. Predictably, the situation is even worse when one of the couple dies and the surviving grand-parent is left totally alone.

It is extremely painful to find a widowed grandfather who feels the need for company and who realizes that his grandchildren have moved forward in their lives and have little time to spend with him. This is the time when the parents will be blamed for not being supportive and for not creating sufficiently strong bridges between the older and the younger generations. Reason will sometimes prevail and grandfathers will usually grant their grandchildren the right to advance in adolescence and find their own interests and people with whom they prefer to associate, but for grandchildren a lonely grandfather can be an incredibly painful figure.

References

Erikson, E. (1950) *Childhood and Society*, New York: Norton.

Jones, E. (1918) "The Significance of the Grandfather for the Fate of the Individual", in *Papers in Psychoanalysis* (Chapt. 38), London: Bailliere, Tudall & Cox.

Rappaport, E.A. (1958) "The Grandparent Syndrome", *Psychoanalytic Quarterly*, 27, 518–538.

Young, M. and Stogdon, J. (2000) "New Age Travails", *The Guardian*, 12 Jan. (supplement).

Mainly clinical

8

ON BECOMING A FATHER

Reflections from infant observation

Ricky Emanuel

An adult female patient recently asked me, "Are fathers absolutely necessary?" It was asked in a tone like that of a small child saying "Do I have to?" Her question was motivated by her belief that there was no such thing as a good father. As such, she had major difficulties in conceiving of a good internal parental relationship which could form the basis for introjective identification with a creative combined object which affected her ability to engage successfully in intimate adult sexual relationships.

Becoming a father, in this sense, for the child, the mother and for the couple is a complex continual process through the developmental cycle, and necessarily a conflictual one, as it necessitates the development for the man of new facets to his personality, functioning and life, as well as the reawakening of conscious and unconscious infantile phantasies and conflicts from his past. No real development takes place without pain, and the ability to tolerate this pain depends on the capacity of the person to contain and modulate it with the help of an internalised container/contained system.

In this chapter, I hope to illustrate some aspects of the developmental process which can either promote or hinder the man becoming the kind of father who is necessary for the baby, and for the family's growth and security. Donald Meltzer writes:

> The father's functions are generally those of supply and protection to the mother–child relationship . . . The parents are seen in the role mainly of providing a protected space where the child may have the kinds of experiences of intimate emotional relationships upon which the evolution of the personality depends . . . The concept of husband (*partner*) as provident

131

manager of the overall space of the family in the community, would seem in keeping with psychic reality.

(Meltzer 1988, p. 65)

From the point of view of the psychic reality of the baby, in a prototypical situation, the mother is filled with projections and evacuations from the baby during the daytime and can seem to be depleted or overburdened in the process. The effect of "Daddy coming home from work" can bring relief to what can often be a stressful situation at the end of the day. Somehow, mysteriously, the mother resurrects in the night-time and appears renewed and available again for the baby in the morning. The father's role in this process is gradually assumed and is intimately connected to his work, the sexual work of servicing the needs of the mother, filling her up with better things, or resupplying her with what the baby needs, and relieving or cleansing her of what she has had to contain from the day. These toileting or feeding functions of the mother are comple-mented by the protective policing function the father is felt to have for the whole family. Daddy's work is thus to be seen not just in external terms of providing for the family materially but also intimately connected to his work in psychic reality and thus the basis for the child's introjective identification of a working father which is necessary for healthy development. The father is also seen as instrumental in turning the baby's view towards the outside world away from the intense intimacy of the mother–child relationship, or as introducing the "third position" (Britton 1989) which is essential for healthy cognitive and emotional growth and development.

I will be drawing on material from infant observation which allows us to see some of these processes in action and their effects on the baby and its caregiver. The technique of psychoanalytic infant observation was developed by Esther Bick (Bick 1964). Bick's original aim was "to help students to conceive vividly the infantile experience of their child patients". Infant observation has now broadened out from its original conception and has become an essential part of many psychoanalytic trainings for both adults and children. The observer visits a family following the birth of a baby regularly for an hour a week (usually for two years), and is exposed to the impact of the baby on the family and the world on the baby in all its varied emotional climates, states of mind and nuance. The observer not only learns at first hand how a particular baby develops in a particular family, but through discussion of the baby in a weekly seminar is also exposed to the detailed accounts of about four other babies whose development is also followed in the seminar. Similarities and differences in the babies and the families are striking, as well as the different kind of impacts the experience has on the observer. The experience is more than "just observation" as it involves the observer in absorbing and holding in mind the whole matrix of the physical and emotional experience of the baby and the family. By using the concomitant counter-transferential effect on him/her in a process akin to Bion's reverie (Bion

1962), as well as the input of the seminar, the student observer tries to make sense of the developing relationships and to construct a meaning for those multiple experiences. It allows the observer to construct imaginatively the internal experience of the baby and the family members. The seminar will always try to remind the observers that these are just constructions and not "facts"; as such, the process of infant observation heightens sensitivity to emotional experience and the value of trying to use observational facts in constructing meanings, whether in clinical work or in other applications.

A full account of the theory and practice of infant observation as described in this chapter can be found in *Closely Observed Infants* (Miller *et al.* 1989) and *Developments in Infant Observation – The Tavistock Model* (Reid 1997). The growth in appreciation of infant observation as both a learning experience and a therapeutic tool in its own right has led to the founding of the *International Journal of Infant Observation and Its Applications*.

The most striking thing about infant observation is that the father is by and large a missing person, except at the beginning of the observation and on occasional visits. There are a few exceptions, when, for example, the father has become the main caregiver in the family or is present for other reasons over a length of time. More usually, we have to intuit the role of the father in the family from observations of the baby or by the way the mother may talk about him. It is significant that the father is such a missing person in the observed family, as it reflects one of the main problems and difficulties in becoming a father; that is, finding a role for himself in the new family constellation. I will start by talking about the birth process itself, and then move onto the different roles which the father may occupy in the family in relation to the mother and the new baby. I will be using examples drawn from infant observation, both my own during my training as a child and adolescent psychotherapist as well as from my experience as a leader of infant observation seminars at the Tavistock Clinic, London.

The impact of birth

It is increasingly common for fathers to be present at the birth of their child, but little has been spoken or written about its impact on them. Only recently have newspaper articles begun to appear where men "share their experiences". I think it has been hidden, as the impact of the birth itself is traumatic for the man as well – though it is hardly acknowledged or spoken about. The sight of the mother in intense pain, with the man relatively helpless to do anything about it despite antenatal classes for men about birth stages etc., is distressing in itself. The emotionality of the whole experience can be awesome and overwhelming. Although birth is so ordinary in one sense, it is so extraordinary in another. The visual and other sensual aspects of the birth itself also can have a powerful impact on the man which can have a long-lasting effect, akin to the post-traumatic stress flashback phenomenon. I think men feel slightly ashamed about this, as they are supposed to be able to take it "like a man" and not be too upset or distressed. Informally, men have spoken about how these images interfere with sexual relations for some time afterwards. The sense of redundancy in the process, even if the man is "supporting" the mother, means that these feelings need to be worked through over and over again, especially with the new nursing couple.

The impact of the new baby

The father, along with the other children in the family, has to adjust to a new situation. In our society the father's role in the earliest days and weeks has been to provide a protective environment for the new nursing couple, as well as to look after the mother. This period can be as vulnerable a time for the father as it is for the siblings. It is easy for him to feel rejected and redundant before he can settle into the new role. He has to find a place for himself. Many men find this extremely difficult, especially if they cannot tolerate the sense of exclusion from the mother–child couple. This stirs up early constellations of feelings, and defences against them, belonging to Oedipal configurations which require reworking through. The man, along with the woman, suddenly has new responsibilities thrust upon him. Most theories of child development are weighted heavily in favour of the role of the mother as primary caregiver and attachment figure. The role of the father "must be appended as an important modulating and potentially modifying force in the field" (Meltzer 1988, p. 59). Meltzer thinks it is the source of some of the most important faults and distortions of both character and psychopathology.

Mothers are somehow assumed to know by instinct what to do with babies, but fathers have to be instructed according to folklore. They often feel clueless and frightened of the potentially screaming bundle.

Perhaps as a defence against the anxieties expressed in the previous extract, some fathers try to deal with the new situation by becoming the confident one who knows:

> Tom (aged 16 days) was lying on a cushion, and as his mother, Laura got up, saying to Tom, "You're OK there aren't you?", Jack, the father, said, "Why, are you going somewhere?", slightly alarmed that Tom might roll over. Laura said, "Well you take him." Jack stood up and reached down to Laura who was on her way upstairs, and expertly took the baby in his arms. Laura remarked on how he did it. The observer asked Jack if it was his first child. He said, "Yes", but that he already felt that he'd been a father a long time. Jack sat back in a rocking chair and rocked, pulling the sheet, tucking it under Tom's toes, making small adjustments to the covers and position of Tom. He

told the observer how glad he was he had waited to take *maternity* leave and how difficult they had found the hospital time. How public it had all been.

In this sequence we see Jack ridding himself of any alarm at being left alone with the baby and becoming an old hand at fathering. Or is it mothering? His slip on the word "maternity" rather than "paternity" suggests a phantasy of getting into the mother's place through projective identification. This became a powerful feature in this family: this father was in danger of "becoming a better mummy than mummy". We will be exploring this situation in more detail later.

It does not mean that fathers cannot perform maternal functions through introjective identification with a good internal mother, and vice versa for mothers performing paternal functions. Meltzer writes:

> Father-liness . . . is a set of feelings, attitudes and consequent behaviour which cannot have a necessary relation to the status of progenitor, nor even of the masculine sex . . . Father-liness can often be simulated, or rather caricatured, by the competitiveness with the mother that interferes, controls, encourages maternal neglect. Similarly the tenderly supportive attitudes and attentiveness of father-liness can be quietly replaced, as the children grow and their sexual attractiveness becomes more manifest, by erotic play and cuddling which easily escalates and also drives the children into secret sexual games and masturbatory habits.
>
> (Meltzer 1988, pp. 64–65)

He continues by pointing out how the changes in patterns of paternal behaviour in Western culture are in severe flux with more sharing of domestic chores and bringing up the children which can lead to a "confusion between father-liness and mother-liness in the man". The threat of redundancy for the man and prolonged periods of unemployment can lead to a "greater gratification of the bisexuality of both partners", but "its consequences for the children are unclear" (ibid., p. 65).

Father as rival

In clinical practice the impression gained is that most fathers who leave a marriage do so after the birth of the second child, closely followed by the birth of the first child. Maybe this is because the first child presents more of a novelty to the family, but in both situations the father can easily feel left out and rivalrous with the baby. In the baby, Oliver, whom I described in *Closely Observed Infants* (Miller *et al.* 1989), I observed the way the father treated me as another new male entering the family may have mirrored the way he felt about his new son's entrance to the family:

135

The first thing that father said to me when he saw me was "so you've come to scrutinise my protégé?" He appeared antagonistic to me, betraying a strong wish to protect his son saying, "I reserve the right not to have an observer as part of my child's experience." This together with his comment that my ethnic background "threw him in his categorisation process" made me offer him the chance to withdraw his consent to the observation. Mother quickly intervened, saying "if he wasn't happy about you observing, you would have been out the door already", and that I "shouldn't worry about him as he is always rude".

(Miller *et al.* 1989, pp. 176–177)

Eventually, I came to feel I was made welcome in the family by the father, but that this was interfered with by negative feelings which emerged despite himself. This may have mirrored the situation of Oliver's arrival. The birth of his son threw him in his categorisation process, as he had to redefine his role to accommodate the new male member of the family. Many of these feelings were projected into me as a safer place for them to be. Throughout the year the father had to go away for his work. Each time he returned his suspicion of me emerged, probably fuelled by painful unconscious jealous phantasies whilst he was away. Several times when he walked in when I was visiting he would apologise for "disturbing our rapport". There was a strong feeling that he felt left out.

Once Susan, Oliver's sister, farted. Father immediately said, "Say pardon me." Mother retorted, "Paul – you'll embarrass her." This comment seemed to embarrass father instead and he said hopefully I was "up wind" and that Susan should have been facing me when she did it. In the same observation while watching Oliver being changed he said to me, "you really do see everything, don't you?" Oliver was put into the bath and whilst in the bath, Susan pulled Oliver's penis. Mother stopped her saying, "That's Oliver's tail – don't pull it." Father saw this and groaned, saying of me, "Susan, don't do that – Ricky is in agony." As I left to go shortly afterwards, with mother saying I should let myself out, father said "Don't steal the silverware."

It was as if all the painful, embarrassing, unwanted bad feelings were to be lodged in me. It seemed father identified me with the baby since we were both males, but at the same time was talking about his own masculine identification and feelings of rivalry, and feeling in danger of something being stolen from him. This may have referred to the loss of his previous position as the only male in the family. Again I and not Oliver was being held responsible.

(Miller *et al.* 1989, pp. 176–177)

There were times however, when the father could not contain his feelings of rivalry and hostility towards Oliver and they spilled out directly:

Once, when Oliver was being breast fed, Father put on a King Kong mask which earlier he had told me in a lot of detail frightened Oliver. He called Oliver as he put the mask on. Oliver turned round and his face dropped. He looked very uncertain but quickly turned back towards Mother and continued feeding. Father said, "Oliver's got his priorities sorted out." After this incident Father played with Oliver, tickling his feet and playing with his toes, tickling him again and then biting his tummy. Oliver grimaced and turned abruptly away from Father who sadly said "You love it when Mummy does that."

It was as if the father's genuine wish to do well by Oliver was continually interfered with by his unconscious rivalry and jealousy. The underlying belief was that only the mummy can really satisfy the baby, and thus there was no real place for a good daddy. The essential paternal function where the father protects the mother–baby couple was inverted.

In this family, the father increasingly wanted me to admire his creations, taking me away from observing Oliver and his mother by showing me his collection of electronic clocks. It was as if he feared all the creativity was held by mother producing the baby as well as being able to breast feed it, so it was difficult for him to find a place as part of a creative couple. It is of course true that the only certainty as far as the parentage of the child is concerned is who the mother is. Judaism recognises this by being matrilineal in the designation of the Jewishness of the child. Psychically, this is true for the position of the father. Only relatively recent DNA testing can decisively settle the matter. It is most reassuring or painful for fathers when the baby is said to have or not to have his features, as deep insecurities can be stirred.

Another way the father's rivalry or envy of the mother's creativity may manifest itself is by trying to take over the functions of the mother and, rather than supporting her, undermine her by being a "better mummy than mummy". This has an insidious effect on the mother, especially if she is post-natally depressed anyway. Such behaviour has a different quality to the father performing maternal functions as it implies the usurping of the mother:

> Tom's father Jack was telling the observer how his mother held the family together. She was the focus, especially at Christmas. After the mother's death, they decided to have a baby. "It occurred to me that now the older generation was going, I must produce the next.'

Like Jack's comment about maternity leave, his statement that *he* rather than *we* must produce the next generation, revealed his unconscious phantasy. During the observation this was repeatedly borne out. The observer noted that as Laura became depressed, Jack took over. Of course this may be necessary, but the spirit in which it is done is all-important. Also it has a chicken and egg quality, as to how much of Laura's depression arose from her feeling pushed out with all feelings of redundancy projected into her. It was not a simple situation, as Laura was reassured by Jack's effective mothering as well. The observer felt that Jack basked in his talent with Tom and that there was a strong sense of collusion between Tom and his father to push the mother out. This was particularly accentuated when the mother weaned Tom and was going back to work, leaving Jack as the main caretaker. The following is an observation of Tom, aged 15 months:

> Laura took out half a biscuit and gave it to Tom who was in Jack's arms looking enthusiastically into the biscuit tin. Jack said sarcastically "that's a generous mummy" and with that sat Tom on the floor with his biscuit. It seemed the biscuit was a disappointment for Tom too as he began to cry again, this time revving up, eyes closed, red in the face. Jack picked him up. Laura came over to Tom and there was a small tug of war between them as Tom held on to Jack and Laura pulled him off. Laura said to Jack that perhaps it was time he went to do the shopping. Jack agreed, he said he could bring back some fruit for Tom. Laura took Tom in her arms and set him on her knee. Tom pulled himself off her on to the floor, crying, biscuit still held but of little comfort. Just occasionally he'd try to put the biscuit in his mouth. Jack returned holding a dried apricot, collecting Tom's beaker on the way. He gave both to Tom. Tom stopped crying when he saw the apricot, he bit on it vigorously, pulling it, stretching the apricot and finally chewing. Laura sat with her head in her hands, twiddling Tom's hair. Jack now had his coat on and was saying goodbye. Tom turned to Jack and held on to him when Jack said goodbye. Laura peeled Tom off Jack. She put him on her knee but he pulled himself off and sat on the floor. Laura was looking thoughtful and said Jack really had taken her place now that she wasn't up in the night to feed Tom or put him to bed. She said she felt redundant but that she could not have carried on breast feeding. She felt she had given him what she could. Since he had been weaned he had slept through the night: she thought he realised there was nothing to wake for. If he did wake Jack saw to him. He was getting lots of attention; Jack was doing very well. As she came to the end of this sad confession of her redundancy, she got up and took hold of a Lego house and said "Now I can break up this house because I made it."

In this observation, Jack gives Tom the impression that he can provide better food for him than his mother, which presumably finds favour with Tom in the context of his weaning. It does not give an impression to him of a mother who has something precious to give him, but instead usurps her position, leaving her bowed and crushed like the Lego house. It almost feels like she has lost the baby *she* "made".

The way in which one parent conveys an image to the baby about the other parent is crucial in shaping the baby's view of the parent. In this observation, the collusion between Jack and Tom that the mother's food is no good may be based on Jack's envy of the mother's feeding capacity and leaves Tom isolated from his mother. It exploits Tom's feelings about the loss of the breast as Jack offers himself up as a substitute. It does not help Tom or Laura work through their own sense of loss.

With Oliver, we have seen how the father felt that only the mother was important to the baby. She colluded with this at times, making the father feel even more redundant.

On one occasion when I arrived at the house, father came in from work and paraded Oliver on his shoulders. Oliver smiled nervously. Father said, "You don't feel like playing but you're pleased to see your Dad." Mother replied, "He couldn't care less: he didn't even notice when you left." Father began complaining of a garlic smell and said it must be my after shave. He then turned to me and began telling me about his gun insurance – in case he accidentally shot someone. He said he would show me his 12 bore shotgun sometime, if I was interested, or else mother could show it to me "next time you are upstairs with her". Mother's statement that Oliver "couldn't care less" about father must have stimulated father's rivalry with me, as it implied he was redundant and excluded. It seemed again that I was being held responsible for making father feel this.

She would tell me not to bother about him whenever he was abrasive in his attitude towards me. This did not help father's fragile brittleness, nor, presumably, foster a feeling in Oliver that Daddy loved him. However, at other times, perhaps feeling guilty as well as wanting to include father more into Oliver's world, mother would talk to Oliver in a positive way about his father. She seemed concerned that father and Oliver should get on well together. For example, while smiling, mother said to Oliver in a deep voice, "I like my daddy the best." She said to me that Oliver looked around when he heard father's voice. I saw little evidence of this except Oliver becoming unsettled and vigilant expecting intrusion from his father or sister.

The feeling of exclusion or inclusion has strong Oedipal roots. The father's ability to cope with being left out must relate to the degree to which his own Oedipal anxieties have been worked through. When the baby feels these anxieties and tries to distance them by relocating them elsewhere, part of the role of the father may be to try and keep the right couple intact. In other words, the father may help the baby realise the facts of its life, that it is a product of the parental couple and not a participant. Tom, for example, started to address his father and referred to his mother as "the other one". A central function of the father is to enable the child to separate from the mother and to introduce the "third position" (Britton 1989) into the mother–baby couple. This allows the baby to observe a relationship without being a participant in it, so that something else exists outside the mother–baby couple. Britton considers it essential if the baby is to learn about the world outside.

Father as the third vertex

It is as if the father has to reclaim the mother as far as the baby is concerned and gradually introduce some space in the relationship between mother and baby. It also enables the baby to be introduced to the world outside the mother and her body. If the father is unable to achieve this, for whatever reason, serious developmental difficulties may ensue. A dream from the patient I quoted at the beginning, who asked if fathers were absolutely necessary, may illustrate this. The dream was reported in the same session as this question, just before the summer break when the patient was going on a walking holiday. We had been working on the issue of her hatred of anything or anyone who interfered with her possessive control of me in the maternal transference:

> In the dream, a woman was walking on holiday with hooks embedded into her feet. It was very painful for her to walk, but she got used to it. Then the patient was given a test, like in school and knew nothing.
>
> In her associations she linked the dream to her walking holiday and her pain about leaving me for the holiday. She also reported a phantasy that the man friend she was going to visit that weekend, to go on a walk and picnic with, would be already preparing her grave in his garden for when he murdered her.

We were able to see how the patient reversed things in the dream and wanted to stop me walking away from her, through keeping me hooked to her, as well as her and I being mixed up and confused with each other. She claimed in the dream to know nothing, especially about the notion that any separation may be "good for her". Her murderous feelings to the father, the man in the phantasy, or the father in me who was removing the mother-me in the transference from her in the break, was barely concealed in its reversed form. The father may turn murderous as well towards her in a primitive form, if the mother is treated in such a cruel manner as in the dream. This process of splitting off and projecting her own feelings into others leaves her in a confused state, not knowing anything. It is precisely the absence of an absolutely necessary good father in her internal world which leaves her in this state.

An essential function for a father is to be a kind of policeman in a good sense, to stop the kind of intrusion into the maternal object represented by the hooks in the dream. This is in addition to his function of looking after the mother and servicing her from the baby's point of view as described above. This is the true meaning of husbanding, used in the sense of husbandry. This is the father who "lays down the laws" of psychic reality, especially as regards the possession of the mother and the need for privacy for the exercise of the mysterious functions of the parental couple. In the absence of such fathering, the mother inevitably deteriorates, as we saw in the earlier example of Tom and Jack colluding to exclude the mother and establish the father and son as the primary couple.

The children's book *Five Minutes Peace* (Murphy 1982) illustrates the absence of this protective policing paternal function. The baby elephant children continually disturb and intrude into the mother's space, pestering her with requests and stopping her having five minutes of peace. There is no father elephant around and the mother gets increasingly exhausted and dispirited, as the children relentlessly intrude, even while she is naked in her bath, to play their recorders to her.

The father's intervention as a third element, and his protection of the mother, can facilitate thought in the child about the world and his place in it.

> Tom got up and went over to Laura and hit her with a beater. Laura said "Oh no Tom, not me." Tom ran over to Jack and buried his head in Jack's knee. He screwed up his face if he was going to cry. Jack said, "Are you full of shame?"
>
> In another episode, when Tom was 19 months, the observer bent down towards Tom to hear what he was saying, and Tom hit her on her face with his hand. Jack sprang to Tom's side and said, "Oh, Tom, that's not nice!" To the observer he said, "He does that to Laura too, she gets quite upset." Tom put his finger in his mouth and peered at the observer thoughtfully. He leaned onto Jack's body and swivelled on one foot. Jack said, "Are you thinking Tom?"

If the parents can be united in the law enforcement, with the father being seen to support the mother, this can be a relief to the children.

> Jack was observing how Tom always put the books back into the box the right way. Laura turned to admire him and it seemed as if their concentration on him made him feel self conscious and he turned around and gave a false laugh. He then took the books and threw them on the floor in a bout of defiance. Both Jack and Laura simultaneously indicated their disapproval. Tom moved away to look for something else.

The father often can intervene in a situation where the mother and child seem to be in a clinch, and provide some space between them. It is a common scenario to find the frazzled mother, having been filled up by the demands of the baby throughout the day, hand over to the father on his return from work. The father has to contain both mother and child in this situation, which can lead to difficulties if the father himself needs some "home comfort" after work. If he can rise to the occasion, a sense of well-being can ensue.

The father's presence can have a containing effect in itself, though more physical containment is sometimes needed:

> Adam, aged 9 months, was sitting on his dad's lap. Dad was talking about how you are supposed to squeeze a baby's forearm if he has done something wrong. He said Adam was still pulling his sister's hair and he was trying to teach him not to by squeezing his forearm. But "all he does is laugh," he said. Adam was laughing now and Dad said "he is mad". He put Adam onto the floor, and he immediately began moving around the room in a manic way suggesting to the observer that he looked drunk. The observer noted to herself that Dad looked stone sober. As they watched him, Dad commented that Adam keeps falling over and said "this is ridiculous". He moved over to Adam and placed him on a duvet on the floor with his bottle, and touched his body firmly with both his hands while Adam calmed down.

This kind of containment, in conjunction with an emotionally responsive maternal presence, can facilitate the development in the child of an idea of parents who keep a watchful eye on the baby.

Introducing the baby to the world

A key role for the father, which most men find they do intuitively, is to introduce the baby to the world. It is interesting to note that in general mothers appear to carry or sit holding their babies in the earliest weeks face to face, whilst fathers tend to hold the baby facing out into the world. Many fathers find that they can only really contain the baby's distress, in the earliest weeks and months, by movement or distraction:

> The observer noted that Tom, aged 16 days, was enjoying his father Jack rocking with him. Jack said that he had discovered in hospital that when Tom was distraught, walking up and down the corridors with him seemed to calm him.

Many of the physical games that fathers tend to enjoy playing with their children in a mutually pleasurable way tend to have elements of separation and return in them – a kind of losing/finding theme, perhaps enacting the necessary separation process mentioned above:

> Dad bought out a yellow alligator and played a game with Adam, squeezing the toy then hiding it round his own back. Adam loved this, followed it,

looking round Dad's head to see where it had gone, and was surprised when it reappeared on the other side. He squealed, calling Dada, and Dad answered Baba. Dad put a folded duvet on the floor and put Adam down near it; Adam crawled onto it and put his cheek on it looking at the observer and smiling. He seemed to love the soft feeling.

It was as if this play allowed Adam to find comfort in the play with his dad, which reassured him that objects can be lost and found again, perhaps referring to the coming and going, and coming again, of both his mother and father into his life. It also enabled Adam to refind the primary sensual comfort of his breast relationship to his mother represented by the way he lay his cheek on the duvet, in a manner so suggestive of how Adam was seen to breast feed. It allowed him to feel he had two parents. Throughout this observation, alone with his father, they played separation–reunion games.

Dad lifted Adam on the sofa and Adam tried to get a pencil from Dad's ear. Dad let him take it. Adam seemed to want to put it in Dad's mouth. Dad kept saying no no, speaking gently. He played with Adam by removing the pencil and taking it out of sight round the back of his head; Adam loved playing this way. Dad let Adam take the pencil. The observer felt nervous watching, because she thought Adam could easily get the pencil in his own or Dad's eye. But Dad seemed not to be worrying about this.

The next game seemed to encompass the idea that contact can be made without the need to intrude into the object, as well as having separation aspects in it. Dad was being a good policeman:

Still on the sofa, Adam moved right into Dad; Dad played another game of saying "no, go away" as he pushed Adam away. Adam laughed as he came crawling into Dad again; and Dad pushed him away; Adam laughed a lot; Adam said Dada; Dad said Baba.

Fathers try and show the baby the world in many different ways. Perhaps their more frequent comings and goings into and out of the household in many families, at least in the early months, suggest to the baby that a world where Daddy goes, often called "work", exists. The father introduces the baby to this world in their play:

Tom pulled himself up and Jack took hold of Tom's hands and they began to walk around the room. Tom steered Jack towards the kitchen but Jack turned him round saying "let's go and see (the observer)." They came back toward the observer, past her, back towards the kitchen. Tom was leaning forward, helping Jack take the weight of his body. If Jack had let go Tom would have fallen face first. The second time he came past the observer, Jack steered him towards the sofa and loudly exclaimed that they had arrived. Tom laughed briefly and lifted his head out of the sofa and turned to the side and looked at the observer. He then stood on his feet and urged Jack to take him round again. Off they went, Jack stumbling slightly.

Here we see the father as literally providing a supporting structure for the baby as he goes into the world. The internalisation of this quality of strong fathering is crucial.

In this next sequence we see how the baby tries to identify with and understand his daddy's work, as well as how the father tries to facilitate this understanding.

Jack collected a file and some letters together and quietly began to write. Tom had moved over to the toys. He took a ball in one hand and a spoon in the other hand and banged the ball with the spoon. He went over to Jack and began to bang the spoon on Jack's file. Jack stopped what he was doing and silently waited. Tom then bent his knees and tried to push the studs on the spring of the file with the ball, he pressed them with the ball then scraped at them with the spoon. This he did for several minutes and seemed to be fascinated by the protruding studs on the file's spine. He then threw the ball away and took out of Jack's hand a bill. He brought the observer the bill. She took it. Jack asked Tom to collect it from her. Tom took it from her and returned it to Jack. Tom then reached for the pen in Jack's hand. Jack gave him the pen. Tom, gazing at Jack, made drawing gestures with the pen on the file. Jack said, "I think I'll do this later." He stood up and Tom went off towards the kitchen. Jack selected a piece of paper for Tom and a dish of fat crayons. He held the paper up and called to Tom. Tom returned to the sitting room and sat down by the paper. Jack went off saying he was going to put the kettle on. Whilst he was away, Tom took a crayon in both hands and used each hand to draw a mark on the paper. He then held two crayons in his left hand and drew with both crayons. Jack came back and held the paper, congratulating Tom on his effort.

Conclusion

Becoming a father is a complex process and one that is never completed. It is something that is highly determined by the quality of the man's internalised mother and father and his relationship with them, as well the external environment he finds himself in. This includes the personality of the woman whose child he fathers, as well as the temperament of the baby he has.

I have tried to show, using examples derived from infant observation, some of the elements that are involved in becoming a father. These include his assuming the role as protector of the mother–child and family space, his containing function for the mother and his work in both internal and external aspects. He also has a crucial role in laying down and maintaining the laws and enforcing the boundaries in both psychic and external reality to encourage separation of the mother and baby and to introduce the baby to the world. Throughout this chapter, I have not emphasised enough, though, the potential joy and privilege in being a father. I also am aware that it is possible and some-times desirable for a father to perform maternal functions, through identification with his internal mother and part of our constitutional bisexuality. However, I have also tried to show that the quality of this identification is all-important, especially if it implies a usurping of the maternal role. It is of course possible and sometimes desirable for the mother to be able to perform paternal functions through identification with her internal father. Single mothers, especially, need to be fathers at times.

We hope that the ministrations of the father enable the child to internalise a good paternal object, in combination with a mother, as the basis of his or her future intimate relationships. This would include the capacity to perform the functions of a good father or be capable of recognising one.

The answer to the question posed by my patient at the beginning, "Are fathers absolutely necessary", must be a resounding yes.

Acknowledgements

I am grateful to Ellie Roberts and Katya Bloom for allowing me to use material from their infant observations.

References

Bick, E. (1964) Notes on Infant Observation in Pyschoanalytic Training. *International Journal of Psychoanalysis*, 45, 558.

Bion, W.R. (1962) *Learning from Experience*. London, Heinemann.

Britton, R. (1989) The Missing Link: Parental Sexuality in the Oedipus Complex. In R. Britton, M. Feldman and E. O'Shaughnessy (eds) *The Oedipus Complex Today*. London, Karnac, pp. 83–102.

Meltzer, D. (1979) *Sexual States of Mind*. Strath Tay, Perths, Clunie Press.

Meltzer, D. (1988) The Role of the Father in Early Development. In *The Apprehension of Beauty*. Strath Tay, Perths: Clunie Press, pp. 59–66.

Miller, L., Rustin, M., Rustin, M. and Shuttleworth, J. (1989) *Closely Observed Infants*. London: Duckworth.

Murphy, J. (1982) *Five Minutes Peace.* Basingstoke, Hampshire: Macmillan Children's Books.

Reid, S. (1997) *Developments in Infant Observation – The Tavistock Model.* London: Routledge.

9

MISSING FATHERS

Hope and disappointment

Biddy Youell

This chapter describes work towards establishing some rudimentary paternal functioning in a woman who, when suddenly widowed, found her defences breaking down. Abuse by her own father had seriously impaired her ability to internalise a benign father and, in the absence of her husband, she could not go on parenting. Her long career as a competent, local authority foster carer came to an end and her relationships with her own children were seriously threatened.

The work described in this chapter is not conventional adult psychotherapy. It began as the kind of parent work which is traditionally offered alongside psychotherapy with children. It developed in a very particular way, and in order to arrive at considerations to do with the themes of this chapter it is necessary to give an outline of an unusual story.

Mrs H did not come to the clinic asking for psychotherapy. She did not come seeking help for herself with her work as foster parent to two abused and disturbed children. If there was any motive in relation to her own needs, it was in an unconscious identification with the children. She was in no doubt but that *they* needed professional, therapeutic help, but when offered weekly appointments for herself, in support of their psychotherapy, she said that surely monthly meetings would be more than enough. The children were difficult to manage but she was very experienced and the decision to adopt them had been made. To her mind, there was very little to discuss.

In spite of her initial reluctance, Mrs H attended weekly appointments and talked about the children's behaviour. She did so very much as a fellow professional, listening politely to my point of view, but at pains to convince me of her ability to manage whatever challenges the children presented her with.

She was, indeed, extremely experienced and I found myself full of admiration for a woman who was taking on such a task and was doing so in a way which really did seem to put the children first. They were going to be given a caring home, to be protected from further abuse, to be provided with the firm, boundaried behaviour management they needed, whilst being given the opportunity to attend the clinic for psychotherapy in an attempt to repair some of the damage to their internal worlds. A very slight feeling of unease at Mrs H's unquestioning confidence was easily quelled. For these two desperate children, it seemed to be a very happy outcome.

Over a period of some months, Mrs H told me about the children's horrific history of early neglect and abuse and the day-to-day struggles which took place as she sought to integrate them into her family. She had two adult daughters and two adolescent sons, as well as an adopted son aged twelve years. Her husband, Tom, had died suddenly four years earlier and she presented his death as something which had knocked her temporarily off track. She was now back in control of things and it felt good. She did not seem to have any difficulty in making decisions about the children, and she clearly found some of my musings unnecessarily complex. She was visibly shaken whenever the children's birth mother came into the picture for contact visits, but these were soon reduced to a minimum and Mrs H looked forward to the adoption as the point at which they would all be free from further interference. My tentative attempts to wonder about any ambivalence about the adoption seemed only to mobilise even more robust certainty in her. The children were going to have a better future.

As the weeks went by, however, Mrs H began to range more widely in what she talked about with me, describing her own children, other children she had cared for, and aspects of her own childhood. She told me a little about her social life and her attempts to make time for a widower who was showing an interest in her. She wanted to give it a try but was very wary of getting involved with anyone. She seemed to be struggling with how wary she felt about her increasing involvement in our sessions. She professed herself as amazed at how much she seemed able to talk and how quickly the fifty minutes went by each week. It became difficult to bring the sessions to a close, and there was less and less material about the two foster children.

At the end of the first year of our work, with very little advanced warning, Mrs H took the children on an extended trip to visit her mother in Canada. She said that she hoped it would cement their position in the family and convince her mother that she had a purposeful and satisfying life in England. She returned from this trip in a broken-down state, telling Social Services that the adoption was off and that the children had to be removed. She gave little explanation. As the shock waves spread through the clinic and the local authority, she did manage to say that it was not because of the children's behaviour (although they had been difficult). She simply felt she could not go on. The professionals responsible for the children were horrified and, at first, disbelieving. Mrs H was their most reliable, most competent foster carer. Surely it was a temporary setback. An offer of respite care was made and when this was rebuffed, they used more persuasive, almost blackmailing tactics; the children would end up in residential care, would never recover from the abuse, and it would all be her fault. It was striking that nothing could mobilise her concern for the children, and the clinic team quickly came to the view that it was better for them to move than to go on living in this bewildering setting. Mrs H took to her bed, coming out only to bring the children to their sessions and to attend her own.

Gentle probing about what had happened in Canada brought her to tell me that her relatives had been very disapproving. They thought her mad to take on such difficult children and she had suddenly felt herself to be alone. "I suddenly realised I was on my own and I couldn't manage. No Tom. No father." She was, of course, referring to the loss of her husband and the resulting absence of a partner for herself and a father for the children. Over time, I came to realise that she was articulating a very much more profound and primitive awareness of an absent, good, internal father.

Mrs H remained in a broken-down state for some weeks after the children's departure. She came to sessions, barely able to walk to the room, shaking, crying and struggling to put a few words together. She was cold and did not seem able to put on warm clothes. She seemed remote, cut off and aimless. She talked only about Tom's death and the parallels between the time when he died and how she was feeling now. There were many similarities, but also some differences. At that time she could satisfy people if she just washed her hair and put on clothes. Now she could not be bothered even to do that. In fact, she did not want to pick up the pieces this time; it had been a mistake to think that she could "get back to normal" by taking on the children. She told me that she had not dreamed at all after Tom's death but she was dreaming again now: terrible nightmares about worms eating away at her and enormous, beckoning black holes. In her dreams, she drove her car into the black hole in a passive, resigned way. There was nothing and nobody there to stop her. However, there was evidence that she had invested some small hope in our contact when she spoke of her fear that she would lose her place in the clinic if she did not have the children and was visibly relieved when we made arrangements to continue.

Mrs H's state of mind was a cause for great concern. She saw no point in going on with life. The children were barely mentioned as she focused more and more on Tom, their marriage, his death and her failure to mourn his passing. She knew she had not come to terms with her loss. She was angry, could not use the life insurance money, could not look at photographs, could not conjure up a picture of him in her mind. As she talked, I gained a picture of a kind, gentle and supremely reliable man. They had such plans for the future. Then he died, aged fifty-one. He went out to work and collapsed. She ceased to function and only got going again because the children needed her and she thought that at least she could be a good mother. Now it was all lost again.

Mrs H believed that a major catalyst and cause of her current predicament had been her developing relationship with her widower friend, Frank. She felt disturbed by how much she wanted his good opinion, how hurt she felt if he did not contact her every day, and how quick she was to imagine them settled in a cosy, married state. It was clear to me, if not to her, that another precipitating factor had been her contact with me. She had been invited to talk about herself to somebody who was prepared to listen and who seemed interested and non-judgemental. I felt responsible for, unwittingly, opening up a well of unmet need in her.

Twelve weeks after Canada, when she was a little stronger physically, she went away again, without warning, and spent two weeks alone in Cyprus, one of the places she had lived in as a child with her mother and brother. Her father had been in the army and had only ever been an occasional visitor to the family home. She had been having flashbacks and wanted to see if she could check out her memories if she returned to the actual places. When she returned, she told me what she believed I must have known all along; namely, that she was herself a neglected and abused child. She painted a bleak picture of a childhood in which her mother treated her with indifference. She had gone out to Cyprus to see the places where family photographs had been taken, always showing her brother close to her mother. If she appeared at all, it was at some distance from the rest of the family group. She remembered beatings and long hours spent in isolation in her bedroom. She described living under a heavy and immovable cloud of disapproval. When she was about five, they returned to England and her father would arrive like Father Christmas with presents from foreign tours of duty.

As my patient grew older, she became suspicious about some of the men who visited the house during her father's absences and she longed for the day when he would return home for good. This he finally did when she was nine years old and she sought solace in his company. He was a popular figure locally and she was proud to be seen with him. She could remember nothing about her parents' relationship with each other and had no memories of them ever really being together. They went out separately. Her mother's men friends continued to visit and women began to appear too. There were sometimes late and raucous parties in the house.

Her father's abuse of her began with a violent rape when she was twelve years old. It occurred when her mother was out at work and was repeated at least once a week for the next three and a half years. She looked to her mother for rescue, but her mother denied that anything was happening. (She had once come into the room.) Mrs H struggled with memories of how she had tried to avoid her father, how she was beaten for trying to get away, and how she eventually stopped fighting and learned to "switch off". "He could have my body but he was not having my mind." She took the money he gave her and tried not to remember that he accompanied the money with advice that she should always be sure and get paid. She was determined not to follow the career path he seemed to have mapped out for her and saved up some money to run away. Perhaps predictably, she rushed into a relationship which turned out to be both sexually abusive and violent. With two small children, she again mustered her resources and left, this time vowing that she would devote herself entirely to their protection. Her mother again turned her away.

She met and married Tom some years later and he became an effective father to the two girls. They then had two sons, before adopting the third. There was virtually no contact with the grandparents and, after Mrs H's father died, her mother moved to Canada. Mrs H was content with her husband, her children and her work. In spite of never talking about her own history, she knew that it was no accident that she chose to foster the most deprived and abused children in the county; she knew it answered a need in her. However, she felt proud that she could manage their behaviour and offer them the protection and unconditional acceptance which she had not had as a child.

This, in summary, is her story. It is one which unfolded over the weeks and months following the visits to Canada and Cyprus and was told against a backdrop of enormous acting out in her external life. Mrs H described the process as dealing with layers, as she systematically dismantled her life and came to her sessions to describe what she had done since our last meeting. Her adolescent children were ejected from home, the house sold, the youngest boy handed over to the eldest daughter who stepped in to care for him. Mrs H had ceased to function as a parent and I began, slowly, to be made aware of her own "parentless" state and, subsequently, to see that it was specifically a paternal function which was lacking.

It is not my purpose here to describe in detail the rest of Mrs H's story, except in so far as the work we subsequently did together serves to illustrate some thoughts on the hopes invested in a father when the relationship with the mother is disappointing and the devastation which can then result if the longed-for father is abusive. My hypothesis is that Mrs H suffered terribly from the absence of an internal couple, and that it was the slow and faltering development of containment in the work which led eventually to the possibility of gradual building and rebuilding of internal structures, through getting back in touch with what had begun to develop during her marriage to Tom. I intend to focus particularly on the aspects of paternal function which became live issues, notably those which might be seen as arising from the super ego. With illustrations from the work with Mrs H, I will discuss the difference between identification with external father figures and the internalisation of paternal function.

Thinking about Mrs H in terms of what I know about her history and what I have experienced in the consulting room, has taught me a great deal about what children face when there is an absent, external father or when a father behaves in a way which challenges normal assumptions and distorts development. Mrs H seems to have been very unfortunate in both parents. Her experience of her mother was of being unloved and unlovable. The absent father

151

in this constellation becomes a potential rescuer, somebody who will intervene and offer something different. A little girl's ordinary Oedipal phantasies take on a particular significance when there is such ambivalence between mother and daughter. Where there is a close, interdependent relationship between mother and child, the absent father may be feared as somebody who will arrive and punish the child for his or her exclusive possession of the mother, but where there is hostility, there is likely to be a further turning away from the mother towards the father.

Mrs H suffered agonies of doubt as to whether she was in some way responsible for what happened between her and her father. Whilst saying that she was not to blame, and being able to take that line most forcefully in relation to all the children she had cared for, she remained painfully uncertain as to her own culpability. She had no notion that she ever felt triumphant about engaging her father's interest in her latency years. She remembered only the relief she felt at being able to get out from under the cloud of disapproval and away from the painful vision of her mother sitting cosily with her brother. She often said that if there was any couple she felt excluded from, it was her mother and brother. She never understood *why* her mother seemed to dislike her so much and so was left with a fear that she must actually have been a *bad* or *horrible* child and that she did not deserve better than she received. She never entirely lost her desire to get close to her mother. After Tom's death, she went out to Canada, desperately wanting to stir some maternal feeling in her mother and to receive some approval, albeit at a late stage in life. Her mother greeted her without warmth, showed no interest in the children and offered no sympathy for the untimely loss of Tom.

She expressed her doubts about her own guilt in terms of whether she could have fought longer or harder against her father or whether she should have refused his money. Her delight at his return to the family home and her enjoyment of his interest in her as a little girl made the betrayal all the more confusing and destructive to her developing sense of self. Where she needed a father who would be an advocate for her with her mother, she found one who encouraged her to distance herself further and then betrayed her trust in the most horrible way. Mrs H's father was absent, then present and abusive, and the complex interplay between her experience with him and with a hostile mother left her with very distorted and unreliable internal objects.

Britton (1998) writes about the importance of reliable internal objects in providing the individual with a sense of continuity and thereby a basis for hope. He suggests that hope is based on an idea of a good mother, whom he characterises as "returning unsummoned and unmerited". This formulation has helped me to think about Mrs H's predicament. In the absence of an internal structure which could provide her with that sense of continuity, she was reliant on massive projection and splitting. After the serial disappointments she experienced with her mother, her father and her first partner, all the liveliness and hopefulness was projected into Tom. After his death, the edifice crumbled and she again found herself face to face with the distortions in her own internal world and at the mercy of the savagery of her internal objects. There were no benign links to either parent and she was left subject to dreams of being drawn into bottomless black holes with the complete absence of a restraining or protective object. In the weeks following her "breakdown" I was conscious of a profound sense of hopelessness. She attended appointments but seemed to expect nothing of me. In looking in more detail at some clinical material, I intend to illustrate this absence of parental function and to highlight ideas of mediation, moderation, advocacy and restraint.

Somewhere along the way, Mrs H had developed a capacity to mother children in a way which is very different from her descriptions of her experience with her own mother. She believed her grandmother to have been a much more friendly and accepting adult presence, and had fond memories of sitting in her much more welcoming kitchen. She also loved school, did well there and earned the approval of her teachers. She remembered being a willing helper on special occasions, an enthusiastic member of sports teams and a determined champion of the small, vulnerable and bullied children. Apart from what she managed to glean from benign sources outside her own home, Mrs H attributed her competence as a mother and foster carer to her bitter determination not to be like her own mother. She knew about multi-generational patterns of abuse and she took strength from knowing that she could break the cycle. She was not going to be abusive, neglectful or promiscuous. Her children would be loved and protected as she never was. All the negative was projected out and she was left occupying the moral high ground. After Tom's death she lost touch with this identity too and seemed to be drawn towards the kind of behaviour she most despised.

In the early stages of the work I found being with Mrs H in the consulting room a very puzzling experience. She slipped very easily into the routine of coming to sessions, and she certainly talked. She would tell me all that had happened in the intervening week and all that was preoccupying her, but there was very little which I felt able to get hold of and think about. I felt unconnected and found that I could not track the transference. I did not have the feeling that she saw what we were doing as any kind of joint enterprise. I often felt that I could have gone through an entire session without saying a word or could even have sent along a substitute and she would not have complained. When I responded to what was being said, or what I thought was being left unsaid, she would listen and then pick up where she had left off. She never minded if I had to change an appointment time, move rooms or take a longer break than usual. While our contract was to think together about the children, traditional parent-work, this did not seem too unusual or problematic. Then, it would have felt inappropriate to have been interpreting in the transference. When the children were gone and my remit changed, I could detect very little change in her attitude to me or in her understanding of our purpose.

153

This is, of course, not absence of transference but transference of a very particular kind. My counter-transference was not that I was being excluded or actively rejected; rather it was of being insignificant, irrelevant, absent. There was no lively expectation that ours was a developing relationship or that her words were taken in by a receptive, working mind.

It is well documented that patients who have been sexually abused often distance themselves, show very little curiosity and do not easily risk becoming attached to their therapists. Mrs H's lack of curiosity was qualitatively different from what I have experienced with other deprived and abused patients. It did not feel as if she were actively defending herself against a contact which might prove abusive so much as that she had no notion of there being a potential for any relationship which might be long-lasting or significant. She had no expectations beyond what sometimes felt akin to her version of competent fostering. It felt as if I was expected to be there, to do my job in a conscientious way and to listen to her, but not to do anything much with what I heard.

This counter-transference experience left me feeling helpless in the months of Mrs H's acting out. While I became increasingly aware of the absence of parental function, I found myself wanting to be prescriptive, to tell her to take better care of the children and to get herself out of what had become a mutually destructive relationship with Frank. In her ever more active pursuit of Frank, she was in search of an object to whom she could cling and with whom she could recreate what she had with Tom. It became clear that he was not Tom and that domestic contentment was not going to happen, but she seemed unable to prevent herself from being open to his increasingly sadistic manoeuvres. She dressed in a provocative way, engaged in what she described as "childish games" and allowed herself to be fooled into renewing the relationship on false promises over and over again. When the relationship broke up, she plotted ways to humiliate him, recognising that she was punishing him unfairly for what her father had done to her, though feeling no remorse. She moved on at great speed to other relationships and repeatedly left herself open to being badly treated. Her children were pushed further and further away and I found myself shocked and worried. Mrs H seemed entirely unconcerned about my reactions. I was not expected to have an opinion. There seemed to be no anxiety about what I might be thinking of her, and no fear of censure.

It was striking that whilst I struggled with what I felt was being projected into me – all the concern for her well-being and for the feelings of the children – at no stage did I feel out of patience. What she was doing was risky, self-destructive and apparently very selfish, and yet at the end of every session I was left feeling sad rather than disapproving. I felt I had been with a floundering, impetuous, angry and demanding, parentless child.

This became my preoccupation as the therapy progressed. Mrs H focused much of her bitterness on her hostile and promiscuous mother. She was desperate for the kind of unconditional acceptance which she believed should come with the job of being a mother. I felt challenged to provide that kind of maternal attention within the therapy, but increasingly could see how desperately she needed to get in touch with capacities which might be described as paternal. I came to see these as what she said she had known in Tom; namely, the ability to slow her down, help her to think, stop her reaching swift and unwise decisions and guard her against harsh judgements about herself or others. I was moved to behave in an overtly paternal way at times: insisting that she see her GP to discuss medication, telling her that the GP and I would need to talk to each other, insisting on being given some facts about the provision she had made for her youngest child. Perhaps my first act of this kind had been my insistence on our meeting weekly rather than monthly; maybe doing so had somehow touched a part of her which longed for a strong, paternal object who would know what she needed. In the weeks immediately after the breakdown, I had picked up the role of advocate for her in the wider network, attending meetings on her behalf, doing my best to represent her and protect her from further pressure. Within the clinic I made it clear that I was concentrating on her needs, and separated her records from those of the referred children in order to protect her privacy. I told her that somebody else was attending to the children's best interests. Perhaps for the first time ever, her own needs could remain located in her. I think I had been registered as a potentially effective object – at the very least as someone who seemed to want to see her. There was nothing of pretence in that. I did want to see her, I worried about her between sessions and developed immense respect for her courage in facing some very horrific memories. For many months she suffered all the symptoms of post-traumatic stress disorder and doubted she would ever recover.

After two years of telling and re-telling her story in therapy whilst re-ordering her life outside, Mrs H brought a dream:

> She was alone on a raft in the middle of a lake. There were mountains in the distance and she knew that some day she would have to go there, but for the time being she was quite comfortable, floating on calm waters. She was enjoying the peace and quiet. A lorry and trailer were waiting on the shore and she knew that somehow she had to get the raft up onto the trailer. She did not know when or how she was going to do it but was not worried. She felt confident. She said that there was nobody actually there in the dream, but she had the feeling that there was somebody there, just at her shoulder, waiting to help.

She said that she was pleased with the dream; she woke up feeling that at last there was evidence that she was recovering from her breakdown.

I was also very relieved to hear this dream; reassured that things were calm and that there was the germ of an idea of a benign object to assist her. There was also evidence of a linked-up parental couple in the trailer and lorry.

155

However, it is now clear to me that in my own relief at reaching calm waters I did not pay due attention to the detail of the dream. I now see that it was telling us something fundamental about Mrs H. When the waters were calm, she had an idea of a benign relationship with an external object, an external father/ husband/therapist, but she actually had not faced the question of how to climb the mountains, or of how to get her raft up onto the safety of the support of the parental couple (lorry and trailer). Her contentment was dependent on the waters remaining calm. She felt safe but was actually without direction or momentum; she was adrift on a raft. All the competence (and all the concern) was projected into an amorphous external figure.

The patient herself described how she cut off from her past as if a rope connecting her to her parents had literally been severed. Once she had left home they did not exist. Indeed, whilst the abuse was continuing she cut herself off, allowing her father, as she put it, access to her body but not to her mind. Much of her emotional life was amputated in the same way. She pledged herself to being a good and protective mother and she managed everything in a very conscious, deliberate and decisive way. In cutting off from the neglectful mother and the absent and then abusive father, she also cut herself off from the potential for development or reliance on helpful and supportive internal objects and structures. During her marriage to Tom, his influence had slowly modified something internally, and as her trust in him developed she allowed him to challenge many of her ways of being. She described this as "taking down one layer of the wall for every year of the marriage". He loved and accepted her for what she was, but also restrained her from being impetuous, teased her when she took herself too seriously and stepped in to mediate between her and the children when necessary. When he died, she cut herself off from memories of him, locked photos up in boxes and tried to resume life as a single parent as if she had never been part of a couple at all.

The absence of Tom in the sense of his apparent ability to restrain his wife from impetuous acts was something we both became aware of in the therapy. Time and again, Mrs H would come with news of another dramatic decision which appeared to have been both made and implemented since our last session. A week after she first admitted to finding her youngest son a strain, he had gone. When her eldest son moved out, he was expected to take absolutely everything with him. Mrs H spoke in terms of "complete breaks", "clean slates" and "new beginnings". It became clear that, for her, a new beginning required a complete severance from the past. There could be no half measures. She stated emphatically that it had been like that since the day she had first left home. She seemed unaware of how her children might be suffering and it seemed to me that she was in identification with a cruel, sadistic internal father, rather than with Tom. I found myself using words like "compromise" and "negotiation" as I held the position of the one who could stop and think. I was painfully aware that most of the thinking was going on after the event, but Mrs H did begin to engage in it and began to laugh at herself a bit as we saw how she repeated the pattern over and over again. For example:

> Mrs H came into the room and sat down. As usual, she took out her small pack of handkerchiefs and, as the tears began to seep from her eyes, told me that she was in a state about Christmas. She was not going to do what the family wanted. She was not going to go to her daughter's. She had told them she would not be available. No way. She wanted to be on her own. She would just go away or take the phone off the hook.
>
> I waited and, as I made eye contact with Mrs H, the shadow of a smile crossed her face. "It's me again isn't it? Typical." We went on to talk about her feelings and fears about a family Christmas. As we did so, various compromises seemed to come to her mind. "I suppose if I had Christmas Eve and Boxing Day to myself, I could go over on the day."

Two years after the fateful visit to Canada, Mrs H decided to go again. She said she was going to confront her mother about the abuse and I felt the familiar rising sense of alarm. However, this time she booked a flight for seven weeks' time, wanting to use her sessions before her departure to examine her own motives and think about the various phantasies she had about this trip. She had restrained herself from leaving immediately and was giving me time to help her prepare. She also talked in a quite different way about a new relationship with another potential partner, saying that she did not want to rush at anything; she was going to try to take it a day at a time and see how it developed.

When the most dramatic acting out came to an end and we had established an idea of taking time to think around her plans, the absence of a mediating function of an internal father became another very live issue within the therapy. Some time after the break-up of the family and the disclosure, Mrs H fell out with both her elder daughters. This triangle of relationships had always been difficult; one or other daughter always seemed to be adrift and was seen as "sulking", "selfish" or "wrapped up in themselves". (Accusations which Mrs H had frequently levelled against herself as she came out of the initial stages of her breakdown.) This sequence of events began when both daughters ignored Mother's Day and she felt that the two of them were in an alliance against her, and in competition with her for the position of mother in the family. She was suddenly estranged from them both and she seemed unable to do anything about it. She was actually very hurt and very worried but she sat back, doing nothing, insisting that they would have to come around. Again, I was left with all the concern, feeling alarmed as I waited, seeing an ever-widening gulf opening up and wondering if anybody was thinking about how the three younger members of the family might be feeling.

Mrs H described herself as stubborn and stupid but refused to shift. I felt myself being invited to sink into the same passivity, and I became very active, speculating as to what she felt would happen if she made a move towards them, speculating about how everybody was really feeling, drawing parallels between the current situation and what I had heard about in her past relationships and, above all, fighting my way past all the angry denial to recognise the depth of hurt, disappointment and fear she was determined not to feel. I talked about the risks she was taking in allowing a rift to develop when she knew how much the gulf between herself and her own mother troubled her. She blandly replied that it was history repeating itself. I thought about the way her daughters were being expected to know about her feelings and needs without being told. They were being challenged, tacitly, to provide Mrs H with the mothering she craved and they were being set up to fail. She felt only their disapproval, whilst I wondered just how confused and alarmed they might be feeling. I wondered aloud about how they might be reacting to the news of a new man partnering their mother and about the way she and her eldest daughter were denying their rivalrous feelings in relation to the shared care of the youngest boy. Nobody moved.

This went on for many weeks. Each week she would engage in the discussion and leave the room in such a way that I would feel some confidence that she was going to sort it out. She would come back a week later and with a defeated smile would tell me that they were still not speaking. Eventually, probably in tones of exasperation, I spoke about how an onlooker felt; namely impotent, enraged and frustrated. I talked about the conspicuous absence of an adult who might, as it were, get the three of them in a room and knock their heads together. I asked if this was what Tom would have done had he been alive. Mrs H smiled with relief, went away and came back the following week with peace talks well underway. I felt that I had jumped into the vacant shoes of the missing father/ husband but doubted whether any of this experience was being internalised. I was worried that her "recovery" (her word) was dependent on the concrete existence of the weekly session. However, from this point on, there was evidence of her taking back some of her own sense of agency and things continued to improve in her external life.

It was not until much later in the therapy that she very tentatively began to think about the enormity of what she had done to her children and to feel guilt and regret for the way she had acted. She felt sad about the two foster children and had to curb her desire to find out where they were and renew contact. She missed her youngest son and wanted him back, but stopped to think what a further upheaval would mean to him and what her daughter would feel if she did reverse the arrangement. She decided that to take him back would be selfish, and she compromised by offering more support and spending more time with them both. It seemed to me that this way of thinking only became available to her after we had observed and talked about innumerable incidents of impetuous action and she had begun to internalise a more thoughtful, cautious object.

After four years, it was clear that there was a much more obvious and accessible transference significance in what was being brought to sessions. She had an idea that she ought to be ready to stop and was suddenly curious about my holidays, annoyed by a change of time and room and very preoccupied with phantasies about how I felt about her talk of finishing. She was aware that she was tempted to leave suddenly. She was worried that if she chose to leave I would never be open to hearing from her again. She was sure that if she said she wanted to go, I would either throw her out immediately or mock her for thinking she could possibly manage without me. The negotiation stirred up feelings about her departure from home at fifteen as well as her husband's sudden death. When I did not immediately fix a date for finishing, she felt very much at sea. There was a lot of material to work with and we had to take care not to move too quickly through it. It felt precarious, as if too sudden a move could sever our connection.

Talk of ending reopened issues to do with the loss of Tom and my patient's inability to mourn. Renewed focus on this, together with the material about separating from me, helped us to understand more of her predicament. It was clear that her failure to deal with loss and separation had not begun with the death of Tom, but was linked with the way she experienced the neglect and abuse of her childhood. There had been some sort of healing in her marriage to Tom and in their joint parenting of their children, but his sudden death had felt like an assault, a repetition of the rape. She felt cut off from helpful objects in a very concrete way: the photo albums remained closed and she was unable to use the insurance money which had become somehow confused with the money her father left in her bedroom. She could not mourn the loss of Tom any more than she had been able to mourn the loss of the hoped-for father. She admitted that she now wanted to walk out of a session one day and never look back. At the same time, she was terrified of doing so.

Steiner (1993) writes that in order to deal with loss, the bereaved patient has to relinquish omnipotent control over the object and mourn it. His suggestion is that in the process of mourning, projective identification can be reversed and the split-off elements reclaimed. Mrs H had reached what Steiner suggests is the first stage in this process in therapy; namely, she was having an experience of containment, of an object capable of gathering up the projections and thinking about them. Anxiety had been lessened but was dependent on the continuing presence of the object. It was at about this time that she brought another dream:

She was in the nearby High Street with her husband, Tom. She left him there and walked along towards the clinic. Suddenly she was in a hilly part of town and could not find the street where she remembered the clinic to be. She became very anxious but kept looking and suddenly the clinic was in front of her. She came into the building, worrying about being late, and felt enormous relief when she found that I was there, waiting in the consulting room with a comfortable chair ready for her.

159

Mrs H was shocked at having a dream with me in it. She also said that Tom very rarely appeared in dreams. It had felt such a relief to have him alive and to leave him in such an ordinary way doing the shopping. We thought together about the getting lost in the streets as being symbolic of the years of turbulence since his death. She said she felt it said something about how important the sessions had become and she doubted her recent confidence about being ready to stop. It seemed to me that in this dream Tom was helping her towards making use of a maternal object in the transference.

In the same session, Mrs H talked about her fears in relation to her new partner. She did not know how much "internal strength" she had got. Was it all lodged in him? Was she becoming too attached to him and could the whole cycle happen again? What if he let her down? I was able to talk in very direct terms about her fears of being without her weekly contact with me and her doubts as to whether she could cope if we were to stop meeting. The very fact that Mrs H was listening to an interpretation in the transference and seeing the relevance of it gave me hope for the future of the work. It felt, at last, that we had a therapeutic relationship in which both maternal and paternal transferences were active, and that there was, therefore, an opportunity to work towards a second stage (Steiner 1993) – that of establishing a more flexible and reversible form of projective identification.

References

Britton, R. (1998) *Belief and Imagination*. London: Routledge.
Steiner, J. (1993) *Psychic Retreats*. London and New York: Routledge.

10

FATHERS AND THE TRANSGENERATIONAL IMPACT OF LOSS

Paul Barrows and Kate Barrows

In psychoanalytic thinking the ability to deal with loss is seen as central to the achievement of mental health. In this chapter we would like to suggest that fathers have a critical – and previously underestimated – role to play in how well this central developmental task is accomplished.

It has long been recognised that the way in which the losses inherent to the Oedipal situation are negotiated may be critical for future development. Britton, for example, writes:

> The initial recognition of the parental sexual relationship involves relinquishing the idea of sole and permanent possession of mother and leads to a *profound sense of loss* which, if not tolerated, may become a sense of persecution. Later, the oedipal encounter also involves recognition of the difference between the relationship between parents as distinct from the relationship between parent and child: the parents' relationship is genital and procreative; the parent–child relationship is not. This recognition produces a *sense of loss* and envy, which, if not tolerated, may become a sense of grievance or self-denigration.
>
> (Britton, 1989, pp. 84–85; our italics)

The father's (sexual) role in this Oedipal drama has, perhaps, tended to obscure the other important (parental) role that he has to play at this time as the one who may be able to help the infant tolerate those feelings of loss.

The losses of the Oedipal position, however, as Klein demonstrated, are fore-shadowed by other, earlier losses. For example, in her paper *A Contribution to the Psychogenesis of Manic-Depressive States* (1935/1985), she argued that such states

161

are the result of a failure to adequately negotiate that prototype of later losses, namely the loss of the breast:

> The first and fundamental external loss of a real loved object, which is experienced through the loss of the breast before and during weaning, will only result later on in a depressive state if at this early period of development the infant has failed to establish its loved object within its ego.
>
> (Klein, 1935/1985, p. 28)

The ability of the infant to establish such an object in its internal world is dependent on a variety of factors, including the nature of the external support that the child receives at this time:

> We must remember that at the critical time of weaning the child, as it were, loses his 'good object', that is, he loses what he loves most. Anything which makes the loss of an external good object less painful and diminishes the fear of being punished will help the child to preserve the belief in his good object within.
>
> (Klein, 1936/1985, p. 296)

Whilst Klein suggests here that a whole range of factors may come into play, subsequent analytic literature has tended to focus almost exclusively on the mother's role in 'making this loss less painful' and in particular on her ability to help the infant through the containment of its distressed feelings (see, for example, O'Shaughnessy, 1964). Little attention has been given to the possible role of the father in this respect.

On the whole, when the father's role *has* been addressed (other than as the third party in the Oedipal triangle), it has tended to be as a support to the mother. By sustaining and containing the mother, it would be argued, she is enabled, in her turn, to nurture the infant. Bick's classic paper on infant observation contains a moving illustration of how crucial this role can be in the case of a mother who was very lacking in confidence in her maternal abilities, and she comments on how 'This supportive behaviour of the father seemed to be an important factor in the gradual improvement in the mother's closeness and tolerance towards the baby' (Bick, 1964, p. 560).

This tradition continues in the work of such recent writers as Daniel Stern, who argues in his latest book (Stern, 1995) that what he refers to as the 'motherhood constellation' (the triad of infant–mother–maternal grandmother) is the primary psychic organiser for the woman at this time. 'It is expected that the father and others will provide a supporting context in which the mother can fulfil her maternal role' (p. 174).

When the infant does, however, face the loss of its primary relationship it is likely to do so in the context of the care being provided by another, substitute carer. The attitude of that carer and the way in which they help (or hinder) the child in this task may be quite as critical to its outcome as the role ascribed to the mother (see, for example, Magagna, 1997, for a discussion of this issue in relation to the role of the nanny).

Fathers, for obvious reasons, are likely to have a particularly crucial role to play in this respect. Not only may they need to help the infant deal with the inevitable loss of an exclusive relationship to the mother, but they may also at times need to intervene to help disentangle an overly involved relationship. Maiello (1997), for example, describes a child being helped out of a symbiotic relationship with her mother by the father: 'The father became more and more important in the child's life. Her language developed rapidly. She called "papa" and said her own name and they often played together' (p. 42). Maiello describes a piece of play in which the father comforts the little girl who is upset that her doll's dummy is for the doll, not for her: 'With her father's support, she could face the loss of the exclusive relationship with her mother and accept the link between two not-me part objects, the mouth and the dummy of her doll. Triangulation in its infinite varieties had become possible' (p. 42).

It is our view that the father's ability to support the child, in the way Maiello describes, will be profoundly influenced by his own history, particularly how he has dealt with losses in his own life, and that in this way he will profoundly influence the developing infant's capacity to face loss.

Empirical support for this view, and the argument that the father's contribution will be quite distinct from that of the mother, is furnished by the recent research of Fonagy *et al.* (1993). They set out to 'measure' the 'ghosts in the nursery' originally described by Fraiberg *et al.* (1975). This research, which demonstrated that the child's attachment status is correlated with the parent's attachment status (as measured by the Adult Attachment Interview), also showed that this may differ according to the parent involved. That is, the child may be securely attached to one parent and insecurely attached to the other. They concluded that: 'There appeared to be no association between the child's relationship to one parent and his or her relationship to the other . . . Evidently, the ghost appeared only in relation to one parent and did not haunt the nursery sufficiently to spoil the child's relation to the other' (Fonagy *et al.*, 1993, p. 972).

This would seem to be a critical finding since it suggests that not only is it not necessarily the case that the relationship to one parent may be modified by the relationship to the other, but it also confirms that the child will have quite separate internal representations of each parent. Much of the recent literature on parent–infant psychotherapy (e.g. Cramer and Palacio-Espasa, 1993) has concentrated solely on elucidating the 'ghosts' haunting the mother's internal world. Fonagy's conclusions underline the fact that the father's 'ghosts' may have just as powerful and specific an impact on the developing child's psyche.

A clinical illustration of this is furnished by the R family, who were seen by one of us (PB) in the context of an Under-Fives Counselling Service in a Child

Guidance Clinic. The family had been referred by their Health Visitor because of sleep problems with their 18-month-old son, Richard. They were described as being 'at the end of their tether', Richard never having slept through the night without them since birth. Both their health visitor and general practitioner had tried intensive input by way of sleep management programmes, but to no avail.

The family was offered a relatively quick appointment and, as it was clear from our initial telephone contact that the father was keen to attend, a time was negotiated that he could manage. When they arrived at the Clinic the father was not there but was on his way and hoped to join us soon. Richard was a bright little boy who came into my room looking around enquiringly. He soon settled in and began to explore the toys. His mother, at my invitation, began to tell me about the problems that brought them to the Clinic. She described how Richard would wake up three or four times in the night, and had done so since he was born. She was concerned to know what it was that woke him up. When I enquired how his waking was dealt with it sounded initially as though she would go into his room to settle him down, and that at times he would settle very quickly, without really having wakened fully, once he had had a little drink from his bottle. She explained that he now had juice or water and that they had phased out milk some time ago as they felt that he did not really need it. She felt that having the bottle was now really more of a habit than a real need.

As we discussed this in a little more detail it became apparent that in fact the parents now rarely tried to settle him in his room, but would immediately bring him into their own bed in order to be able to get some rest themselves. This did not mean, however, that he no longer woke through the night, but that if he did so he would very quickly drop back off again knowing that they were there.

The father arrived at this point, some five to ten minutes into the session, and greeted Richard very warmly, clearly enchanted by him. We explained what we had covered so far, and the father went on to add that they had tried all sorts of things to help Richard stay in his room having had advice from both the health visitor and the GP. He too, like the mother, expressed concern about what it could be that was waking Richard up, although neither seemed to think that it was a matter of him having bad dreams. The father joined in playing with his son throughout our discussion and Richard responded by often taking toys over to show to him.

I asked about how and when Richard actually went off to sleep, and learnt that in fact once he had been put down in his cot one of his parents always remained with him until he had fallen asleep. I commented on the fact that this meant that he had therefore not had the chance to develop his own resources and get himself off to sleep, so that when he did wake in the night he had no experience of getting himself back to sleep. I asked about his earliest infancy and the mother explained that as a baby he had fed every two hours. She had breast fed him for six weeks and then moved quite quickly on to bottle feeding and then to solids, largely, it seemed, out of worry that he was not getting enough. It appeared that Richard's crying had regularly been interpreted as a demand for more food (and they had felt this was confirmed because it did indeed stop him crying), but of late they had begun to question this and to wonder whether there might have been other explanations such as wind or colic. He had regularly had a bottle when he woke at night, but now they wondered if he really needed this or whether his regular pattern of waking had just become a continuation of his habit of being fed two-hourly. They added that they were desperate about getting more sleep, and that at times they had left him with maternal grandparents for a few days to have time to recover. The grandparents had had the same difficulties with him.

I commented on the fact that they seemed very concerned that *something* was waking him up and that therefore something was wrong. I then said that it was, however, known that in fact children do frequently wake, or at least half wake, through the night as seemed to be the case with Richard. Often, however, they will then get themselves back to sleep, perhaps just turning over and drop-ping off again. I suggested that perhaps the question we needed to look at was not so much *why* he woke up so much as what happened then. Why did he call out? How did they respond when he did?

I asked more about how they felt when he did call out and the father quickly stated that he could not bear to hear Richard crying. It soon became clear that Richard's mother would have left him for longer and that it was his father who would intervene. I asked the father to tell me a little about his own family. I learnt that he is from Spain, and that he has two older sisters and a younger brother – he was, therefore, the first-born son. He described his family as very close and said that he had been the only one to 'escape', having left Spain at 22. I asked if this had been difficult. He said not, but that there was something very claustro-phobic about the family and he had been determined to get away. His father had told him that he would be back within three weeks – so he had deliberately bought a one-way ticket to prove him wrong and had been in England ever since. He did not regret his decision, but his mother had been 'gutted' when he left.

Richard was playing with a toy phone and the father told him to speak to 'gramps', explaining to me that they called his father every week. His mother, he told me, had died about three years ago so that she had never seen this grandson. When I asked about their decision to have children, he went on to explain that initially he had had no wish to have children. It had only been with his mother's death that he had found himself wanting to do so. I asked him how he understood this, and he replied that with the death of his mother he had lost something very precious and that he had felt the need to replace this. Richard filled, or at least partially filled, the void left by the loss of his mother. He emphasised how precious Richard was to him, and how he could not bear to hear him upset. He could see no reason why Richard should be upset or uncomfortable.

This information seemed to throw some light on the difficulties the father experienced in implementing the advice given by the health visitor and others. The distress at separation expressed by Richard's crying touched on powerful feelings in the father to do with the way he had had to tear himself away from his own family in order to achieve some degree of separateness. It would also seem that Richard came to represent, in some way, the paternal grandmother – a very precious object – who should not be allowed to experience suffering, perhaps from guilt at her 'gutted' response to his departure. One can only speculate that this response might be indicative that other earlier separations would have been felt to be unbearably painful and that, in consequence, the father himself had little help in managing those feelings. The 'ghost' of the paternal grandmother seems to have loomed large in this nursery.

It was not possible in this first session to explore all these possible ramifications. I did comment on the fear that they, and particularly the father, expressed; that is, that they would be doing Richard some real damage by leaving him upset. I also underlined the fact that in going off to sleep with them present Richard could not develop his own resources and so had to turn to them in the night. The father took up this point at the end of the session and said that he thought they needed to go away and find a way of helping him to get off to sleep by himself. He also said quite openly that he felt he needed reassurance that they would not be harming Richard by leaving him.

It did not prove possible to explore any further the issues raised around separation for this father, since when they returned two weeks later the situation was vastly improved. Twice Richard had slept right through the night, and on the other occasions he had remained in his cot and been reassured by them simply calling out to him. They went on to tell me that they had decided to leave him in his cot when going off to sleep and remained nearby to reassure him. On the first night he had protested for several hours and the father had eventually gone in to him (to the mother's considerable relief), but the next night he had not protested for long and since then had gone off quite readily. The father agreed that he had found it very hard and the mother jokingly said that she had had to keep reassuring him that Richard was all right – had indeed been having to reassure the two of them, Richard and his father! They felt they did not need any further help at this stage.

In this case we can see quite clearly how the father's difficulty in facing loss was projected into the child, leading to an entangled relationship with both parents. Even when not quite so directly involved, a father's own difficulties in this area may interfere critically with his capacity to help the child face the impact, not only of such inevitable losses as that of the more exclusive relationship with the mother, but also the many other losses that a child may have to face.

When there has not been the possibility of resolving such difficulties early on, as in the example of Richard, they may profoundly influence the individual's subsequent development. In the case of Miss Y, her father's own history of tragic loss in his childhood seems to have left him ill-equipped to help her deal with her feelings of loss and separation, and in consequence her development had ground to a halt.

She was referred to one of us (KB) in her late twenties with bulimia, suicidal thoughts and extreme withdrawal from life and people. Although Miss Y did express her desperation about herself when she came for her initial consultation, when her analysis started it soon became clear that she was entrenched in a retreat which she was terrified of leaving, and which at times she felt to be far superior to other modes of existence. She talked about how bad she felt about having thrown away all her opportunities, particularly in her education and her social relationships, but then went on to talk of dieting and of filling herself up with books. As she spoke she took on an arrogant tone, saying how she can have such intense experiences with books that she can't see how people bear to live their boring lives, with mortgages, children and jobs, although there must be some 'compensations'. She had withdrawn from a painful awareness of lost opportunities. Her retreat was a place which seemed to her to be superior to the realities of life, which she was looking down on as though she now had no needs of her own and nothing to lose.

As the analysis progressed she gradually became aware of the barrenness of her retreat. After eight months of analysis she talked of not having minded too much seeing her mother and mother's boyfriend at the weekend. This was in contrast to her previously having refused any contact with them as a couple. She seemed sad, however, and talked of her fear of not being able to remember anything for an exam. Then she said that she was thinking of being like Robinson Crusoe on his island, surrounded by books and all that he needed. This seemed at first a calming thought. But then she thought of how arid this actually felt, it was more like Napoleon, imprisoned on St Helena – or was it Elba? Where once there used to be green and fertile vegetation and goats, now it seemed a barren place. She imagined him confined to the grounds of the house, riven with the wish to get away. I said that she wanted to be like she thinks Robinson Crusoe is, make herself an island, feel that books are all that she needs. But then she feels barren and bleak, trapped like Napoleon, shut away from life. She agreed, crying, and said that it doesn't work.

In this example Miss Y attempts to make herself an island where there can be no loss. In Miss Y's island retreat she models herself upon a father who is apparently invulnerable to loss, who can meet his own needs on his intellectual island. This sounds like Miss Y's account of her actual father, who apparently had no friends outside the family and whose books and study were his retreat. However, she became painfully aware of the fact that this could also become a prison, a life-sentence; that this was a bleak solution to the vicissitudes of relationships and of loss, of not having all that one needs.

Miss Y's feelings of exclusion took the form of extreme misanthropy. She hated people in general, in the street, on the bus travelling to and from her sessions, and she professed utter callousness towards anyone with needs. Children, old people, victims of violence were all subject to cold and sadistic scorn. This seemed related to her feelings of rivalry, envy and possessiveness and to be intensified by the fact that she cut off her own needy aspects from possibilities of receiving concern and support. Her callousness also served another purpose: there was then no need to feel upset about the damage or loss of life which she so scorned – there was nothing and nobody whose loss could affect her.

Miss Y's fear of contact with someone who could stand neither her ambivalence nor her feelings of loss seemed of central importance to her withdrawal from contact. For instance, early in her analysis there were several sessions which seemed helpful, following which she was able to have a meal and socialise with people, something which she had previously been unable to do. She seemed heartened, but then feelings of exclusion came up and she felt that her positive feelings were getting lost. She told me that she used to love animals as a child and wanted to keep all sorts of pets. Her first pets were goldfish and they developed a fungus; two of them died. She remembered 'screaming with terror and a sort of frustration' when she discovered that two of them had fin-rot, and her father said that she should not keep pets if she was that upset before they even died. I interpreted her fear that I might not stand her feelings about things getting killed off inside her. She then remembered moving house aged ten and going back to stay with her best friend. When she came home she was terribly unhappy, crying a lot. Her father said that she shouldn't go any more if she was that unhappy when she came home, so she tried to shut out her feelings and bury herself in books. She did not have any more close friends until after her father died, when she formed an intense friendship with another girl at school. However, she could not stand her friend's other attachments, even to her parents, so she broke off the friendship. I commented on her fear that I would not stand her upset feelings between the sessions, nor her feelings about my other attachments, to my family and others. She described her father as finding her upset feelings 'irritating and annoying', as though he had no place for them. He was a very 'moral' person and could not tolerate any jealousy or squabbling; Miss Y said that it 'made him go all sad'. She felt inadequate and despairing because she knew that she could not be 'mature' enough to please him. This was something which she also feared in relation to me.

It seemed of crucial importance in relation to Miss Y's withdrawal from relationships that at a point when she was distressed about the loss of a friend, or the illness of her pets, her father could not help her to stand her feelings. It seems likely, moreover, that this deficit was already a feature at the time when she lost the special, feeding relationship with her mother and had to cope with her mother's subsequent pregnancies. She had often expressed acute hostility towards her mother's relationship with her younger siblings and with her father. The damage to her pets may have represented her anxieties about what her feelings could do to her parents or siblings. It seemed that there had been no one to help Miss Y come to terms with her feeling that if she were to care about people she could also damage them, which then led her to withdraw from live contact and her fears of consequent loss.

The persistent impression of her father as unable to tolerate feelings, particularly feelings of loss, made sense much later on in Miss Y's third year of analysis. She told me how when her father was eight years old and he was looking after his younger sister in the garden she fell into the pond and was drowned. He felt that his father never forgave him and his mother never recovered. These grandparents seemed to Miss Y frighteningly stern and disapproving. She used to dread visiting them and felt that she should sit still 'as though she didn't exist'. In feeling that she should not exist she seems to have identified with her father's younger sister. She frequently expressed this in terms of feeling that she was not meant to have a life like other people: on one occasion she thought of hermit crabs who lay their eggs in the sand and when the young hatch out they have to get to the sea. Only one or two survive out of thousands, and she felt that she was one of the ones who was not meant to survive. One of the factors in her internal environment which militated against the survival of her needy self was her father's inability to bear her feelings of loss. This seemed linked to his inability to mourn his own losses. The ghosts of his sister and of his own uncontaining parents were present in the analysis, as were his childhood feelings of intolerable grief and guilt. Miss Y could not turn to her father to help her to cope with the feelings involved in separating from her mother as her father's experience of undealt-with loss prevented him from being able to help her to deal with her feelings in their own right. Therefore she attempted to retreat to a position where she would be undisturbed by emotions which might cause fear or disapproval in her father or his internal objects; she was haunted by his ghosts. Into this internal father she also projected her own intolerance of feelings of ambivalence or of loss.

Fundamental to emotional development is the capacity to relinquish sole possession of external objects and to establish them within the psyche. This entails being able to tolerate the ambivalent feelings generated by the recognition of the object's independent life and relationships with others. Hence the ability to stand loss is not only a function of the ability to tolerate feelings of grief, but also to tolerate feelings of ambivalence towards the relinquished object and the damage that is felt to have been inflicted by this ambivalence. If there is no chance for these feelings to be contained and worked through, then they cannot be integrated into the personality, which is consequently impoverished and restricted, as in the case of Miss Y. A wide range of feelings were unavailable to her, lively feelings as well as aggressive ones. In this way, intolerance of loss can lead to intolerance of life.

However, in the course of her analysis she recovered from her bulimia, established a sexual relationship for the first time and became able to pursue a career – she managed to allow herself to have the essential things in life which

169

previously she had been afraid to have because, in the words of a Shakespeare sonnet:

This thought is as a death, which cannot choose
But weep to have that which it fears to lose.

The childhood loss suffered by Miss Y's father seems to have contributed to his difficulty in helping her to bear the feelings of loss and separation inherent in normal development. His subsequent death in her adolescence, at a time when she was beginning to rebel, prevented her from having another chance of working through earlier conflicts related to separation, as well as facing her with another loss which she was not equipped to bear.

We believe these clinical examples illustrate the critical role that fathers may play in determining the future psychological development of their children. As Phares and Compas (1992) note: 'paternal behaviours, personality characteristics and psychopathology are significant sources of risk for child and adolescent psychopathology' (p. 403). Further, it appears to us that it is more specifically the father's capacity to help the child negotiate the essential developmental task of coming to terms with loss that is a key factor, forming as it does the cornerstone for future mental health. That capacity is in turn determined to a large extent by the father's own experiences of loss, and particularly, as the work of both Fraiberg *et al.* (1975) and Fonagy *et al.* (1993) has emphasised, by his capacity to construct a coherent narrative of those losses. These conclusions are borne out in a recent paper by Walters (1997) in which she demonstrates that significant loss in the father's own background is often an important factor in the clinical presentation of children. 'Painful early experiences may also make it difficult for fathers to be open to recognition of difficult experiences in their own children and thus harder for them both to parent and to recognise problems that might require clinical intervention' (p. 420).

It is at the time of weaning – of the infant's first major experience of loss – that the father will often be most naturally the object called upon to help the child process the attendant feelings. When his own losses are unresolved he will probably lack the necessary emotional resources for this task. On the other hand, when things go well, he may be an invaluable resource to his infant.

The father may be helped in this task by the fact that he must himself, at this stage, renegotiate earlier losses as he 'loses' his previous identity for his new parental/paternal role and also, to a degree, 'loses' his wife to the baby and her new role as mother. Just as the mother's loss of identity may prepare her to be in tune with her baby's primitive anxieties, so the father's experience of loss may prepare him to help his infant face the loss of an exclusive relationship with his primary object – as well as recognise the gains inherent in this same experience as he reaches out to new relationships.

References

Ballard, C. and Davies, R. (1996) 'Postnatal depression in fathers'. *International Review of Psychiatry* 8 (1): 65–71.

Bick, E. (1964) 'Notes on infant observation in psychoanalytic training'. *International Journal of Psycho-Analysis* 45: 558–566.

Britton, R. (1989) 'The missing link: parental sexuality in the Oedipus complex'. In R. Britton, M. Feldman and E. O'Shaughnessy (eds) *The Oedipus Complex Today* London: Karnac Books, pp. 83–102.

Britton, R. (1992) 'The Oedipus situation and the depressive position'. In R. Anderson (ed.) *Clinical Lectures on Klein and Bion*. London and New York: Tavistock/Routledge, pp. 34–45.

Cramer, B. and Palacio-Espasa, F. (1993) *La pratique des psychothérapies mères-bébés*. Paris: P.U.F.

Fonagy, P., Steele, M., Moran, G., Steele, H. and Higgitt, A. (1993) 'Measuring the ghost in the nursery: an empirical study of the relationship between parents' mental representations of childhood experiences and their infants' security of attachment'. *Journal of the American Psychoanalytic Association* 41 (4): 957–989.

Fraiberg, S., Adelson, E. and Shapiro, V. (1975) 'Ghosts in the nursery: a psychoanalytic approach to the problems of impaired infant–mother relationships'. In *Clinical Studies in Infant Mental Health*. London: Tavistock (1980).

Klein, M. ([1935] 1985). 'A contribution to the psychogenesis of manic depressive states'. In *Love, Guilt and Reparation*. London: Hogarth Press.

Klein, M. ([1936] 1985) 'Weaning'. In *Love, Guilt and Repartation*. London: Hogarth Press.

Magagna, J. (1997) 'Shared unconscious and conscious perceptions in the nanny–parent interaction which affect the emotional development of the infant'. In S. Reid (ed.) *Developments in Infant Observation*. London: Routledge.

Maiello, S. (1997) 'Twinning phantasies in the mother–infant couple and the observer's counterpoint function'. *International Journal of Infant Observation* 1 (1): 31–50.

O'Shaughnessy, E. (1964) 'The absent object'. *Journal of Child Psychotherapy* 1 (2): 34–43.

Phares, V. and Compas, B. (1992) 'The role of fathers in child and adolescent psychopathology: Make room for daddy.' *Psychological Bulletin* 111 (3): 387–412.

Stern, D. (1995) *The Motherhood Constellation*. New York: Basic Books.

Walters, J. (1997) 'Talking with fathers: the inter-relation of significant loss, clinical presentation in children and engagement of fathers in therapy'. *Clinical Child Psychology and Psychiatry* 2 (3): 415–430.

11

FATHERLESS SONS

Psychoanalytic psychotherapy with bereaved boys

Suzanne Blundell

Introduction

In this chapter, I explore the internal world of bereaved boys who faced adolescence without their father. Furthermore, in the majority of the cases I shall present, when the father was alive he had been absent from the family and therefore had been unable to establish a proper relationship with his son. I would like to reflect on the extreme difficulties of mourning the death of an absent father and the resulting emotional struggle to cope with being an adolescent and finding a mature male identity. I base this chapter on individual psychotherapy with a number of bereaved boys aged between twelve and eighteen years.

The referral process

The referrals come from a variety of sources, such as teachers, social workers, doctors, foster parents and, of course, mothers. Some older adolescents refer themselves. The case material shows that the timing and the process of referral are often important to note in understanding the conflicts of the young person and the referrer.

My patients have not only had a serious bereavement, such as the death of their fathers, either recently or earlier in their lives, but they also present a wide range of problems besides grief. The most common disturbances are drug abuse, school phobias, depression and learning difficulties. These disturbances are not only the result of their grief taking a pathological course but also because the boys referred to me all had serious problems long before their fathers died. They lived in poorly functioning families where the father was absent long before his death. Some had abused alcohol, had been violent towards members of the family or engaged in offending behaviour. The death of some fathers was apparently due to their psychopathology and, as I shall show, this made the whole process of mourning and coming to terms with the father's death extremely difficult for these young boys.

Deciding the appropriate therapeutic intervention depends on what the young person and the primary carer are able to manage. For instance, I have found that the mother and her adolescent son can be extremely ambivalent about the son receiving therapy, especially if the mother is not offered support in her own right. In many cases there is a very powerful and immediate transference by the mother and her son in response to my treatment recommendation, especially individual therapy sessions for the adolescent boy. I shall expand on this theme later.

There are a number of factors which influence the referral. The death of the absent and 'pathological' father stirred unbearable feelings in the mother, who was the referrer in most cases. They described a history of parental and familial discord many years before the father's death. In short, the mothers and the boys obviously needed help years ago but it was only the father's death and the impact this had on the adolescent and the relationship with his mother that legitimated and prompted the request for help. The actual death gave them a concrete reason for their sons' disturbed behaviour, and it gave them a focus to think and talk about their distress which was complex and deep rooted and well beyond ordinary mourning. I wonder whether some mothers referred their son following the father's death so that they could repair the damage done by the father when he was alive. Before the bereavement they may have felt that 'things' might sort themselves out one day or, alternatively, that there was nothing they could do either for themselves or their son. The death of the father put an end to years of misery and fear and gave them hope of a new beginning for themselves and their son.

However, the father's death also stirred intense feelings of guilt in some mothers for having chosen an unsuitable father for their son and for not having been able to change the father and, ultimately, for not saving him from death.

I think that a crucial factor in prompting the mother's referral was the impact the death of the father had on their perception of the son's move from being a child to becoming an adolescent in the context of being a lone parent. The mother–son partnership of latency appeared unable to stand the forces unleashed by the combination of the concrete loss of the father and the needs of the adolescent boy. Unconsciously, the mothers feared their sons were failing in the age-appropriate developmental tasks associated with acquiring a mature male identity. For instance, two mothers, whose sons were both twelve years old and were meant to start secondary school around the time of the father's death, brought their sons to the Centre because the boys refused to go to school after their father died. These mothers felt anxious and guilty about their sons' unyielding regressive behaviour and their 'Oedipal' longing to stay with their mothers. On the other hand, unconsciously, the boys felt that they were doing what their mothers wanted by continuing to be their 'partner' as they had been in childhood. The whole matter of a boy's separation from his mother is therefore marked by extreme ambivalence on both sides – the mother wants the son to remain loyally attached to her and show signs of developing as a 'normal' adolescent boy; the son wants to be separate and be part of the adolescent group, but is pulled towards continuing his special relationship with his mother out of loyalty and because he feels poorly equipped to cope with the tasks of adolescence.

As is often the case in bereavement, one loss often brought other secondary losses in its train, which played a role in prompting referral for help. One boy, whose father paid for a private education for his son while living separately from his family, had to leave school and go to a rougher state school after his father's death because his mother could not afford the fees. He therefore lost his schoolmates and his teachers at the same time as losing his father. Another boy had to go to a foster home after his father died because his mother, who suffered from serious depression, could neither cope with her husband's death nor with her son's increasingly difficult behaviour. Hence this boy, who was fourteen, lost his father, his mother and his home.

Case material: the effect of the death of the previously absent father on the son

I have suggested that boys who lose fathers already absent in their lives prior to the death are bound to have additional problems as a result of the bereavement. Adam was twelve years old when his mother referred him to the Centre shortly after his father had died suddenly abroad. His mother sought help because Adam seemed more and more withdrawn and hostile towards her, isolated and unhappy. The mother explained to me that she met Adam's dad when she was very young, but that they had been separated since Adam was four years old. The father had had little contact with his son until one year ago, when he started to form a new relationship with him, taking him on holiday and outings. Adam's mother recognised that he had lost his father just at the age when he had started to bond with him for the first time since early childhood and just before adolescence. It was a cruel and untimely interruption. Even though it was obvious to me that Adam needed help, like many twelve-year-olds referred for therapy or counselling, he communicated little and was often bewildered and defensive in his sessions. I therefore encouraged him to draw. Adam drew a man with strong muscles on his arms and legs, broad shoulders, a stiff collar around the back of his neck to protect him and a mouth that turned up on one side and down on the other, which gave him an air of superiority and ambivalence. When I asked Adam what sort of man he had drawn he said that it was a 'forest man'. He went on to explain that the man was saying: 'I am stronger than you.' He also explained that there were bears in the forest and that 'forest man' could fight the bears as he was stronger than they were..

I understood Adam's drawing as a picture of a fantasy father. I thought he wished to have a father who was strong and unbeatable and who could survive even the most dangerous situations in life's jungle. I also thought that his wish to identify with this father was in order to assist him to find his male identity. The fantasy father was created in order to cope with the difficulty Adam had in talking about his real father, who had not survived a fatal accident, and was dead and not strong. The father drawn by Adam was of such an idealised and imaginary nature because Adam had very little experience of his actual father and therefore had little concept of a real role model. My understanding of Adam's choice of a 'forest man' and a 'hunter' as a representation of his father has been deepened by Bettelheim's analysis of the meaning of fairytales. Bettelheim (1976) says,

> In the unconscious the hunter is seen as the symbol of protection. It is a suitable image of a strong and protective father figure . . . In his dreams and daydreams the child is threatened and pursued by angry animals, creations of his fear and guilt. Only the parent hunter, so he feels, can scare these threatening animals away . . . hence the hunter of fairytales is not a figure who kills friendly creatures but one who dominates, controls and subdues wild, ferocious beasts. On a deeper level, he represents the subjugation of the animal, asocial, violent tendencies in man . . . the hunter is an eminently protective figure who can and does save us from the dangers of our violent emotions and those of others.
>
> (Bettelheim 1976, p. 205)

These lines from Bettelheim seem a very accurate description of what Adam wished from his father, and indeed what many other male patients without fathers are truly missing – namely, a protective shield to modify their own aggressive and violent emotions. It therefore seems very important for these bereaved boys to have some male role model amongst their family or friends, be it an elder brother, an uncle or a stepfather. It seems evident from working with these boys that the ones who suffer most are the ones who only live with females, especially boys who live alone with mother. It is much harder for a boy to work out aggressive feelings with people of the opposite sex, and more dangerous too.

The creation of an idealised and omnipotent father in their drawings has been a common feature of working with bereaved boys whose fathers were physically absent before their death. They appear to need to create a father to identify with which is based on their own wishful fantasy rather than reality. Adam's forest man hid his father's abandonment of the family. Maybe another wish was to remember him as a strong individual who spent his time on his own looking after the forest and was in control of the beasts of the forest, rather than as a man who abandoned his baby son, his wife and went off with another woman and then suffered a sudden tragic death.

As I said, the creation of an idealised and omnipotent father in their drawings and in their minds is a frequent feature in working with bereaved boys. It is also interesting to note that the transference relationship with me tends to be equally idealised in such cases. Even though I am a female therapist I often felt I had a very positive and powerful influence on the boy's psyche and, no doubt, came to stand symbolically for the absent father. This feeling of a positive transference was also mirrored in my own feelings. For example, I often grew very fond of these boys – I liked them without knowing much about them or even being able to do much traditional psychodynamic work through talking. In other words, I often became like an 'unreal' idealised father. Adam, who talked little but did lots of drawings, was reported to be doing increasingly well at school by his mother. In art, he apparently surprised his teacher by his increasing and rapid drawing skills. While, at the beginning, I often felt that Adam came to the sessions with nothing to say, after a few months I noticed how his drawings became more and more sophisticated and complicated and how he used them to communicate his feelings. The strong 'forest man' turned eventually into a big whale with strong teeth, rising above the sea and shouting to a sea bird about to dive into the waves to eat a little fish 'leave it alone or else . . .'. I interpreted that the big whale father was trying to protect the little baby fish from getting eaten up by a nasty bird. The question was, could Dad protect the fish child or not? In the next session, Adam drew the answer. It was a bad end as in real life. The bird killed the fish. The whale's threat was in vain. I felt that Adam was able to change his idealised state of mind into more realistic, angry, devouring feelings where the big whale Dad was unable to save the fish child and became a useless object. Adam was able to get in touch with a lot of important feelings and show them to me in a symbolic way through drawings which to him felt safer than talking about the awesome reality of a dead father who cruelly left him as a young boy and then totally as an adolescent.

It is also interesting to note that the boys who internally stick to an idealised, potent and strong father are often the ones whose mother seems to have good memories of their past relationships with their husband, even though they may have been separated from them years ago. It is important how the mother feels towards her separated and dead husband since their son unconsciously picks up his mother's attitude towards her ex-partner. Adam's mother, for example, said to me when she referred her son that she had been very fond of her husband and his death upset her more than she would have imagined. A good loving bond between mother and father, even if it does not last, seems crucial to a boy's capacity to be able to mourn a father who has been available for a very short time but who has left an important memory in the son and, more importantly, in the mother who continues to live with the son. A mother who has had a satisfying sexual and personal relationship with her husband and the father of her son automatically unconsciously feels differently towards her male child than a mother whose relationship with her husband was unhappy. She will possibly see him as more loving and potent as feelings are inevitably projected from parents into children.

Some boys, whose fathers were absent or emotionally damaged before their deaths, created an idealised father in order to defend against feelings associated with loss and abandonment. Other boys could not talk about their father or his death with me and would get very upset and angry with anyone who criticised their parents. John, for example, preferred to think about day-to-day problems such as schoolwork, girlfriends, drugs and his new foster home, even though he was referred because of a major 'bereavement'. When he came for help he was having difficulties in learning at school and he had absconded from home and truanted from school regularly. He was intelligent and sensitive and his behaviour was a natural cry for help which his social worker understood and which prompted the referral. She also placed him in a caring foster home instead of leaving him with his mother. His father had been a drug addict, which led to his death, but social services only removed the boy from a very unstable home after his father's death. His father's death was indirectly John's salvation as it gave him, at the age of fourteen, a stable home for the first time in his life. It also led to individual psychotherapy. Even though he rarely acknowledged this, he took the chance given to him after his father's death and, unlike many boys of his age, he regularly came to his sessions, at first with his social worker and then on his own.

Only after a year was he able to start facing his most disturbing and painful feelings that were to do with being the son of a dead and addicted father and a highly disturbed mother who was alive but too ill to care for him. In most previous sessions he had talked about his current preoccupations. He wanted to concentrate on how to cope with life rather than to think about the death of his father and his mother's psychopathology. After he was more settled in his new foster home and increasingly able to face reality, he started to think about both of his parents.

John felt there had been a natural bond between his father and him, partly because his father, in spite of his drug addiction, was more affectionate and emotionally available, when he was drug-free, than his depressed mother. He felt very sad because deep down he missed his dead father much more than his surviving mother. He started to work through many feelings with me of love, guilt and anger.

A son identifies with his father, and adolescent boys can feel very abandoned if their father dies. They may feel very angry with their mother because they want her to be a father. This may be one of the reasons why John was able to start being angry with his mother and not his dead father. Another very important reason why it was much harder for him to explore his feelings towards his father objectively was because his father was dead. He could visit his mother and do some proper reality testing as he developed and became more mature, but his father was dead and the memory and feelings about him stayed the same as when he died and John was younger and less mature (he was just thirteen). There was probably also some healthy reality in John's wish to forgive his dead father and work on his anger towards his live mother instead. Bowlby (1960) distinguished between functional and non-functional anger. He thought that whenever loss is permanent, as it is after a bereavement, anger is necessarily without function. With a dead father there is no more concrete reality testing to be done, no emotional development to be had, no making up or arguing. John wanted his father as his role model in spite of his many faults. He told me that his father had said to him when his mother was in bed at twelve o'clock in the morning, unable to get up because she was so depressed, that he never wanted John to become like his mother. He also said to me 'You know, I can't be good for my mother because I am not like her.' Hearing this made me realise John's strong need to have a male role model.

Time and again it is evident how bereaved boys tenaciously pursue their wish to identify with their fathers in order to find their own identity when their father is dead and has been largely absent.

The father of another patient, Richard, aged twelve, died of liver failure when Richard was eleven. The father had not lived with Richard and his mother since Richard was aged two years, nor did they have much contact. Nevertheless Richard supported his father's home baseball team even though he lived far away. This seemed to be a sad and unrealistic way of following in his father's footsteps, a desperate external connection when he had no internal way of linking with his dead father. All he had internally were gruesome images, which he preferred to keep at bay and not talk about. Unlike Adam, he was unable to find anything good about his father as a real person or to idealise him, which left him feeling empty and depressed.

His mother seemed to have always been locked into a perverse and damaging relationship with Richard's father and therefore was unable to convey to her son something worth while about a sexual couple or a relationship between a man and a woman (either consciously or unconsciously). She was also very disturbed and full of disappointment, anger, guilt and depression. Even though she initially referred her son for therapy because he was unable to return back to school after his father's death, she later undermined his therapy as soon as he was back at school because she could not tolerate the idea of a third person (the therapist) coming between her son and herself. I became like a dangerous father/husband who had to be got rid of, just as her husband had been got rid of by her when Richard was two years old.

After a long summer break, Richard's mother telephoned me to let me know that her son had taken up drama lessons at the same time as his session. When I said to the mother that maybe at this point in time the sessions were more important than drama, she replied: 'I was surprised that Richard said he wanted to come back to the sessions.' Later on, I agreed with Richard that it was acceptable for him to end therapy now since he could always return when he was older. He had attended sessions for over six months. He missed his last session because of family commitments, this left me feeling desolate and undermined. Richard's mother could not tolerate a good ending between her son and myself and I was turned into a 'monster' father. Richard was not able to say goodbye to me, which seemed to connect with the way he had been unable to say goodbye to his father. Richard's mother let me know about the many faults she had noted about her son's therapy, which left me feeling impotent and wronged – just like I imagine Richard's father had felt.

I was later able to meet Richard one more time. He told me that he had just tripped over a paving stone on his way back from school, which seemed symbolic of a boy who felt dangerously lost without a father or a therapist. Perhaps he was also trying to convey how vulnerable he felt about the future. This case is a sad example of how a dead, absent and disturbed father combined with a disturbed mother can hinder therapy with an adolescent boy. However, I was able to tell Richard that he could come back for help at any time of his own accord. I felt that he had had a good experience with me and he was quite likely to be able to refer himself at a later date.

In his sessions, he had often preferred to draw rather than speak. He drew a male figure that represented his father. The picture was horrific, and frightened Richard. He had drawn a man who was exploding. Out of his mouth came the word 'Help'. Looking at this picture together, I interpreted to Richard that he might have drawn his father, who seemed to be dying a cruel death, shouting for help. The boy stared at the picture and could not believe he had drawn it. The picture seemed to have come straight from his unconscious feelings; no words could have described this boy's fantasies about his father's death as accurately and immediately as this drawing. He had drawn a father who was shouting for help as he was exploding, but there was no one there to help him. Richard told me that he felt that he should have saved his dad and he was cross with his mother for sending his father out of the house. Richard felt very guilty about his father's death. With hindsight I can see that the male figure shouting for help might also have been Richard, who felt he was being driven mad by his mother's possessiveness and disturbed behaviour and needed a third person (i.e. perhaps a therapist) to help him.

A further difficulty for Richard in coming to terms with the death of his father was that, like John, his mother was very depressed. She had been unable to come to terms with her ex-husband's death, her rejection of him as a man and father, and her guilt about having chosen such a damaged father for her son.

179

Richard was unable to return to school for a whole year after his father died, even though he had had very little contact with him for over ten years. Richard felt that due to the fragile state of his mother that he had to look after her and could therefore not be absent from home during school hours. However, with the help of therapy he was eventually able to attend school regularly.

Difficulties regarding the emotional development of fatherless adolescent boys

Adolescent boys who grow up without a father have to cope with a whole range of added difficulties in their development. I have already briefly mentioned difficulties in finding their male identity due to the lack of a role model.

Many young boys felt abandoned even before their fathers died due to divorce, separation or the emotional unavailability of the father as a result of alcoholism, drug abuse or depression. When the father was alive the son may have harboured the hope that contact with him would be restored one day; but death has a finality that abandonment does not. It is the end of all hope and the beginning of mourning something they never had. But how does one mourn something one has never had?

These boys have great trouble mourning their lost fathers because, as I mentioned earlier, they have great difficulty in letting go of an idealised father. Even when the father has been absent for many years prior to his death, they may still unconsciously hope that he will return either in person or in spirit. Their way of differentiating between a live and dead and absent father may be blurred.

They are full of unrealistic ideas of what their father was like, why he died and why he left them in the first place. Mishne (1979) writes that parental abandonment is a unique form of loss and narcissistic injury and that abandoned children may suffer from lack of empathy, depression, feelings of emptiness, delinquency, addictions, uncontrollable rage, pathological lying, hypochondriacal preoccupations and grandiose fantasies of themselves.

Because of their lack of a proper father image they have extra difficulties in establishing their identity. Without a living father to refer to for comparison, these boys have to invent much of their own identity. This adds an extra burden to adolescence, which is permeated with the task of finding one's identity.

While most bereaved children eventually find solace by collecting information about their dead father, either concretely by accumulating facts about his life or emotionally by talking about their feelings in order to help them develop, these boys find collecting information in order to work through their grief extremely difficult. Very often they have little factual information and they know deep down that what they would find would be unbearably painful and make them feel impotent. They therefore tend to operate in extremes, either being pseudo-strong, aggressive and delinquent, or lethargic, heavily depressed and hopeless. Adolescence is an age of intense feelings and the added pressure of unresolved grief often leads to extreme difficulties in keeping a healthy balance and makes it harder for them to function normally on a daily basis.

Sometimes the boys do not succeed in finding a good balance between feeling vulnerable to death and strong enough to survive, and they start to delude themselves. Fred, aged sixteen, whose father died of alcoholism, deluded himself that nothing could harm him. He drew a picture of himself with cigarettes coming out of his ears and hands like potent penises and the words 'cool man' coming out of his mouth. Out of his brain came an air bubble saying 'sex and drugs and food'. I felt this was a boy in danger of testing the limits more and more by taking and experimenting with drugs, being promiscuous and generally tough. He may want to prove to himself that he is the one who can take risks and win, that he will not be affected by bad luck, that he is not like his father and will never die no matter what he does. However, unconsciously, he may also fear that he will develop in the same way as his father. With the help of therapy, I hoped to find the right balance to put him in touch with his own vulnerability without making him feel impotent. This boy said several times that he wanted to be a bad boy outside but a good boy inside. He was telling me that his outside and his inside do not match. This is often the case with adolescent boys who have a disturbing internal image of their own father and try to be tough externally. The result is that they can feel very alone and are unable to make or keep friends of their own sex as well as girlfriends. However, with the help of therapy they often have a chance to unwrap some of their internal feelings (i.e. to admit and understand them in their own time in a safe environment away from the pressures of external life).

Bereaved boys are in great danger of developing a 'false self', especially when they feel they have constantly to deny their real origin – namely, coming from a father who was unstable and abandoning and then died. They cannot show off with their fathers, as boys like to do; instead they may show off themselves by acting dangerously and irresponsibly. Because their life story is tarnished, every new intimate relationship, especially with the opposite sex, is in their own minds threatened by ghosts of the past.

Fred, for example, whose mother was alive but suicidal and whose father was a drug addict who died as a result of his addiction, had endless problems whenever he met a new girlfriend he fancied. As he was living in a foster home, it was obvious that his parents had not been able to care for him, and his past had been very distressing and abnormal. One day he met a nice girl in a pub, but was so frightened of her knowing anything about his parents or his background that he invented a complete lie, saying that he was living in America and was visiting England. He lied in order to deny his origins and what he felt was his shameful past. He wished to be seen as coming from a great country, like America, rather than from the East End and two very ill parents, one of whom was dead. Fred had a long and very painful path in his therapy in coming to terms with his past and to accept that it was not his fault that he was born into such a difficult family. As a result of his therapy his future may be more hopeful than his past.

As I have already noted, the emotional development of fatherless boys is especially complicated if they live alone with their mother.

In extreme cases, boys who live alone with their mothers, and therefore find it difficult to have an internalised alignment with a male role model, can be in danger of serious role confusions. I treated twelve-year-old George, who felt that not only did he have to do what his mother did but also, because she was depressed, what mother could not do. He cooked for her, did the shopping and cleaned the house. He was a 'mummy' instead of being an adolescent boy. George's appearance was similar to his mother's. He was obese like her and his movements were very unmasculine. He even slept in his mother's bedroom. George had been denied any male role model. He was an only child and lived with his mother and maternal grandmother. Even though, like many other boys, he loved football and was keen to draw endless footballs and football teams, his drawings of footballers showed a worrying lack of vigour, muscle and potency. His male figures had hunched up shoulders, which made them look hesitant rather than determined. They had huge floppy heads and faces with spots and big babyish frightened eyes, and one had a baby's tongue sticking out of his mouth. One of these figures had the head of a rabbit and another was hiding half his face behind a wall. Their bodies were rigid and thin and weak. Looking at all George's figures, especially the lower part from the waist downwards, worried me. They gave me the impression of having no penis, or a very tiny one, and their bottoms were very tight and narrow. Their legs and arms lacked muscle and tension and none of the footballers kicked any of the balls surrounding them.

George drew similar people again and again in order to show me his feelings of impotence, vulnerability and anger. It was hardly surprising that George felt this way. His mother made no effort to hide from her son her resentment towards her ex-partner. She desperately needed George to be loyal and exclusively available for her. However, she felt guilty about this since she could see that he was failing to grow up as an ordinary adolescent boy. George showed how stuck he felt by repeatedly drawing the same pictures. Unlike Adam, George's emotional life could not develop until his mother was able to accept her son's needs to be separate, including the physical need for a separate bedroom. I encouraged George's mother to get help for herself in order to help her child.

Tragically, George, like many boys who have lost a father and whose mother cannot allow the symbolic presence of the father, was unable to learn about heterosexual relationships or triangular relationships and had great difficulty resolving Oedipal feelings. He was unable to end the symbiotic relationship with his mother because she could not survive without him. Therapy with such boys is often a hazardous undertaking since the therapist is likely to be perceived by the mother as a threat to their relationship with their son. It is still important, however, to try to respect the parent's feelings and wishes and, ideally, not only increase the communication between therapist and child but also foster the development of an understanding between child and parent. After all, it is the child and parent who have to find a way of living with each other daily and not just for 50 minutes a week during sessions.

Concluding remarks

The study of bereavement in children and adolescents from a psychoanalytic perspective has focused on when the child develops the capacity to mourn (Freud 1917; Bowlby 1960; Klein 1940; Furman 1964) and the impact of loss on his development. In this chapter on bereaved boys who often barely knew their dead father, or whose fathers were very disturbed when alive, the impact of a life without fathers on their development was great. There is widespread agreement that the death of a parent is likely to interfere with the child's development and can affect the individual at later stages of development (see Nagera 1970). The main developmental impact of the loss of his father on the boy entering adolescence concerns the lack of a restraining Oedipal rival, which intensifies anxiety and guilt (Burgner 1985). The boy may have incestuous fantasies or project these fantasies on to his mother. Anna Freud ([1958] 1969, 268) suggested that the emergence of and the intensity of the adolescent's sexual and aggressive drives lend 'a new and threatening reality to oedipal and pre-oedipal fantasies which had seemed extinct but are, in fact, merely under repression' earlier on.

The role of the father in the initial stage of male adolescence as being a 'buffer' between the adolescent boy and the mother cannot be underestimated. Blos (1965) described the preadolescent boy as turning decisively away from the opposite sex when puberty stirs. He described a leading fantasy of the boy at this stage of adolescence as fear of 'the archaic mother' (p. 148). The boy fears castration in relation to this omnipotent woman who is endowed with impulses to devour and destroy the boy. On the other hand, he often has a surprisingly positive relationship with his father. At the early stage of adolescence the boy's aggression is directed towards his mother, whereas later in adolescence it is directed towards his father. In early adolescence (eleven to thirteen years), the boy sees the father as an ally rather than as a rival and he draws great reassurance in coping with castration anxiety from a father who is actually strong or is imagined to be strong. Thus coping with the re-emergence of the Oedipal situation is a crucial task for the adolescent boy and, as we have seen, the absence of the father to assist in this task can seriously interfere with the boy's capacity to tackle other tasks of adolescence. Bereaved boys whose fathers have been absent from their lives before they died are doubly disadvantaged. Firstly, they miss the support of a 'real' father. Secondly, because they have never known their father they are unable to incorporate and identify with his image (Grossburg and Crandell 1978). A common observation of adolescent boys whose fathers live a separate life but remain in contact with their sons is the son's need to identify with his father. The absent father can act as a defence against incestuous urges towards his mother. The bereaved boys I described were often unable to make such an identification because they had never known their fathers enough to form a realistic internal picture of them.

Clearly the role of the mother and her relationship with her bereaved son is a crucial factor in whether the boy's development becomes pathological or not. Freud (1910) noted the possibility of the mother using her children to meet needs formerly supplied by her partner and the 'maternal seduction' which may ensue. The danger of being too close to mother, as I have described, is particularly worrying in adolescence due to the child acquiring a mature sexual body. In the cases I presented, difficulties in the relationship between mother and son were an important factor in treatment being sought, and in some instances treatment broke down – particularly where the mother was very disturbed and was therefore over-dependent on her son.

However, some boys who were unable to continue therapy for long enough may well be able, due to having had a short but good enough experience, to ask for more help at a later date.

For many 'fatherless sons', long-term therapy can fill an internal gap and provide them with an internal voice that can help them to find their identity, assist in distancing themselves from the mother and give them a chance to lead a more fulfilling adult life, a life they may never have had had they not felt able to ask for help because of the actual death of the father. In many cases, ironically, the actual death of a very disturbed father has helped them to move forward in a more positive way by giving them and their mothers permission to admit how hard their lives have been for years.

Some mothers may get much-needed help for the first time because of their husband's or ex-husband's death, and this can indirectly help the growing adolescent boy.

References

Bettelheim, B. (1976). *The Use of Enchantment: The Meaning and Use of Fairy Tales.* London: Penguin Books.

Blos, P. (1965). The initial stage of male adolescence. *Psychoanalytic Study of the Child*, 20, 145–164 (New Haven: Yale University Press).

Bowlby, J. (1960). Grief and mourning in infancy and early childhood. *Psychoanalytic Study of the Child*, 15, 9–52 (New Haven: Yale University Press).

Burgner, M. (1985). The Oedipal experience: Effects on development of an absent father. *International Journal of Psycho-Analysis*, 66, 311–320.

Freud, A. ([1958] 1969). Adolescence. In *The Writings of Anna Freud*: Vol. 5 *Research at the Hampstead Child-Therapy Clinic and other papers*. New York: International Universities Press, pp. 136–166.

Freud, S. (1910). Leonardo Da Vinci and a memory of his childhood. *Standard Edition*, 2. London: Hogarth Press.

Freud, S. (1917). Mourning and melancholia. *Standard Edition*, 14, 237–260. London: Hogarth Press.

Furman, R. (1964). Death and the young child. *Psychoanalytic Study of the Child*, 19, 321–333 (New Haven: Yale University Press).

Grossburg, S.H. and Crandell, L. (1978). Father loss and father absence in preschool children. *Clinical Social Work Journal*, 6, 2, 123–134.

Klein, M. (1940). Mourning and its relation to manic-depressive states. In *Contributions to Psycho-analysis*. London: Hogarth Press, pp. 311–338.

Mishne, J. (1979). Parental abandonment – a unique form of loss and narcissistic injury in clinical social work. *Journal of Clinical Social Work*, 7,1, 15–33.

Nagera, H. (1970). Children's reactions to the death of important objects: A developmental approach. *Psychoanalytic Study of the Child*, 25, 360–400 (New Haven: Yale University Press).

12

IDENTIFICATION AND DIS-IDENTIFICATION IN THE DEVELOPMENT OF SEXUAL IDENTITY

Marcus Johns

Drink to me only with thine eyes,
And I will pledge with mine . . .
        Ben Jonson, 'To Celia'

The development of sexual identity and gender identity is a prolonged and complex process which is at the heart of psychoanalysis. It was sexuality which precipitated Freud into his investigation of the human mind and it is sexuality which is the foundation stone of psychoanalysis. From his *Studies in Hysteria* (1895), through *Three Essays on the Theory of Sexuality* (1905), then *A Special Type of Choice of Object Made by Man* (1910), *The Ego and the Id* (1923) and then, shortly before his death in London on 23 September 1939, to *An Outline of Psychoanalysis* (1938), Freud emphasised the primacy of sexuality as a wide concept that was present in childhood and was to be distinguished sharply from genitality. This wider concept of sexuality is driven by the instinctual energy which represented the body's somatic demands upon the mind; an energy he called libido. The mind has to deal with the conflictual demands upon it, which are both conscious and unconscious, by mental activity which allows satisfactions whilst at the same time having defences against anxiety which may be overwhelming (A. Freud 1936). The central element of the conflicts to be dealt with is a man's love for his mother together with his jealousy of his father, which stand in opposition to his affection for that very same father. This central element he delineated as the Oedipus complex, realising that the Greek legend of King

Oedipus represented that universal struggle that every man feels within himself and has to resolve in his own particular and unique way.

During the course of growing-up, in order to resolve this nuclear complex, the boy has to make an identification with his father. Freud described identification as the earliest expression of an emotional tie with another person. Hence the little boy exhibits an especial interest in his father and takes him as his ideal; he would like to grow like him and be like him. This normal earliest identification was seen to be modelled on an infantile feeding fantasy of devouring what was loved; the child could have the omnipotent fantasy that one could become what one desired to be by swallowing the rivalled loved one whole and becoming him in a cannibalistic identification with his strengths and potency (Freud 1921).

An example of this cannibalistic identification is seen in the struggles of a small boy shortly after his third birthday. He is being settled to sleep in his own room by his father who was wishing to return to our adult company. The child was unhappy at his exclusion from the adult party and was angrily complaining at his father that he had nobody to sleep with him. During his complaining he picked up one of his small plastic toys from his bed. This toy was a tiger with a wide-open mouth and prominent teeth. In his resentment he angrily screwed the jaws of the tiger into his father's neck. The father, endeavouring to cope with the resentment, tried to defuse the situation by making it more of a game and said to the child 'Now you are eating me up'. The boy smiled and triumphantly stood up in his bed moving his body slowly and ponderously as if he had suddenly become a giant or a King Kong figure. In this manner he marched up and down his bed telling his father that he, the son, had become a puppet man and, moving his hand as if he were controlling the strings of an imaginary puppet, told his father that he would control him. This was in line with his current chosen career after having had an entertainer at his recent birthday party who had given a string puppet show and was hence known as The Puppet Man. During the exchange it seemed that the little boy had made an omnipotent identification with the father by eating him up and swallowing him whole so that he then saw his own self representation as swollen by the total incorporation of his father's body, hence concretely inflating the child into a giant adult figure. In so doing he turned the tables on his father, both in order to control the father, who would now become his puppet, and also to rescue himself from the frustration and indignity of his controlling father. However, after some minutes of enjoying this triumphant solution the boy terminated his march, sat down and sadly said to his father: 'But with you inside me all my bones would break'.

At this point his body relaxed and he settled to sleep with his favourite blanket and allowed his father to rejoin his mother in our adult party. The omnipotent identification based on the fantasy of total physical incorporation by swallowing up was not sustained by the child. His contact with reality allowed him to face both the unrealistic nature of the identification and the consequent danger that such a gargantuan engulfment would be for his small frame. The danger was that to swallow his father whole, python like, would mean having a foreign body so large inside his own small frame that his own would be disrupted and ruptured by the inflationary effect of that larger body. The reality sense coming from the awareness of bodily limitation, emphasises the fact that the first ego is a body ego (Freud 1923, 26). The boy battled with the pains of exclusion and frustration, maintaining his hold on reality and an awareness that 'his eyes were bigger than his stomach'. He was able to keep the appropriate relationship with his father, who was both loved as well as hated, whilst at the same time being sad at the painful reality of the differences between boy and man, and coping with the disillusionment at the failure of the omnipotent fantasy.

In this exchange between father and son there does not seem to be any doubt that the boy sees himself as a male, both in his omnipotent identification with The Puppet Man that could not be sustained because of the demands of reality, but also in his ordinary relationship to his father. This ordinary relationship is one in which a gender identity is the function of the knowledge and awareness, whether conscious or unconscious, that one belongs to one sex and not the other:

> This sense of core gender identity in the normal individual is derived from three sources: the anatomy and physiology of the genitalia; the attitudes of parents, siblings and peers toward the child's gender role; and a biological force that can more or less modify the attitudinal (environmental) forces.
>
> (Stoller 1968, p. 65)

This essential gender identity is the bedrock upon which a sexual identity may sit. This allows that a male or female may have a homosexual or heterosexual identity whilst still knowing that they are, and must remain, essentially male or female.

The temporary identification that was made by the child with The Puppet Man father, through the fantasy of an oral incorporation by swallowing him whole, depended on the use of omnipotence and denial under the pressures of desire, rivalry, jealousy and anger. It is not related to reality or to a function of the ego but is only an expression of the id. The ego, temporarily swamped by the power of the id's desires, abandoned some of its reality testing functions in order to enjoy the triumphs over the father. It is as if the ego momentarily 'closed its eyes' to the environmental forces of external reality. If the ego had permanently relinquished such testing of reality then the oral incorporation would have introjected The Puppet Man into the self-representation, where it could have remained to achieve a need satisfying 'perceptual identity' and a delusional state subject to the omnipotent mechanisms of the primary processes (Freud 1900, vol. 5, 601). But, for this child, the ego did not remain permanently out of touch with reality but recovered and reinstated its reality testing functions. The child was able to inhibit and undo the omnipotent mechanisms by the application of secondary processes, primarily at the behest of vision, both perceptual and conceptual. The permanent change brought about in the psychic structure was the growth of the 'thought identity' of the ego (ibid., 602), an increase in the stability and permanence in the capacity for conceptual vision, dependent on the painful acceptance of reality and resulting in an increased capacity for negotiating with it.

This growth of the ego involves a different form of identification to that of omnipotently swallowing the father whole. The identification giving rise to ego growth is more reality based and is an identification with the *functions* of the object, its thoughtfulness and containment of conflict and frustration, rather than being based on the totality of an oral incorporation fantasy. This identification with the functions of the father is a continuation of the 'primary identification' of the child with the mother which is itself 'a direct and immediate identification and takes place earlier than any object cathexis' (Freud 1923, 31).

How does this primary identification come about if it is not based on an object cathexis and an oral incorporation? If one considers the work of Axelrad and Brody and their brilliant film series (*Mother–Infant Interaction*, 1967–1970, New York University Film Library), it seems clear from the *manner* in which a child performs a cognitive task in later life (i.e. rapidly, playfully, thoughtfully, anxiously, tentatively, etc., when finding a hidden toy at nine months and posting shapes in a posting box at 12 months) that the infant makes an identification not only with the mother but also with the *manner* in which the mother negotiated her interaction with the child during the infant feeding situation. If the mother fed the infant in an excited and entertaining way, then the two-year-old posted shapes in a similar way. If the mother fed the infant slowly and deliberately then the two-year-old posted shapes slowly and deliberately. This detailed identification would not be possible unless it was carried out primarily as a function of sight. Is Freud referring to a primary identification which is the direct and immediate result of seeing the parent and that this is differentiated from the separate identificatory activities of early oral incorporations of part and whole objects? Mouth and eye co-operate in their responsive receptivity and seem to supplement each other with intensification of sensory imagery, and sometimes to substitute for each other (Greenacre 1957). Greenacre emphasises that the build-up of the body image, especially the genital parts, proceeds through the combined agencies of touch and vision rather than a real internalised incorporation through the mouth. The essential function of vision in the development of the sense of self is discussed by Wright (1991).

The primary identification that occurs between infant and mother applies for all infants. This means that both boy and girl two-year-olds will perform tasks in ways that are related to the mother's earlier feeding behaviour. This behaviour during feeding is dependent on, and a reflection of, the mother's conscious and unconscious attitudes towards her infant. Hence the infant is not only imitating her behaviour but is also responding to the explicit and implicit fantasies that the mother will have about the infant. There will be identifications, both with the mother and also with what is communicated from the mother about her imagined infant, which will exist within the mother's fantasies, consciously and unconsciously. The child will tend to become like the mother but also like that infant of the maternal fantasies who may be more or less related to the real and genuine child that is in the mother's arms. As the infant develops, other identifications with the father, and the father's fantasies, take place, but for the male child to secure both its gender and sexual identity there has also to be a degree of dis-identification from the mother of its earliest primary identifications (Greenson 1968; Tyson 1989.) An essential part of this process is the mastering of the envy of the mother's capacity to procreate and give birth (Kittay 1998).

Identification with the father contingent on dis-identification from the mother

I will now present some clinical material in order to show how the role of the father is essential in securing the son's dis-identification from the mother. This is achieved by the father's ability to facilitate distancing and thought, and what happens when the father fails to support the appropriate distancing of a son from his mother but instead is felt to demand the continuation of a subservient position of a mother/son symbiosis to the father's own authority.

The patient is a professional man in his early thirties who had come into analysis because of depression, an inability to complete work projects and hoping to find out if he was homosexual or not. His masturbation fantasies were homosexual. The family live in the USA where his father was a successful man who had built up his own business which he had started as a motor mechanic. His mother was a nurse and she had been an athlete when at college. During early years of comparative poverty the mother's sister had lived with the family and the accommodation necessitated the patient sharing her room.

Father had wanted to be an engineer, but had been unable to go to university. He was very competitive with those engineers who had been to university, disparaging them by belittling them as incompetent and impractical and emphasising their dependence on him for the practical solutions to what he considered were their grandiose ideas. He is a generous though controlling and controlled man, sometimes erupting with fury when there is a small mistake in the assembling of machinery. He is generous to his family members but retains overall control of the family's assets.

It appears that from birth my patient was designated by the family to be an engineer and that there were conscious and unconscious fantasies for him to achieve this goal. For as long as he could remember, even as a very small child, he was referred to as 'Dan the engineer' at the instigation of his father. His father had set plans for his son throughout childhood. The patient remembers his father as being warmer than his mother in moments of physical care of the patient, but also to have been distant, working long hours in the machine shop away from home. The father also seems to have been overly concerned about his son's genital development, as the patient remembers his father repeatedly examining his genitals when he was a child in the bathroom. He was also aware that his mother would have preferred him to have been a blonde, blue-eyed girl. He was a child talented in music and art but had accepted the family's wishes to train as an engineer as if they were his own, becoming the model 'little adult' child to be exhibited to friends and family. He was advised to come to England to work in a specialist engineering company. His father set him up in a flat and furnished it for him. It was unclear as to whether the flat was for the family or the patient. The patient had been befriended by his boss, a middle-aged woman whom he admired and valued highly. When he came to analysis he was failing to complete work assignments, though the company continued to employ him because of their awareness of his capacities. He identified himself closely with his boss in her approach to engineering problems and their solutions.

After coming into analysis he began to be able to complete work projects, though he found it difficult to develop a project beyond the planning stage as he hated doing the detailed drawings necessary for manufacture. Hence he felt that he never produced anything in the way that his practical father had done. Gradually freeing himself from the engineering demand for detailed drawings and the internal conflict with his productive but controlling father, he became more creative. He had always been interested in the use of light and textures in assembling and manufacturing, and now started using his undoubted visual ability to produce constructions of moving and interacting elements which could change dynamically from appearing charming and pretty to dark and threatening. His original intention was that these constructions could be shown publicly as works of art, but in the event he felt that they were too personal to him, his internal world and his analysis, for public viewing. The constructions were ways for him to view different elements of himself set at a distance. These could be viewed from different perspectives by placing them outside himself whilst still retaining their links to his own affective states.

During the few months of his analysis prior to the sessions I shall describe he had moved off the couch to sit on the chair and was surprised that I had continued the analysis. He had thought that I would either get furious at his temerity in altering what he saw as my constructed framework or else he would have a friendly chat with me that would not involve analytic work. As he became more comfortable with his own thoughts and conflicts he decided to undertake a more major work. At the same time he decided that rather than make some proposed alterations to his flat he would move to a flat which he felt would be more suitable for his character, age and lifestyle. He had already changed the furniture which had been provided by his father. He telephoned his father in the States to tell him that he was going to sell the flat and buy a different one. His father exclaimed, 'How can you do this to me, you'll be the death of me'. My patient was furious but completely deflated, and although he tried to continue with the purchase of the new flat he was terrified that he would receive news that his father had died. Hence he could not proceed with his move, despite the analytic work. He decided to stay in the flat and to proceed with his work. The work was to be a construction using particular perspectives to view the female body dispassionately, 'much as a surgeon needs in order to do his work' but juxtaposed to a different perspective which was exciting, provocative, shocking and openly sexual.

For some years he had been able to engage in some engineering projects as part of peripheral work under the aegis of his boss with whom he had been intimately linked, though this was always dependent on his fantasy of being her star apprentice. He now wished to escape from this situation and break the apron-strings that held him in order to complete his own independent project.

On this particular session, the week following his capitulation to his father's control over the flat, he came into the session more alive than I had ever previously seen him. He was furious. He had been with his boss the previous evening when unexpectedly she had designated him as the leader of her own project, whilst completely ignoring a previous conversation that he had had with her concerning his independent work. Being the leader designated by her also involved him in representing the other workers on her project at an important meeting the following day. He was indignant about her trapping him into these positions when he had already told her of his intention to separate. He felt she was pacifying him in the same way that politicians do, appearing to agree with the independent growth of others but actually only pursuing their own agenda and not letting any individual go forward separately. He felt himself to be a volcano of fury wishing to smash things. He said, 'All the people on her project have lost interest and I am now supposed to lead them, enthuse them and do what she should be doing. She wants to be equal with everyone, but actually she is not and she shouldn't pretend to be, she is actually very controlling and belittling. She pretends to be equal and asks for criticism but she cannot stand it at all. When the workers tell her about their dissatisfaction with her project she blackmails them with guilt by saying "so you don't want to do it and want to give it all up". He felt that this was said to provoke their defensive response of 'Oh no' when really everyone wanted to respond 'yes'. He was delighted with another American there who said to him 'She's just like my mother, I'm back at home not having tidied my room or finished all the food on my plate'. My patient felt that all he could do was to employ an ironic sarcasm in playing at being her obedient slave. He was furious at the subjugation he felt at being placed in the situation of having no choice whilst also being ignored.

At this point I was thinking to myself that the patient had projected into the boss not only a paternal figure but also his internal maternal figure with whom he had been previously identified but was now trying to dis-identify from. The link to the maternal figure was clear through the American friend's comment about his mother. Certainly that aspect of the patient which wanted to verbalise his mockery was safely located in the other American so that the patient was relieved of the responsibility for some of his own rage. The anxiety about exposing his anger and presumed fear of retaliation resulted in him playing at being the obedient slave who is in reality mocking the authority of the parent (mother/father). I was also thinking how did this material relate to the transference; for instance, had I missed some communication from him that resulted in some inexpressible anger towards me? However, I could not convince myself that such a transference inter-pretation would be either correct or helpful and thought it would probably be unhelpful if it was felt to be deflecting his rage away from his boss in a protective or defensive way. I also felt that I was being expected to contain the anxiety about the rage rather than the rage itself and that this was also a communication function of a projection as well as a wish for a container function.

He continued by telling me that he had had a dream that night and explained that it was not a recurrent dream but a dream on a recurrent theme. In the dream he was in his flat in a respectable and good class part of the city. There is a violent revolution going on in the city of which he is aware. It is frightening, and he and his rich neighbours are worried about the envy of the mob. The common people, peasants, are in the streets smashing things up and the violence is coming nearer. Then they are at his flat coming inside and using the bathroom. Then it wasn't so frightening, they didn't smash up his flat and he was able to make friends with them. He understood that these violent people were reflections of himself that he was frightened of, but there was some sense of this being said not only as understanding but also to distance himself from their feelings. He then said that he hoped his boss would make it easy for him to leave.

It now seemed clear that in the dream he had split off and denied the violent aspects of himself and had projected them into the peasants whom were now identified with the violence. However, even then the situation is not safe enough as when the splitting is diminishing, so that those aspects of himself are coming back home 'into the flat', they are made safe by 'using the bathroom'; that is, by being evacuated out in a physical and concrete way. I suspect that he has also just done the same thing in the session by using his understanding to make the feelings safe by evacuating the intensity of his experiences. I felt that I was probably the boss who was supposed to make it easy for him by not expecting him to expose those feelings that he did not want to recognise as parts of himself, and that if I did that I would provoke more rage.

I said that I thought that he was referring to a recurrent theme in the analysis which we had seen before. This theme is one where he sees himself as the little prince of the family who was always so good and nice that he felt himself to be above the common peasants whom he despised. It was only these common peasants who had to deal with envy, frustration and violence, whilst he could be an onlooker distanced from these feelings and above such things. I said that he was now very alarmed to find these feelings were more his own and were inside him as a result of the analysis which was causing a revolution in his life. I said that I thought that he wanted to accept these feelings as his own but perhaps could only do so by some friendly pacification, and that he had tried to do this by using his understanding and by hoping that his boss will make it easy for him rather than confront him. He laughed, and said that of course she would not make it easy for him and that he would have to deal with his anger.

I now felt that he had to some extent distanced himself from any feelings about me and the analysis, but that it would detract from his experience of the feelings with regard to his boss if I were to persist with some reference to myself even if I could formulate it clearly. I also felt that I would be in danger of being identified with an aspect of his father, who was felt to be antagonistic to the patient's own development.

He continued by saying that he was not sure how the day would go as he was feeling so angry. He felt that he had to leave the engineering project, but the boss had said that she was not sure how he could do his own creative work outside the company, implying that he needed her. He emphasised that he did not need her and could approach people independently. He explained that he had received all that his boss could give him. He had been with her too long. He had depended on her a great deal when he first came to England, and she had helped him a lot. He still liked the way she worked, her friendship and when they worked together, but now he knows what she is going to say and what she is going to recommend. He added that he needed something different now. He was vehement that he did not need to be told that he needs her in order to do his own project.

I was now certain that this was a transference communication about his feelings about the analysis, but I felt that I could not find a way of communicating this to him which would not be dull and wooden and allow him to confirm to himself that as with his boss, he knew what I would say and had heard it all before. However, I thought that from what I knew of some of his feelings about his mother I could link it to what I had thought had been split off and projected into the other American and his mother.

I said that he, like his American friend, felt that his boss was like a mother whom he wanted to be like but who also wanted to keep him attached to her in a dependent position – perhaps like his own mother who would still bake him Brownies which she sent over with various relatives when they visited. He liked the attention of his boss as he liked the cookies from home, but felt angry and humiliated by her attitude towards him, as if he was a little boy who was terrified of offending her if he refused her special gifts.

I now thought that what might have been projected into his boss was a combination of both parents, which included both his internal representations of an infantilising mother along with that of a controlling mechanic boss father who wished to keep him fused with his mother rather than coming between them to promote separateness and independence and supporting a dis-identification from the mother.

194

I said that he felt that his boss was not only a smothering mother but also a mechanic father who was saying that the patient must not work independently of him, but has to do what he says as he felt an engineer has to do what the mechanic says. He was nodding as I said this and came to the end of the session. We ended the session with him saying that he was unsure how he was going to cope with the meeting and determined to separate himself from his boss's project.

Following session

He told me that after the previous day's session he had gone in to work and attended the meeting to represent the project work as had been requested by his boss. The meeting had gone on for some time, about three hours, and had been monopolised by the more senior management who ignored him when he tried to speak. The meeting was in a dilapidated room and had been mainly about shortage of funds.

He continued to explain that at the end of the meeting one of the people had turned to him to ask if there was anything he wanted to say, and they also commented that he had been quiet during the meeting. He had then erupted and told them how angry he was with what he was getting from the company for what he put in. He had walked out of the meeting, gone home and then sent an e-mail to his boss. After he'd sent the e-mail he had a telephone call from his boss, even before she'd seen his e-mail. She had been concerned about how he was feeling and what he had said. He explained to her that being with the company was making him ill, and was making him feel belittled and humiliated. She asked if it was something that she was doing; he said that it was not, but that it was only the company. She said that it sounded as if it felt like a prison to him, and he agreed. For the first time ever he intimated to her that he was seeing someone about his feelings (i.e. was in psychoanalysis). She kept asking if it was something she was doing and he repeated that it was only the company. She had seemed to understand, and he felt that he could resign from the project and remain friends with his boss. He felt that he had found a courteous way out.

Though I saw this as being about the analysis I could not find a way of interpreting it in a way that would not have sounded mechanical, automatic and rather dead. I certainly felt that I would be a mechanic(al) father needlessly intruding. What I did feel was alive was his avoidance of the direct angry engagement with his boss and his fear of her response to him.

Hence I commented on his subterfuge in avoiding a direct confrontation with her about his resentment and disappointment, and how he had skirted around the issues by putting it down to the company. He quickly said that his rage had gone into the e-mail in which he had complained of her controllingness and her conflict over her own authority. He had been much more attacking and scathing than during the telephone call and he had told her to take the e-mail as only one side of his feelings about her. He hoped that they would continue to be friends when he had separated himself from her and the company.

Though I felt that he had experienced my comment on his subterfuge as critical, and had come in quickly to defend himself as if from a charge of cowardice, I did not take this up as I also thought that he was owning the violent feelings that were usually projected into the peasants and wanted me to understand that.

He proceeded by telling me that he'd had another dream last night. In the dream he was comforting a little girl because he knew she would be upset by the arrival of a new baby. He had his arms around her, kissing her and reassuring her that she was still special.

He went on to say that he was pleased to feel that he can now leave the company. He explained that he had been able to telephone a specialist company in the States about his own project and arrange to send some things there. He emphasised how he wished to work creatively with someone in partnership rather than be doing what his boss tells him. He said that what he needed was a mentor who would help him develop his own ideas. He vehemently told me that he was not a child. He was angry that his boss always had her favourites and controls them by getting them to feel that they are special, and that is what he had allowed himself to become.

His wish is to have a strong supportive mentor father who will help him in his dis-identification from his mother. Though this is a battle with his boss it is also about his relationship with me with his wish that I support him as a mentor father, but also his wish to remain my favourite as a mother but at the cost of independence and potency.

I said that he felt that he would only be his boss's favourite if he remained the passive, accepting little baby princess in the dream and that he would lose his place with the boss mother if he gave up being the special child to some other baby to become the next favourite. I now said that I thought he also saw me as a boss who had the analysis as my project and that he felt that it was not his. I said that I thought that he was frightened to confront me with his resentment as he was terrified that if he was not seen as the good accepting patient in this analytical project, which he felt would need him to be lying passively on the couch agreeing with my interpretation, then he would not be what he thought would be my ideal favourite patient and he would then be in danger of losing his sense of being special to me. He nodded and described how his aunt idolised the new baby of his cousin, and how he felt she was being sickeningly sentimental about it. He didn't know what he would do when he went back to the States for the coming holiday as it disturbed him greatly to see her treating the baby in the way she did – as if it were a lovely doll – without apparently seeing it as having a personality of its own.

Though he had nodded his agreement with my interpretation I was left feeling that he had gone away from the direct confrontation with me and was taking the conflict out of the analysis by returning it to the relationship with his aunt.

196

I now said he was terrified of my not seeing him as a real person, but only as a doll patient, passive to my analysing. I added that he felt I resented his own activity, and that in his mind I was only thinking of myself and my own projects, idolising my ideas and thoughts, as if it was my analytic project that he felt he had to support.

He then commented that he was anxious that his boss would feel that he had been using her and that now he had got what he wanted she was to be discarded.

I started to say that I thought that he was worried that if she did make the connection between him getting what he needed and then leaving her she would be angry at his use of her and the company and that he was frightened that she would then accuse him of selfishness. Whilst I was talking he became very angry, waving his hand to brush me away and silence me, saying that he didn't want to think about it. He impatiently asked why did I go on digging away at him. He felt I was just like the dentist. I was silent for some minutes and he then said, 'People use people and that's that'. I started to say that he was frightened of being accused of using his boss when he again interrupted and said that *she* had used *him*. I went on to be more specific and say how he feared being accused of misusing people in an inappropriate way. This surprised him, and I then linked it to his anxiety about an ordinary and proper use of me, to which he added that I also made use of him. However, he said he felt his boss did misuse him. He couldn't stand her manipulating and blackmailing. He returned to talking about his boss by saying how cold she was in her attitude, focusing on one element in detail and that it became a sterile exercise. It is dull and repetitious for him. He now explained that he was worried about feeling so angry because he has to go to another meeting today as the representative for his boss and he doesn't like being aware of the ugly violence he finds in himself.

I said it worried him to feel so angry with me when he felt that I was a cold, pain-creating dentist analyst with boring repetitious unfeeling interpretations. He said in a resentful tone that his boss would always take what someone said and take it up as a good idea. I said that when I had just used what he said he felt I took it up as a good idea, but that perhaps this was then a feeling of having his ideas stolen. I linked this to an oft-voiced complaint that his father wanted his shirts, his watch, his windsurfer, his car, etc. He disagreed. He explained that the situation with his boss was different in that she always saw potential in something, and he emphasised the word 'potential'. If anyone put forward an idea she would say 'there's potential in that'. However, he felt that she saw it as having potential for her rather than for him. She would not see the distress and conflict in the workers which accompanied their ideas and had been put forward tentatively. She would only take advantage of their insecurity to set up some project of her own.

I felt that he was continuing to describe a 'boss' whom he had projected into me, and with whom I was now identified, and that I was experienced by him as callously disregarding his pain and conflict for my own self-interest. There is a change from his anxiety about his self-interest to his accusation of the boss's/my self-interest.

I interpreted that he felt I took advantage of his distress and that he experienced me as taking him as potential for my own psychoanalytic project, rather than helping him by being in touch with his pain and conflict. He immediately agreed that he did see me like that. He explained that he often had the thought that maybe I was going to write about him. He had read books with papers in about patients. He thought perhaps he was giving me new ideas and I would be writing about him in a cold, academic way, more intent on improving my professional standing than being in touch with his pain.

Now, at the end of the session, before the weekend, he told me that he would not be here for the last session before the Christmas break as he was flying back to the USA. As he went out of the door, he smiled with his usual charm and said that I could then have a free morning.

I felt slightly irritated and realised that he had just avoided a confrontation with me over abandoning the last session. I thought that he had projected into me the misused worker who was to be given a day off whilst he had gone off as the boss involved in his own projects.

His next session was after the weekend

He came in and told me that he was angry about the meeting at work and followed this with a list of things he was angry about. He was angry at a telephone call from his uncle, angry with his brother, angry with a woman friend, and then he commented with a wry smile that he seemed to be angry with so much these days. He was angry with his uncle who had kindly offered him some engineering work and then, when he had politely refused it, had accused him of not wanting to work and having it easy. He was angry with his woman friend because she was preoccupied with her own anxieties and so possessive of him and others that he could not get her to divulge the address of another woman he was interested in. He was angry at his work team because they were now using his dissatisfaction as a focus for putting pressure on the company to change things in the factory. He said that it was good to have his complaints taken seriously, and his boss was realising that her team were all angry at her somewhat obsessional and controlling approach to their group project.

He explained that it had become clearer to him that he wanted to try and make a video of his home state of Virginia which would have the storyline of a son's 'discovery' of his mother's sexual activity set in the context of an engineering industrial complex. This idea had been stimulated by seeing a painting of a young woman bathing, an athletic Virginian. The device that he would use would be the dialogue and relationship between the adult son and a celibate Benedictine monk. The monk was important as he said that monks have to illustrate their illuminated manuscripts in great detail, drawing the Virgin Mary, Mother of God, and therefore have to divorce themselves from their feelings to avoid being aroused whilst visualising and painting the details of the woman's body. Though the frame of the film would be engineering it would not be structured in the controlled way that his boss would have him make it – a project for her benefit. It was personal to him. He felt that he had to be separate from her now. He was looking forward to going back home. He had things to research there. He feels at home in his own State and therefore can get in touch with people without embarrassment. He said that he was feeling better in himself.

I commented on how he wanted to bring together the two aspects of himself. These were the painful realisation of his mother's sexuality with his father and that she was not only the idealised virginal athlete of his childhood, and to link this with the monastic him that had had to divorce himself from any awareness of arousal with regard to the woman's body as he had when sleeping in his aunt's room. He feels more comfortable with his psychological state and less embarrassed at what he 'sees'.

He then said that he had been to see his masseur over the weekend and had felt that it too was different. He had gone to visit him because of something more positive in his attitude to life, not just because he was lonely. He had taken him a present as a friend, though of course he does pay him a fee. He wanted to emphasise the friendship for the man beyond the professional. I was about to comment on the transference when he continued 'I also went for a haircut. My hair was washed by a young man. I was very aware of his care and his gentleness of my hair and skin and ears. Gently and softly drying me, full of care and very maternal. Not just roughly touching my hair and then moving me out. I enjoyed it and found it stimulating. Actually I got an erection and was excited. But it was a different sort of erection to my compulsive masturbation. It's quite clear to me now that my compulsive masturbation is full of anger and resentment, against everybody, my mother, my father, whoever, just looking for the big male body and the big penis. This was quite different'. He explained that he felt moved and loving and could remember something of what he had been like when he was with Hillary. (Hillary had been his much-loved girlfriend for some years during his adolescence who had been taken from him by his best male friend, and is the name of the wife of his President.)

He talked further about his sense of owning his own State and having to resist the disapproval of both his uncle and his father if he persisted in distancing himself from his father's specialist engineering and went ahead with his own interests.

I said that he was pleased to feel he could own his own State, as owning his own state of mind, and that it was like being able to own his own mother and his interest in her as well as his interest in the State of Virginia. However, it then disturbed him to find himself having an erection from the stimulation of motherly handling, and that he was terrified of what his father would say if he found him with an erection as a boy enjoying being handled by his mother; hence it was safer to experience it through the man.

He nodded and was thoughtfully silent. After a while he continued to say that the Benedictine was becoming more and more important in his story. He said he knew it was linked to him but felt that he could use it without it being too obviously personal and autobiographical. He wanted to emphasise that the monk had a need to distance himself from women. He wanted to indicate that something had occurred during the childhood of the monk, otherwise why would any man become a monk? He told me that he was thinking of himself sharing his room with his aunt and his awareness of her dressing and undressing every night. He explained how he would have to roll over and look the other way.

I said how he felt he had not only to look the other way but had also to create an internal blindness so that he was not supposed to see anything in his mind's eye; though, as he had said some time ago, doors and walls were no barrier to his all–seeing internal eye.

He agreed, saying that that is what the monks have to do; they have to create an internal blindness when they are painting. Much of their work is very detailed so their visual acuity and perception is very good. They were very good artists but they could not allow themselves to have feelings about the bodies that they were illustrating. There was beautiful detail in the illuminated manuscripts, but they could only paint the Virgin's face and hands. Her body was presented as dead and wooden; so different from the sculptures of classical times where the body is enhanced by the drape of the clothing so that one is aware of the breasts and the body even though they are hidden. He said he knew this was about him and the importance of being bathed and handled.

I linked this to the importance he had attached to the painting of the Virginian and his awareness of his own sexual excitement and erection that he was alarmed at exposing to his father, and was troubled by his father's repetitive examination of his genitals in the bathroom.

He said that he felt that he could use these aspects of his life in the creative way that he had found with me, but now also wanted a partner to work with as well as an analyst. To some extent the analyst was experienced as a new relationship which could be used to assist separation and differentiation. (The demand to have an appropriate and usable relationship with a father is beautifully described in Nick Hornby's novel, *About a Boy.*)

The analysis followed a fluctuating course with the patient oscillating between moves towards heterosexual contact and defensive retreats into compulsive masturbation that would last for hours and drive him to despair and suicidal ruminations. He was able gradually to separate himself from what he had perceived as the mother's unconscious demand that he be her beloved daughter into whom she could project herself and through whom she would realise her frustrated ambitions and desires. He experimented with different careers, but then was able to return to engineering with great pleasure when he was able to establish a particular way of working which was his own and largely free of that imposed by his father. This allowed a healthy identification with his father's effectiveness. In his own field he became very successful. He temporarily established a tender and sexual relationship with a woman and was sad when their personalities clashed in such a way to make a permanent relationship impractical. He maintained some heterosexual interest but with intense genital anxiety which continued to push him towards the safety of homosexual fantasising.

Factors militating against a secure sexual identity

There were many elements that made it unusually difficult for this patient to achieve the normal dis-identification with his mother and establish a secure identification with his father and a stable heterosexual interest. (Both parents have important roles in the psychological development of the child (Phares 1996).) It seems that this patient had an exceptional inborn visual capacity, along with a capacity for deep sensitivity and responsiveness. This included a special awareness of colour, form and space, and later an awareness of complex personal relationships. In discussing creative and talented people Greenacre suggests that 'The increased sensitivity permits an unusual degree of projection of empathy to operate readily with both male and female forms, often supported by vivid fantasy life. There is thus a predisposition to bisexual self-awareness, sometimes even producing personal confusion' (Greenacre 1963: pp. 19–20). The personal confusion of this patient was further compounded by the belief within the family that he was an ugly boy and by the mother's disappointment that she did not get the little girl she was hoping for. An unconscious aspect of the mother's unfulfilled wish may have been instrumental in placing him within the aunt's bedroom, where his sexual curiosity was stimulated but required suppression because of the closeness and lack of privacy. Further suppression was supported by the disapproval of the mother and aunt towards the sexuality of the grand-father. These pressures pulled the boy further into the identification with his much-loved mother whom he wanted to please. It seems that the father was not able to intervene between the boy and his mother and aunt to enable a separate bedroom and a separation from their powerful fantasies.

His drive towards a sexual identity was further confused by his father's fantasies of the sort of son he was going to have: a son to fulfil his ambition of being an engineer, though at the same time he denigrated engineers. An identity that would be imposed on the son which the son would try to accept, both out of love for the father and also out of fear; fear that his independence would kill his father and also an intense castration anxiety engendered by the excessive proximity to his aunt, combined with his father's repeated examinations of his penis. The father's relationship to the mother served as a further model of authority and subservience with implications for the patient in retaining a particular identification with his mother in order to remain safe. This also protected him from exposing his own intense aggression and resentment at his father's domination.

References

Axelrad, S. and Brody, S. (1967–1970) *Mother–Infant Interaction*. New York University Film Library.

Freud, A. (1936) *The Ego and Mechanisms of Defence*. Hogarth Press, London.

Freud, S. (1895) *Studies in Hysteria*. Standard Edition 2. Hogarth Press, London.

—— (1900) *The Interpretation of Dreams*. Standard Edition 4, Standard Edition 5. Hogarth Press, London.

—— (1905) *Three Essays on the Theory of Sexuality*. Standard Edition 7. Hogarth Press, London.

—— (1910) *A Special Type of Choice of Object made by Man*. Standard Edition 11. Hogarth Press, London.

—— (1921) *Group Psychology*. Standard Edition 18. Hogarth Press, London.

—— (1923) *The Ego and the Id*. Standard Edition 19. Hogarth Press, London.

—— (1938) *An Outline of Psychoanalysis*. Standard Edition 23. Hogarth Press, London.

Greenacre, P. (1957) Early Physical Determinants in the Development of the Sense of Identity. In *Emotional Growth*, Vol. 1, 1971, I.U.P., New York, pp. 113–127.

—— (1963) *The Quest for the Father*. I.U.P., New York.

Greenson, R.R. (1968) Dis-Identifying from Mother: Its Special Importance for the Boy. *International Journal of Psycho-Analysis*, 49, 370–374.

Hornby, N. (1998) *About a Boy*. Victor Gollanz, London.

Kittay, E.F. (1998) Mastering Envy. In N. Burke (ed.) *Gender and Envy*. Routledge, London and New York, pp. 171–197.

Phares, V. (1996) *Fathers and Developmental Psychopathology*. John Wiley & Sons, New York.

Stoller, R.J. (1968) *Sex and Gender. The Development of Masculinity and Femininity*. Hogarth, London.

Tyson, P. (1989) Infantile Sexuality and Gender. *Journal of the American Psychoanalytic Association*, 37, 1051.

Wright, K. (1991) *Vision and Separation: Between Mother and Baby*. Free Association Books, London.

13

THE ADOPTIVE FATHER

Denis Flynn

Introduction

Most accounts of adoption give very little space to the adoptive father. Whilst rightful emphasis is given to the adopted child or adoptee, to the natural or birth parents, and to the adoptive mother, even specific discussions of the adoptive parents give the father only a small mention. In short the adoptive father is a bit of a nonentity. Such an attitude underlies our current notion of adoption in western culture, and expresses a primitive emotion and thinking, a "myth" in Bion's sense, indicative of a level of growth and certain preconceptions and fragmented forms of thinking (Bion, 1962b: 63, 67) The adoptive father holds much the same sort of peripheral place in the adoptive family that Joseph, overshadowed by the infant Jesus and his mother Mary, holds in the Holy Family. Yet this lack of emphasis is markedly different from the family as understood by Freud, where the Oedipal conflict underlies all relationships, and where the role of the father is central. Freud's relationship to his own father, in historical reality and in his central early works (in particular *The Interpretation of Dreams* where many important dreams are about his own father), underlies the development of his theory of the Oedipus complex. Later, from 1905 onwards, the doctor experienced the father is central to the development of the concept of transference, the main psychological mechanism of understanding in psychoanalytic treatments.

The comparative neglect of the adoptive father is in part due to the absence, until very recently, of cogent and fully expressed psychoanalytically informed views about the role of the father within the family. Yet the very marginal view of the adoptive father flies in the face of the intuition and experience of many who work in the field of adoption, who see the role of adoptive father as crucial in practice to successful and unsuccessful adoptions alike.

I believe, and will outline in this chapter, that *the adoptive father* has a key role in the development of the adopted child in so far as, firstly, he *supports the nurturing of the adoptive mother*, which focuses around the physical and emotional developing needs of the adopted child, and, secondly, he *actively creates meaningful links for the family*, for the child and the adoptive mother, about their relationship, his part in it and with other members of the adoptive family, and, thirdly, he *actively creates meaningful links for the adoptive child about his/her personal history*, including about his/her adoption and the connections to the natural parents.

I shall look first at some historical and cultural perspectives on adoption, then at the changes of view of adoption which stem from the philosophical ideas of the Enlightenment – in particular, calculations about needs and wants, and how these ideas have pervaded the psychoanalytic literature on adoption until very recently. I shall fill out my own psychoanalytic view of the adoptive father, with reference to some more recent psychoanalytic studies on adoption, and give some case illustrations from psychoanalytic work with adopted children and adoptive parents.

Historical and cultural perspectives

There is no universal or singular view of adoption, so that within different historical and cultural contexts there can be widely differing philosophies on it. I believe our modern views on adoption have lost, in many ways, some of the richness of this cultural heritage. I shall make just one historical comparison: with the Roman concept of adoption, which is especially important for under-standing a central feature of the role of the adoptive father which is missing in our present concepts of the practice of adoption. In the Roman world the philosophy of adoption involved conferment of privilege and high rank, essentially of status. Interestingly much of our terminology of adoption is Latin, the words "adoption", "parent", "father", "mother", "family", and so on. (An exception is "child", from the old English, and originally old German root, "cild", although "infant" is derived from Latin.)

Adoption occurred in the Roman world not because of the neediness of the child, nor because of the neediness of the adoptive family, but as a means by which very worthy individuals were sponsored by a very senior figure (for example a senator or governor of a province) so that they could be groomed to take on the privileges and responsibilities of office. The central figures in it were all men, especially the adoptive father, whose action in adopting a boy or young man was a symbol of his substantial importance and position. One of the special features of Roman law was the principle of *patria potestas*, the power of the father, which involved the lifelong authority of the father over the person and property of his descendants, and was the outcome of the family organisation of a primitive society. (Compare here Freud's discussion of the power and authority of the father in primitive and mythology society in *Totem and Taboo*.) This authority in its earliest form could be quite total, although it was modified in later centuries, and included the power of life and death, control of the marriage of son or daughter, and power of transferring them to another family or selling them.

Trajan is an example of an adoptive father in Roman times. As a successful soldier and provincial governor, he adopted another Spaniard and his great-nephew, Hadrian, who was then a very promising young man, a soldier from a lower-ranking provincial family. Hadrian joined with Trajan in his military successes as he conquered the Dacians, whose territory he constituted a Roman province (modern Romania), and a large part of the Parthian Empire, reaching the Persian Gulf. Trajan was Roman Emperor AD 98–117. We know something of the relationship between the two men from literary sources and interpretation of the dramatic sculptures of Trajan's column in Rome. When Hadrian, with many successes of his own, succeeded Trajan as Emperor in AD 117, he put his main energies not into further conquests to extend the Empire but into improving its internal cohesion. As a former provincial Hadrian knew of the real dangers of incursion by barbarian invasion, and the dangers of maladministration, corruption and chaotic use of power and authority in separate corners of the Empire, so his energies went into creating links and connections, to strengthen the body of the Empire as a whole. As part of his task he organised afresh the imperial bureaucracy, placing men of the equestrian order in high posts formerly held by freedmen. He codified the Praetor's Edict and made it the fixed law of the whole Empire. He spent many tireless years travelling all the provinces, visiting amongst others Britain, where he built the famous Hadrian's Wall, from the mouth of the Solway to the mouth of the Tyne. This work, continued by others later, effectively ensured the survival of the Roman Empire for a further three centuries.

What I am hoping to bring out in this historical analogy is the importance which Trajan conferred on Hadrian by his adoption. It meant a major increase in Hadrian's status during Trajan's lifetime, and, after his death, his succession as Emperor. Hadrian accepted the privilege of his adoption by Trajan, and lived up to his early promise by identifying with and devoting himself tirelessly to his "adoptive role", making the Empire more safe, internally coherent, and promoting long-term effective good government within the Empire.

There are a number of other cultural attitudes towards adoption which are similar in emphasis to the Roman, of which I shall mention just a few. Among the Marquesans, adoption occurred at the request of the adoptive parents and independently of the wishes of the biological parents (Linton, 1936). The Hopi developed a system of adoption which existed in parallel with blood ties, so that everyone within a tribe was related to everyone else by blood or adoption (Thomson and Joseph, 1944). In Manus, adoption became a way of strengthening the economic status of the family; yet the relationship of the adopted person was always somewhat tenuous as, in times of crisis, the adoption might be repudiated in favour of blood ties (Mead, 1956). Interestingly, as with Roman adoption, many of these cultures view adoption at least in part as a matter of societal gain or an issue of economic and societal cohesion, in part emphasising the power and status of the adoptive parents.

Contrast these cultural views with a more modern view of the child who does not belong and is not wanted in Ibsen's *Eyolf* (1894). Halfway through Act One, Eyolf, aged nine, wishing to overcome his personal defect (lameness) and become a soldier, and aware of the sterility of his parents' marriage, his father's depression and his parents' forgetful indifference to him, slips out to the garden. By the end of Act One he has been seen drowned, lying on his back with his eyes open staring upwards, his crutch floating on the water, before he is swept away by the "undercurrent" deep in the fjord. The awful truth dawns on the parents that the undercurrent of family life, their marital difficulties, and in particular the father's failure to be a father (emotionally withdrawn and falsely preoccupied, getting nowhere with writing his life's work, a book ironically called "The Responsibility of Man"), has meant that in real active terms they have neglected their son, whose death, a second accident, like the one that crippled him, occurred in the midst of their indifference. Eyolf left the home after the Ratwife left, and his following her is deeply symbolic of his being got rid of like the loathsome rats, who follow the Ratwife to be drowned in the fjord. The rest of the play painfully unravels the complicated reasons for their failure and neglect, including the father's near incestuous connection to his "sister" Asta, confusions of identity between her and Eyolf, "big" Eyolf and the poor substitute "little" Eyolf, the hate and disowning of the child as "only half mine", the blaming of the child for their problems – "the evil that lies in the child's eye". The forgetting of Eyolf is just one sign of their failure to address and find the meaning of their relationships – "I forgot him completely", "He slipped right out of my mind. Out of my thoughts."

ALLMERS   . . . our child never really belonged to us.
RITA   No. We never loved him.
ALLMERS   [*quietly*] The crutch.
          . . . While he lived, our cowardly, furtive consciences would not let
          us love him because we could not bear to look at the – thing that
          he carried – . . .

(Ibsen, trans. 1968, p. 264–265)

And yet, powerfully, it is the crutch which is left floating on the surface of the water after Eyolf drowns. Eyolf has a physical handicap, but he is experienced as emotionally handicapped – much as the adopted child may be seen. The family is experienced as incomplete, and there is a pattern of inadequate emotional relationships.

The philosophical ideas of the Enlightenment

Our modern philosophical understanding of the place of adoption in the family and in society is tied up with issues about needs and wants. The child who is abandoned or given up by his/her parents *needs* a substitute family. Parents who have not been able to have a child of their own, whether through infertility or some other cause which prevents the satisfaction of their perceived *needs* as individuals or as a couple, *want* to take on a child to be their own. Society, which sees itself responsible for looking after abandoned or unfortunate children, *needs* a social provision which can best secure the future development of children. The child without a family *wants* a family like other children around have. A voluntary contract, the adoption, gives the child a permanent place within a new family.

This view of needs and wants, and of a voluntary legal contract, stems from the philosophy of the Enlightenment, from Rousseau, Hobbes and Locke, which sees rightful political authority to lie in a society whose citizens agree upon a structure of needs and wants, where authority, and sovereignty, rests upon the agreed will of the people (Locke), and where the agreement which underlies the structure of satisfaction of agreed needs and wants is formulated in a social contract (Rousseau). No longer is a God-given right or an hereditary principle adequate. The utilitarian theorists, Bentham, Mill and Sedgewick, embedded such thinking within our social arrangements, so that any particular social provision is deemed to be in the interests of the people if a calculation of conflicting needs and wants can be set up to show that the greater happiness of the greater number is provided for.

There are such potential conflicts of needs and wants at every level in adoption, between the birth family and the adoptive family, between the adoptee and the adoptive family. Up to the present, such difficulties are still inherent in the procedures and legal provisions surrounding adoption. As with all areas of child care law and administration in Britain the final test having taken into account the other parties and considerations, is the provision "in the best interests of the child"?

There have been huge advantages which have stemmed from this modern philosophy of adoption. However, on a philosophical level there can also be serious flaws in this approach, since such calculations of needs and wants are after all not exact calculations at all. There are different and potentially conflicting human values which come into all of this, which spoil the simplicity of the calculations (cf. in particular Smart and Williams (1973) and Quinton (1973) for extensive arguments on J.S. Mills's (1863) thesis). Setting up such calculations of needs and wants on their own does not work. In deciding issues about important basic values (e.g. honesty, integrity, procedures about establishing truth) this philosophy gives no guiding principle to follow. Important values can be overlooked and other important elements ignored or left out, including a perspective on adoption which gives the adoptive father a strong contributory role.

Viewing adoption as a calculation of needs and wants is most unsatisfactory. It makes more likely views which stress the neediness of individuals and how their wants are well-guided or misguided. It lays stress on the neediness of the child, as abandoned or unwanted, or the neediness of the adoptive parents as bereft without children. It stresses mothering, fears of it or failings in it as applied to the birth mother, and the need to be or capacity for it as applied to the adoptive mother. It neglects the father, the natural or birth father, because when it is a calculation of the child's needs he is seen as already out of the picture, having let the mother and child down; it neglects the adoptive father because he is not deemed so central to the nurturing needs of the adoptive child.

These ideas from the Enlightenment and the Utilitarians began to influence social institutions and law-making just as the first adoption laws were being introduced in Western societies. In modern Western civilisation an adoption law was first passed in France in the Code Napoléon, initially modelled on ancient Roman law. Other laws followed in Spain, then in the United States and Great Britain, but gradually there was a shift in emphasis from protection of the rights of the adoptive parents to a policy based on the supposed welfare of the child (Schechter, 1967). These laws increasingly began to incorporate modern philosophical thinking about needs and wants.

The literature: defect and narcissistic disturbance

Although the adoptive father is absent from the psychoanalytic literature on adoption, there have been two important relevant themes: the discussions of defect and narcissistic disturbance in adoptive parents or the adoptive child, which I shall look at first, and discussions of the quality of relationship and capacity for dialogue between adoptive parents and adopted child, which I shall look at next.

For a long time the adoptive child who presented with problems was viewed as having them because of his adoption. The ratio of adopted to non-adopted children who presented at clinics was higher than the ratio of adopted to non-adopted children in the population. So the conclusion was drawn that adoption was a problem per se. This conclusion ignored the contributory fact that adoptive families have already had and continue to have better access to social and psychiatric agencies. Now, we believe that no special syndrome or disturbance is associated with adoption (Blum, 1983). However, there can be pathology in adoptive families, and there are inherent traumas in adoption itself which affect subsequent relationships. Also in the child's inner world, adoption may function as an organiser, a focus for various anxieties to do with feeling unloved, rejected, damaged, undervalued – all things which equally may occur in non-adopted children.

In some situations in adoptive families, problems are projected onto the adoptive child, as if he or she, or their birth family, are their cause. The child can be seen as coming from "bad seed", which may refer to the abnormal sperm or eggs of the adoptive parents. The adopted child may become the black sheep of the family. This sort of aggressive and destructive fantasy can cause the irruption of difficulties and enactments at points of crisis.

All parents, and especially adoptive parents, who have a child from a different biological family have to deal with the instinctual sides of human life, and with the ambivalence of their children, at all stages of development. Unresolved instinctual conflicts in adoptive parents amplify normal developmental conflicts in the adopted child and antecedent issues of the abuse which the child may have suffered before going for adoption. Parental anxiety may lead to attempts to repress the child's expression of his instinctual urges, and if this fails to reject that instinctual part and attribute it to the biological parents. A process can occur by which the "defect" is attributed to the biological parents. This can be exacerbated by the perceived absence in adoption of the incest barrier and to the effect, real or perceived, of increased seductiveness in parent or child. Early separations and multiple placements prior to adoption, and the inherent difficulties to be experienced by the adopted child and the adoptive mother in establishing an emotional bond, cause further problems.

There is a stress in the literature on the vulnerability of the adopted child, viewing themselves as unwanted and facing inevitably a narcissistic blow, and there is stress too on the adoptive parents being unable to recognise the reality of this narcissistic blow in the child and also being unable to come to terms with and work through the aspects of their own original difficulties which led to their adopting a child. They are in essence a narcissistic blow for the adoptive parents. This may be related to infertility, or psychosomatic conflicts affecting fertility. Resultant confusions occur about issues of potency, self-worth and identity, sexual conflicts, guilt, etc., or "injured family narcissism": a concept used to describe a family which cannot accept its adoption of a child, because in not producing a child biologically the family cannot idealise itself (Blum, 1983).

Compensatory fantasies can pathologically safeguard injured narcissism, in adoptive parents or the adoptive child. The latency boy whom Sherick (1983) describes had very ambivalent feelings about his adoptive father, and in the transference his analyst, as adoptive father, was treated as a "dogcatcher". When there was a shift away from the ambivalently cathected easily provoked adoptive father, as the analysis dealt with his masturbation, competitive wishes and castration anxiety, the boy began to see how his narcissistic compensatory defences were used against his sense of vulnerability. Now in the transference the analyst, as adoptive father, was seen as the "coach" who could help the boy achieve his wish for praise and recognition, albeit on a grandiose scale.

Many papers on adoption deal with the family romance fantasies (the wish for "a better or happier family" in place of one's own family), which Freud (1909) wrote about. Burlingham (1952) and Anna Freud (1965) have commented on family romances as being ubiquitous during the latency years in which the latency child has to deal with the disappointment of the preceding Oedipal stage. Typically, in the fantasy of natural children the biological parents are denigrated and the wished-for parents are idealised. For adopted children matters are less straightforward. For the adopted child, the issue of his or her discovery of and knowledge about their adoptive status, including when and what they know about their birth parents, is crucial. Children react differently and idiosyncratically to the knowledge of adoption, but it comes to be associated with some defect or stain. In latency or younger children the apparent lack of interest can belie the inner existence of intense curiosity and speculation. The full impact may not be felt until later, at school or in adolescence with the emergence of new or different instinctuality, sexuality, individualised aggression, and issues about identity, especially personal identity. There are a number of different transformations throughout the life cycle, and at these times the adopted child may need special attention or help, and there is a particular and ongoing role for the adoptive father.

The quality of relationships and dialogue in the adoptive family

The more recent psychoanalytic literature on adoption sees the quality of relationships and dialogue in adoptive families as crucial and of foremost importance for the success of adoptions. Anna Freud crucially links, in her study of adoption, the need for affection (for the unfolding and centring of the infant's own feelings), with the need for stimulation (to elicit inherent functions and potentialities), and with the need for unbroken continuity (to prevent damage done to the personality by the loss of function and destruction of capacities which follow invariably on the emotional upheavals brought about by separation by death or disappearance of the child from his first love objects) (Yale Law School seminar, quoted in Schecter, 1967).

Yet it is very difficult for adopted children and adoptive parents to talk about adoption, and rather as with theories about sex and childbirth, children arrive at their own version of events (Hodges *et al.*, 1984). They do not publicly disclose their thoughts about such matters, or at least not in any elaborated way. Several surveys of adult adoptees reveal a wish on their part to have known more about their origins (e.g. Jaffe and Fanshel, 1970; Triseliotis, 1973; McWinnie, 1976; ABAFA, 1980). Most studies indicate how a circle of silence is set up by the reluctance of parent and child to raise the question of adoption.

The most commonly cited etiological factors in adoption-related disturbances are the child's learning about his adoption and the adoptive parents' ambivalence (Frankel, 1991). After that the important factors are the quality of the disturbing anxiety in the adopted child and their sense of the level of investment in them by the adoptive parents. Learning about adoption is itself a kind of mourning process in which the child progressively modifies his conviction that he unequivocally belongs to his adoptive parents (Brinich, 1980). All adopted children have to negotiate this and those who succeed do so by engaging in a finely tuned co-operative effort with their adoptive parents.

Nickman (1985) sets a different tone from that in most psychoanalytic studies in his opening sentence, "Adoption is acknowledged as a vitally important institution in our society . . ." (p. 365). He refers to studies such as Hodges *et al.* (1984) which highlight the issue of non-communication, including passing over what the child thinks, causing resentment towards the adoptive parents (Triseliotis, 1973; McWhinnie, 1976; Raynor, 1980). Most of the literature is about loss and problems of bonding. But little has been written on the topic of parent–child dialogues about their meaning and feelings at any point in time about adoption, in the school years and later. Yet a child's understanding of adoption does not grow by gradual accretion beginning in the earliest years; rather, children commonly display an apparent early acceptance and understanding of the situation. This "understanding" shifts between six and eight years to a more complex attitude characterised by worry and questioning, in accordance with the cognitive growth which has occurred in the intervening years. Adoptive parents often make the mistaken assumption that "telling" automatically leads to "understanding" on the part of the child (Brodzinsky, 1990). Natural children in a family can also suffer from the same failures of dialogue (Jacobs, 1988). He describes the impact on a natural sibling of his having three adopted siblings, how he tended to play down any differences, and how his fantasies about adoption reduced his confidence in the truthfulness and reliability of his parents. Nickman argues that the major intervention which can help an adopted child grieve for these various losses is dialogue and discourse about adoption, which should begin at an appropriate age and continue intermittently throughout the various stages of development. Parents who cannot "connect" with their children about adoption, in particular those who deny difference, fail to help in important ways and thereby add another dimension of loss to the child's experience. The dialogue should be ongoing in an open communicative atmosphere, and not terminated at some arbitrary point when parents, uncomfortable with the subject, decide that their job is done.

A new psychoanalytic view of the adoptive father

I believe that *the adoptive father* has a key role in the development of the adopted child. First, he *supports the nurturing of the adoptive mother*, which focuses around the physical and emotional developing needs of the adopted child. Second, he *actively creates meaningful links for the family*, for the child and the adoptive mother, about their relationship, his part in it and with other members of the adoptive family. Importantly, too, he *actively creates meaningful links for the adoptive child about his/her personal history*, including about his/her adoption and the connections to the natural parents.

Underpinning this view of the adoptive father are Bion's view of the intrapsychic functions of linking, expanded in his 1959 paper "Attacks on Linking", and his theory of containment, and Britton's (1989) view of the linking function of the father, in relation to the primitive formation of the Oedipus complex.

Bion describes how powerful and destructive early processes of projective identification can be employed by the psyche to attack objects that serve as a link. I believe that the early broken links in attachment for the adoptive child can at times reach this level of primitive fragmentation, and that there can be an interplay between early external developmental issues, including the fact of adoption, and primitive intrapsychic processes. Britton, as well as Bion, argues that if the third position is not possible, to "bring his parental objects together in his mind would result in explosion and disintegration" (Britton, 1987: p. 97) For adopted children this is crucial, as sooner or later they attempt to bring together in their minds a sense of themselves, their knowledge of their natural parents and their adoptive parents. For there are two, or more, sets of parents and actual fragmented relationships to integrate, making the possibility of an "explosion" or "disintegration" in the mind of the adopted child more likely and progression to a thoughtful, more depressive, position harder.

The role of the adoptive father in creating links to assist the adoptive child has to happen at every level. The adoptive mother concentrates on creating a bond and seeing to the nurturing needs of the adoptive child. In the course of this nurturing process, the father should have the task of being a third object, providing a different way of thinking, which becomes a boundary to limit the intensity of contact between mother and child. He has to facilitate a period of "primary maternal preoccupation", in Winnicott's terms; and he has to protect the mother by realistic observation and intervention. He has to foster the processes of bonding and attachment of mother and child, otherwise attachment problems will arise within the new relationship for adoptive child and parents alike.

At another level the adoptive father is in a special position to keep some continuous focus upon the adoptive child's connection to the natural family. His task is to handle a dialogue with the adoptive child at appropriate points in the child's development, to create a necessary space for the adoptive child so as to sustain links to the natural family, in thinking or in reality. It is important that the adoptive father can deal with his own envy of the adoptive mother's special position with the child and with his own narcissistic hurt since this child is not his natural child. Like all fathers, he needs to resist the wish to intrude between mother and child, and at times, when nurturing and bonding issues are foremost, to wait to fulfil his own role. His knowledge of his own narcissistic hurt may enable him to be in touch with that of the adoptive child. Something needs to be continuous and emotionally alive between the adoptive father and the adoptive child, and indeed with the adoptive mother and the rest of the adoptive family, so that a kind of emotional deadness does not proliferate, which can lead to the formation of what Quinodoz calls a "hole-object" inside the adoptive child.

Danielle Quinodoz's important paper (1996), "An Adopted Analysand's Transference of a 'Hole-Object'", looks at how an adopted person experienced a "hole-object", in respect of what was missing in her experience of life about her adoption. Her analyst became aware of this unknown element of experience through awareness of her counter-transference, and an appreciation of the true nature of the patient's transference. In my view, the adoptive father needs to work in relation to the adopted child to know, not just what may be known by the child and experienced by him, but also what may *not* be known and the child's reactions and experience of that.

Quinodoz's more recent paper (1999), "The Oedipus Complex Revisited: Oedipus Abandoned, Oedipus Adopted", looks further at these issues. She draws attention to the obscurity of Oedipus' adoptive parents, Polybus and Merope, rulers of Corinth. Oedipus loved his adoptive parents and missed them, but, importantly, he did *not know* they were *not* his natural parents. Quinodoz found, in analysis of adopted and non-adopted patients, that there can be psychically both natural and adoptive parents, but a failure to work through affective relations to each can bring a severe conflict of ambivalence. Quinodoz sees three possible consequences of ambivalence: one, where affects of love and hate are *fused*; two, where the patient might *link them while distinguishing them*; three, where the patient might *distinguish the affects but not yet be capable of linking them* (Quinodoz's italics). This third occurrence can bring severe consequences such as vertigo, accidents or suicide, which Quinodoz sees as a failure of "*dichotomisation*" (French: *dedoublement*); that is, of separating out psychically natural parents and adoptive parents. My view is that there also is a fourth type of conflict, which is pre-ambivalent and originates out of more primitive processes of splitting (as described by Klein, 1946), where *there is a not knowing, or additionally in Bion's terms a −K, or a confusion and disintegrative diffusion of affects, and an inability to link* natural and adoptive parents. The adoptive father will need to help the adoptive child with the task of making sense of these deepest confusions.

Case illustrations

I shall now look at the linking role of the adoptive father in my psychoanalytic work with two adopted children and their adoptive parents. In my first illustration, the adoptive father was a white high ranking professional, who with his wife adopted two black children, Andrew and Virginia, into their family. I saw Andrew for twice weekly psychotherapy for seven years, from the age of nine until the age of sixteen, and had regular meetings with his adoptive parents throughout this time.

In psychotherapy, at home and at school, Andrew had shown an early false compliance, which hid severe early neglect and deprivation. There was a known-about but unknown and off-the-scene black natural father, and a white natural mother who now was elsewhere. Unworked-through issues about childlessness affected the consistency of the adoptive mother's usual capacity for caring, sometimes making her somewhat abrupt and harsh. The adoptive father's own father was himself renowned in his profession and a man of influence, though the adoptive father had chosen a different more modern field of work. In all of this there was a double difficulty for the adoptive father. He felt a sense of not being accepted in his own family, and for a time was fostered nearby but separately from the family of his natural father. In a sense the adoptive father experienced being excluded and not being adopted himself. What came through in my work, both with the boy and his adoptive parents, was that this adoptive father, despite his natural personal warmth and immense intellectual ability, continuously struggled to think and help his adoptive son and his wife to think, and to make meaningful emotional links, in particular during times of crisis, about the boy's experience, particularly the changing emotional impact of his adoption.

At nine, Andrew was an atypical latency child, more verbally able than most, but at first without a capacity to use the toys available to play. He was described as intelligent, witty and personable, but he had a distressingly depressive view of himself: "I'm rubbish", "I belong in a bin". He had suffered considerable trauma and was referred because of rages at home and at school. He was haunted by fears of insects, killer bees and tarantulas, and of many ordinary situations, and by beliefs about his underlying destructiveness encapsulated in a story from his family of origin, whereby he saw himself as responsible for a fire in the family house before he was taken into care. This happened when he was three, and he was adopted at five. His adoptive father described something which showed how Andrew himself broke the links which could make sense of his experience; he described Andrew's "ability to cocoon himself from past events in his life both recent and distant, and refuse to discuss them at all, as if they had no impact upon him". This persisted to a smaller or greater extent throughout the time I saw Andrew, even as he also actively sought to find out information and understand what had happened to him. There was an ongoing conflict at a primitive level, and, in a contradictory way, of continuously linking and unlinking his experiences. His younger sister, Virginia, with whom he was adopted, was highly disturbed at first, but thereafter was more secure than Andrew, despite some difficulties at times.

In some ways the adoptive father and mother could make links which helped Andrew make sense of his past, in particular his feelings about the children's home he had been in, his normality as an adopted child with other children locally who were not adopted and "minor" incidents of racial abuse, his feelings about his natural mother and his natural sister adopted elsewhere. However, conflicts could erupt from misunderstanding and intolerance, and incidents between Andrew and his adoptive parents could all too readily assume a concreteness which seemed to make thinking impossible, and frequently resulted in violent disruptions of family life. At such times the adoptive father and mother increasingly saw Andrew as "strange" and were hopeless about their ability to care for him. They then became excessively dependent on me for out-of-hours thinking and support in such a way that I became a surrogate for the adoptive father, sometimes to such a degree that I felt they wiped out any sense of my own personal and family life and needs. There were particular problems when the adoptive mother had an hysterectomy, and about Andrew's feelings about his natural father, both of which I shall come to, which created special difficulties for the adoptive father.

Nine months into treatment Andrew could express his anger at my attempts to think and make links with him. He wrote to me after a disturbing outburst before and during the previous session, "I felt very angry on Friday. It all started when we got there. I felt angry that this man was spoiling my week for me and taking out my feelings from the boxes that are arranged in shelves inside me." He enclosed a poem:

Mr Flynn

He makes me mad when I feel bad,
I think it's Friday time to die,
but why does this man say to me,
Now what happened on that day?
I feel I could say bug off go away,
and he'd say,
Can you tell me something about,
the ruddy week?
I think what a cheek,
I'd tear down all the houses
if I could get away, and
not hear him say now,
what happened on that day?

This trait in Andrew of wishing to withdraw completely into himself continued. Two years later when he broke his arm he told me with irritation how he was sick of the children at school (and me in the session) asking him about it. He wished he just had a notice to say he had broken his arm. Yet such things as a broken arm, which gave others the opportunity to initiate and create contact, temporarily opened Andrew up more. The day after his plaster came off, and he was less noticeable, Andrew told me that his teacher had said his face mask had gone on again.

As he made progress in the psychotherapy he could be very in touch with me, secure and confiding, aware he could have a favourite place, like the place in the picture on my wall which he took as my favourite place. He could talk about racist taunts at school, him being called "pooface". I thought and interpreted he could think about differences, and about his natural mother and his origins. Some of the time he could glorify his own phallic rivalry and competitiveness. Once he heard children in the background and he was wistful. I asked him what he felt. Andrew said he wondered if "he was like that". I understood him to mean, "as a child who would cry out and may not be heard or responded to". The issue of being heard was a very alive one for him. Andrew now confided that he had eaten cornflake packets sometimes as a child (because of hunger and not being heard).

His adoptive mother's forthcoming hysterectomy brought out anxiety and fear in Andrew. In the transference he tried to ensconce himself in the room and the house, like trying to get back into the womb, but his puzzled and confused feeling was, how could he as a black boy get back into a white womb? It seemed hard to remember that Andrew's natural mother was in fact white. He wanted to have a white father, like me and his adoptive father. When he was able to talk about his hurt, such as when he was upset when he had a tooth-break and pierced his brace, he did so in an open and more direct way. He spoke about his dad having nervous problems from bottling up his feelings about his family. He thought that his adoptive mother and father did not want him to contact his first mother and father. He talked about how what happened to him was his first father's fault. He searched for and got more information about his past, but felt overwhelmed by the information he received from the children's home. As he was more expansive with me, and trusted me as the adoptive father in the transference to help him make the links, his guilt lessened about his own part in events and he became more confident and imaginative in his play, discussion and associations.

When his anxieties about his mother's hysterectomy increased and his parents cancelled or changed around some sessions with me, he became increasingly alarmed. This tended to bring out a kind of compulsive materialism in him, which had a wearing-down effect in his parents: wanting this bike, that pair of trainers, another fishing rod and so on, as if he had regressed to a non-parental pre-care anarchic state. I found that as the adoptive mother herself became more preoccupied with her health and with herself, the adoptive couple could not contain Andrew's increasing distress together. The adoptive father became literally dependent on every aspect of my thinking, rather than continuing his own attempts to keep talking to Andrew and helping him through the crisis. In many ways I had been like the adoptive father to Andrew, making links and establishing

216

emotional connections, which until now had paralleled what he, the adoptive father, had been doing and trying to do. We all struggled on for another two years after this before Andrew's actions again involved a wider range of services such as psychiatry, the police and social services. His psychotherapy ended at this time. This seemed to mark the temporary breakdown of the adoptive family as a unit to contain the problems and the substitution of a wider more institutional non-personal framework around Andrew. It was a repetition of the breakdown in his natural family, when he went into institutional care.

In my second clinical illustration I shall describe a different outcome despite the odds against it. This is a child, Brian, who suffered not just deprivation and emotional abuse but also severe physical abuse in early infancy. On being adopted, and for some years afterwards, his behaviour was severely disturbed, getting him expelled from school and taxing everyone's capacities, especially his adoptive parents' and his psychotherapist's, to the limits. I saw this boy mainly twice weekly for five years, between the ages of five and ten, and met his parents periodically at two- to three-monthly intervals. I found in the psychotherapy that again and again I became the abusing natural father in the transference, or the weak and distancing mother, reflecting aspects of both his natural and adoptive mother as his work in psychotherapy differentiated each of these more. His natural mother had been complicit and collusive with her abusing partner and locked in a narcissistic trap of contemplation of her own beauty, which her son had inherited. His adoptive mother could become bewildered and fogged-out in response to this child's very disturbed behaviour, but a determined and strongly loving inner self, with support from her husband and good communication between them, meant that he steadily improved. All this happened despite the adoptive mother developing and being treated for a major cancer, which hospitalised her at times. The adoptive father gently questioned whether his adopted son was being affected by the past or by the present. He talked to and guided his son, whose improvement meant an inner change and a capacity to think and feel, with considerably more self-control, which represented an internal capacity to link together fragmented aspects of his past and present experience.

The adoption had happened very quickly, and the adoptive family only had three days' notice before placement of Brian at eighteen months. Brian's adoptive father felt Brian looked odd with his big lips and thought he would never be able to love him. They felt Brian attached to them too easily, shallowly or adhesively. His adoptive mother returned to full-time work six months after his placement. Brian did not talk until he was three. Despite the adoptive father's initial response to Brian, and I think perhaps because he reacted to looks, and something about his seductiveness and narcissistic processes and conflicts, he in time became more tolerant than his wife and more aware of Brian's inner anxieties.

In psychotherapy with Brian, contradictory harsh and affectionate interchanges alternated with baffling rapidity, reflecting his internal state and the confused and abusive treatment he had received. A recurring theme in his play was the rhino versus the crocodile, in which the crocodile (me) was pushed, mauled and crushed. He got under my skin, pierced my tough professional (crocodile) hide, and provoked near-abusive anger and retaliation from me and guilt about holding him too tightly when he hit me or tried to touch me seductively. At such fraught times Brian could not accept any reasonable boundaries of conduct. We each struggled with the guilt of what happened. All of this occurred in the adoptive family too.

One session he brought a brightly coloured umbrella, using it to fly "as free as a bird". He hurt his finger and wanted (inappropriately) a cuddle from me. Then he found a large roll of sellotape, and put it in his pocket wanting to keep it. There were tears of severe hurt as he was not allowed to. Eventually I decided to allow him to keep it, so that we could talk about it, which we did. He told me there were frogs in the pool at school and so it was closed. His dad had got rid of a frog in a pool. Much of what he said was confused and puzzling. I interpreted that I thought he felt not wanted here, and at home sometimes, and saw himself like the frog intruder that his adoptive father and I tried to keep out.

Such understandings of his deep sense of hurt at rejection and abuse helped him make sense of why he found himself feeling and acting as he did, and to bring it under more control. Brian could then talk about his natural mother, his memories of her, and say he did not understand why she did not love him. Later too, as this was worked over and over again in the psychotherapy, with immense strain both inside and at home, he could differentiate me and his adoptive father from the abusing natural father. Brian told me of his first dad leaving when he was one, because he needed someone to look after Brian. It all sounded rational and sad, some of it borrowed from information from records that Brian knew. Much of this work his adoptive father did in his caring personal contacts with Brian, in a way that paralleled and fitted with the work of the psychotherapy. Brian now improved at home and at school.

Conclusion

I have outlined in this chapter how the adoptive father has a distinctive role to help provide a thinking space about adoption, which includes thinking about issues to do with adoption throughout the development of the adoptive child, in a way which gives the adoptive child an experience of consistency and continuity. It allows the child to bring together complex areas of their experience, about their natural family and their adoptive family, and it enables them to view their natural and adoptive parents separately, and, in a singular way, to view themselves and their adoptive status in a full and positive light.

When problems arise in adoptions there can be a feeling, whether in a therapeutic situation or in the family, that nothing makes any sense. Important links cannot be made and instead there is a "hole-object" in Quinodoz's sense. As in my first case example, violent enactments by the adopted child against the adoptive parents can have many levels but may be rooted in previously fragmented Oedipal relationships which cannot be recognised, especially by the adoptive father who can feel deskilled and out of role, leaving the adoptive mother and the family exposed. Conversely the anger which meets the adoptive child's outbursts can have a vengeful quality, showing the adoptive parents' own problems and disappointments, and taking revenge on the Oedipal couple and the natural parents, thereby creating more destructive confusion. The adoptive father can feel deskilled and there can be a carry-over of negativism towards the natural father onto him, as having no real place or role. Such attacks on the Oedipal couple weaken the possibility of acquiring more meaning in the adoptive family and the adopted child's intrapsychic functioning.

For the adopted child to grow psychically in their new adopted family, *the family has to communicate to the child their value and real place within the family*, and *communicate the real value of the family to the child*. The stress should not be upon the neediness of the adopted child or of the adopted parents or family, though the deeper consequences of these needs, especially unmet needs, have to be remembered. The growth of status for the adopted child in the adoptive family is not necessarily or simply social, intellectual or material, but involves a capacity to help the adopted child to know their psychic reality, including the fact of adoption and its consequences. Viewing the adoption as a positive increase in status for the adoptive child and the adoptive parents, and a status that involves an enriched capacity for emotional understanding, is what is important. The standing of adoption and the position and role the adoptive father takes is crucial. The adoptive father has an active role to make meaningful links for the adoptive child and the rest of the adoptive family, and also a symbolic function to represent the value and status of the family to the adoptive child – in essence of an intact Oedipal couple – and thereby to allow for the consistent growth of meaning in the child's mind.

References

Access to Birth Records (1989) ABAFA Research Series.

Bion, W.R. (1957) "Differentiation of the psychotic from the non-psychotic personalities", *International Journal of Psycho-Analysis* 38, and in *Second Thoughts* (1967), Karnac, London.

Bion, W.R. (1959) "Attacks on linking", *International Journal of Psycho-Analysis* 40, parts 5–6, and in *Second Thoughts* (1967), Karnac, London.

Bion, W.R. (1962a) "A theory of thinking", *International Journal of Psycho-Analysis* 43, parts 4–5, and in *Second Thoughts* (1967), Karnac, London.

Bion, W.R. (1962b) *Learning From Experience*, in *Seven Servants*. Aronson, New York (1977).

Blum, H.P. (1983) "Adoptive parents: generative conflict and generational continuity", *Psychoanalytic Study of the Child* 38, 141–163.

Boardman, J., Griffin, J. and Murray, O. (eds) (1986) *The Oxford History of the Classical World*. Oxford University Press, Oxford.

Brinich, P.M. (1980) "Some potential effects of adoption on self and object representations", *Psychoanalytic Study of the Child* 35, 107–133.

Brinich, P.M. (1995) "Psychoanalytic perspectives on adoption and ambivalence", *Psychoanalytic Psychology* 12(2), 181–199.

Britton, R. (1989) "The missing link: parental sexuality in the Oedipus complex", in R. Britton, M. Feldman and E. O'Shaugnessy (eds) *The Oedipus Complex Today*, Karnac, London, pp. 83–102.

Brodzinsky, D.M. *et al.* (1990) *Open Adoption*. Oxford University Press, New York.

Burlingham, D. (1952) *Twins: A Study of Three Pairs of Identical Twins*. International Universities Press, New York.

Flynn, D. (1987a) "The child's view of the hospital: an examination of the child's experience of an in-patient setting", in A. Heymans, R. Kennedy and L. Tischler (eds) *The Family as In-Patient*, Free Association Books, London.

Flynn, D. (1987b) "Internal conflict and growth in a child preparing to start school", *Journal of Child Psychotherapy* 13(2), 77–90.

Flynn, D. (1988) "The assessment and psychotherapy of a physically abused girl during in-patient family treatment", *Journal of Child Psychotherapy* 14(2), 61–78.

Flynn, D. (1992) "Adolescent group work in a hospital in-patient setting with spina bifida patients and others", *Journal of Child Psychotherapy* 18(2), 87–108.

Flynn, D. (1998) "Psychoanalytic aspects of inpatient treatment", *Journal of Child Psychotherapy* 24(2), 283–306.

Flynn, D. (1999) "The challenges of in-patient work in a therapeutic community", in A. Horne and M. Lanyado (eds) *Handbook of Child Psychotherapy*, Routledge, London.

Frankel, S.A. (1991) "Pathogenic factors in the experience of early and late adopted children", *Psychoanalytic Study of the Child* 46, 91–108.

Freud, A. (1965) *Normality and Pathology in Childhood Writings 6*. International Universities Press, New York.

Freud, S. (1900) *The Interpretation of Dreams*, Standard Edition 4 and 5, Hogarth Press, London.

Freud, S. (1914) *On Narcissism*, Standard Edition 14, 73–102, Hogarth Press, London.

Freud, S. (1909) "Family romance phantasies", Standard Edition 9, 236–241, Hogarth Press, London.

Harvey, P. (1937) *The Oxford Companion to Classical Literature*. Clarendon Press, Oxford.

Hobbes, T. (1651) *Leviathan* (Fontana edn, 1962, William Collins and Sons, London).

Hodges, J. *et al.* (1984) "Two crucial questions: adopted children in psychoanalytic treatment", *Journal of Child Psychotherapy* 10, 47–56.

Hodges, J. (1990) "The relationship to self and objects in early maternal deprivation and adoption", *Journal of Child Psychotherapy* 16(1), 53–74.

Ibsen, A. (1968) *Little Eyolf* (Michael Meyer, Trans). London: Methuen.

Jaffe, B. and Fanshel, D. (1970) *How They Fared in Adoption: A Follow-up Study*. Columbia University Press, New York.

Jacobs, T.J. (1988) "On having an adopted sibling", *International Review of Psycho-Analysis* 15(1), 25–35.

Klein, M. (1945) "The Oedipus complex in the light of early anxieties", in *Collected Writings*, Vol. 1 (pp. 370–419), Hogarth Press, London.

Klein, M. (1946) "Notes on some schizoid mechanisms", *International Journal of Psycho-Analysis* 27, and in *Collected Writings*, Vol. 3 (pp. 1–24), Hogarth Press, London.

Linton, R. (1936) *The Study of Man*. Appleton-Century, New York.

Locke, J. (1690) *Two Treatises on Civil Government* (Everyman edn, 1924, Dent and Sons, London).

Mead, M. (1956) *New Lives for Old*. William Harrow, New York.

McWhinnie, A.M. (1976) *Adopted Children: How They Grow Up*. Routledge and Kegan Paul, London.

Mill, J.S. (1863) *Utilitarianism* (Everyman edn, 1910, Dent and Sons, London).

Nickman, S.L. (1985) "Losses in adoption: the need for dialogue", *Psychoanalytic Study of the Child* 40, 365–398.

Quinodoz, D. (1996) "An adopted analysand's transference of a 'hole-object'", *International Journal of Psycho-Analysis* 77(2), 323–336.

Quinodoz, D. (1999) "The Oedipus complex revisited: Oedipus abandoned, Oedipus adopted", *International Journal of Psycho-Analysis* 80(1), 15–30.

Quinton, A. (1973) *Utilitarian Ethics*. Macmillan, London.

Salo, F. (1990) "Well, I couldn't say no, could I?: Difficulties in the path of late adoption", *Journal of Child Psychotherapy* 16(1), 75–92.

Schechter, M.D. (1967) "Psychoanalytic theory as it relates to adoption", *Journal of the American Psycho-Analytical Association* 15, 695–708.

Sherick, I. (1983) "Adoption and disturbed narcissism: a case illustration of a latency boy", *Journal of the American Psycho-Analytical Association* 31(2), 487–513.

Smart, J.J.C. and Williams, B. (1973) *Utilitarianism: For and Against*. Cambridge University Press, London.

Raynor, L. (1980) *The Adopted Child Comes of Age*. George Allen and Unwin, London.

Rousseau, J.-J. (1762) *The Social Contract* (Everyman edn, 1913, Dent and Sons, London).

Thompson, L. and Joseph, A. (1944) *The Hopi Way*. University of Chicago Press, Chicago.

Tizard, B. (1977) *Adoption – A Second Chance*. Open Books, London.

Triseliotis, J. (1973) *In Search of Origins – The Experiences of Adopted People*. Routledge and Kegan Paul, London.

Voltaire (1759) *Candide* (Editions Gallimard, 1972, Paris).

— 14 —

FATHERS AND DISABILITY

Clifford Yorke

Introduction

Many psychoanalysts have written about children with chronic illness or physical disabilities, and discussed the different ways the sufferer and his[1] family cope with the *psychological* effects of these misfortunes. In particular, the handicapped child's psychological development forms the subject matter of numerous papers in the child analytic literature. From the Anna Freud Centre alone, many publications have drawn attention to the psychological effects on development of total and partial blindness, deafness, haemophilia, congenital deformities, and other disabilities including amputation of a limb for bone cancer.[2] Like many papers to be found elsewhere, these contributions include in their survey the effect of the disability on the child's family. In particular, the impact of a damaged child on parents – especially the mother – has been widely reported. The psychological effect that a sick child may have on a healthy sibling has been a subject of discussion, notably by Kennedy (1985). As for sick or damaged parents, it is an everyday matter to discuss the effect on an infant of a mother's post-partum depression or long-standing incapacity; examples abound in routine clinical practice. The effects on the family of uncommon or unusual conditions have been the subject of fascinating studies – for example, a clinical study of a man raised by deaf-mute parents (Arlow, 1976) was followed by an account of psychoanalytic work with a child brought up in comparable conditions (Bene, 1977). These papers are of particular interest in that *both* father and mother were irremediably damaged. But in general the significance for a child's psychological development of a chronically ill or disabled *father* has received less attention than the psychological effects on child care of damaged mothers. It may be of value to comment on something of what is known about the subject, and to illustrate various points with appropriate vignettes.

222

The mother's disabled partner

Clearly, not all disabilities are sustained by the father *after* a marriage or partnership has been established. As a young psychiatrist who was then untrained in psychoanalysis, my attention was drawn to the power of the repetition-compulsion when I treated a woman who had twice married tuberculous husbands and nursed them through their deathbeds. Less dramatically, perhaps, many women (and men, for that matter) choose damaged partners and have children by them, often for reasons of which they themselves are unaware. Although the disability may not be a significant motivation for the union, where it *is*, and where it satisfies a need in the mother, her attitude towards her husband or partner, as well as his disability, may have important consequences for their children. This may be true for children of either sex, even though boys seem the more likely to suffer if the mother's choice of a damaged husband is in part guided by hostility to men, whether conscious or not. Nor does the mother necessarily share her life with a damaged father – in such instances the hostility may be quite overt. The following example springs to mind.

An unattached woman of 37 desperately wanted a child, and realized that her childbearing years were passing. She resolved to be a single parent and raise a child without a father's assistance. She chose to be impregnated by the most damaged man she could find and never, thereafter, saw the father again. She remembered her own childhood as deeply unhappy. She was the first-born of three children. Her father, a self-righteous martinet in his behaviour towards her, seemed only to value his sons. She was treated as a lackey from an early age, and subjected to aggressive reprimand and humiliating injunction. By contrast, her brothers were excessively indulged. The father's attitude to his wife was one of disparagement: she was afraid of him and, although she herself showed no overt hostility to her daughter, she acquiesced in the face of her husband's attitudes and did little to defend her.

The patient's hatred of men was abiding. Consciously she wanted a daughter, but a son was born from the one night union with the crippled man. The mother tried to be caring in bringing him up, but did whatever she could to feminize him, encouraging girls' interests at every end and turn. Determined not to be weak like her mother, she tried to put pressure on him – a pressure that often conflicted with the care and consideration she consciously wanted to give him. The boy's endowment refused to support the sought-after feminine role, and the difficulties faced by the mother in the part she felt obliged to play made her increasingly desperate and led her to seek help.

When the boy asked his mother about his father, she told him he would not want to meet him because he was "so terribly damaged". The cruelty of this remark (bordering on the conscious) led the boy into a series of potentially dangerous accidents. Of the many matters clarified in treatment were the controlling masculine identifications that were so much in conflict with her conscious ideals, and the unhappy fact that she could find no relief for her conflicts of sexual identity. She wanted to be loved as a woman and mother, but despised the femininity that had brought her so much anguish; and in as much as she wished to be a man, she consciously hated that aspiration. Indeed, in choosing the damaged partner, she took revenge on the father, and gave her son someone of whom he could not easily be proud. For present purposes, it seems enough to indicate that the damaged father was omnipresent.

We all know that, in general, the choice of partner rarely rests on the woman's wishes alone. A man may, for example, want to settle down with the woman who nursed him in hospital. If he has recovered from his illness and, physically, is fit and well once more, the partnership would have no special claim on our attention. But if the husband has remained chronically ill the situation may be very different. In the case of an intense love match, such a union may satisfy unconscious and mutually compatible needs in both partners and, *from their point of view*, turn out well. But that may not be the case for a child born of the union, as the following example may illustrate.

The father of an eight-year-old girl (who was in analysis) suffered from a neurological illness that afflicted him severely – frequently, but intermittently. He had to rest at unpredictable times. The child never knew how she would find him when arriving home from school, and her pre-school years were marred by the restrictions so often imposed on her. Her play was severely curtailed, and she was told that under no circumstances must she make a noise in case it awakened the ailing man. Furthermore, the mother devoted her nursing skills to her husband's care, much to the envy and resentment of the daughter who felt neglected. Her attitude towards, and feelings about, both her parents had profoundly affected many aspects of her development. To be loved you had to be ill, and though her illness was psychological it was none the less real to the family. This aspect of the disturbance represented little more than the epinosic gain, but the ramifications of the patient's complex psychopathology need not concern us here.

A point of departure: the healthy father

Before pursuing these matters further, it may be useful to keep in mind something of what psychoanalysts know about the role of the *healthy* father in what, these days, must be called the "traditional" family. For a long time this was not a matter that attracted much comment in the literature: far more attention was paid to the role of the mother, except in the Oedipal phase. Freud himself often wrote about the significance of mothers in the early development of children. In 1931, for example, he emphasized the long pre-Oedipal attachment of the girl to her mother, and further discussed female psychological development in relation to the mother and child in a succinct and highly informative way in the "New Introductory Lectures" (1933). Although he talked a great deal about fathers, as is well known, he had more to say about their role in the *Oedipal* stage of development. But he *did* discuss the significance of the pre-Oedipal father, and an excellent summary of these contributions may be found in Dorothy Burlingham's (1973) paper on the pre-Oedipal infant–father relationship. There she considers Freud's writings on the father as a (pre-Oedipal) object of love, admiration, and identification; as a provider of bodily care; as a "powerful or omnipotent Godlike being; as a great man; as a protector; and as a punishing figure, a threatening castrator, and inhibiting authority" (pp. 26–30). But Burlingham was well aware that times were changing and that the role of the father was changing with them. As she herself put it:

> We have occasion in our own times to observe far-reaching alterations in the roles of father and mother. I refer here to what is happening in many young couples, especially in the United States, who espouse the Women's Liberation Movement, which so often means liberation from the chores of household and child care. I also refer to the changes brought about by what is called "planned parenthood" and the pill.
>
> (Burlingham, 1973: 26)

But that was in 1973, and these changes have long since crossed the Atlantic and spread very rapidly. Today, a family in which the father goes to work and the mother stays at home to look after her own child or children, at any rate for their first few years, has ceased to be the norm. The various, and often varying, social circumstances in which children are *not* brought up in this way have to be taken into account.[3] It is now almost the custom for both parents to work and, increasingly, to work full time. What, in 1973, was called "women's liberation" has long taken over the older name of "feminism" and given it increased militancy. It is ever more strongly contended that, if the child *did* need one parent to care for him at home, there was no good reason why this should not be the father and that the mother should be the breadwinner. *Even if this were true, it would hardly apply to fathers who were chronically ill or disabled.* For all that, the belief that differences in sexual identity are of little or no significance outside the narrow concerns of anatomy has grown apace, and has had considerable effects on child-rearing practices.

Taking cognisance of some of these changes, Colette Chiland, in 1982, acknowledged the importance of Dorothy Burlingham's contribution at a time when the psychoanalytic literature on the father's pre-Oedipal role in child care was exiguous, but felt it necessary to take "a fresh look at fathers". In the summary of her paper, she has this to say:

> The concept of a purely dyadic relationship between infant and mother is now as unacceptable as the concept of a stage of normal autism. The father

is present, often in the flesh, and in any event in the mother's psyche. The impact of the father's mothering or of his absence on the child probably depends on the internal and external relationships between the parents and on those each has with the child.

(Chiland, 1982: 377)

However, Chiland was by no means unappreciative of Burlingham's paper, and considered the author "captive neither to phallocentric[4] nor to feminist prejudices" (p. 367). Certainly, what Burlingham had to say about pre-Oedipal fathers remains of considerable interest even in the light of changing social circumstances. It is based not only on a study of the literature as it stood at the time but also on direct observation of fathers' attitudes and responses to sons and daughters; from the analysis of young men who were in treatment at the time their children were born; and from the work of those departments of the Hampstead Clinic (as it was then called) that dealt with infants and young children. It is difficult to address the subject of the handicapped father without bearing in mind the many points Burlingham made about the healthy one.[5] Of these I shall mention but one or two, for those who may not be familiar with the paper. They are, I believe, worth restating; but I shall add to them a little, and supply a few clinical illustrations.

Traditionally (it is hard to avoid a word that, in this context, is so often used pejoratively), the mother–infant dyad was considered to be at the centre of the bonding process and was regarded as the foundation stone of the capacity to make close personal relationships.[6] In this, the father was thought to have little part to play, especially in the first few weeks. His interest was primarily in the mother, of whom the baby, in the father's mind, was still part. (This remains true for many fathers today, but fathers have always differed in this respect.) Some feel the baby as their own from the very beginning – in one case quoted by Burlingham from the moment of conception.

Fathers may feel themselves unwanted and of little use in the child's earliest years; not infrequently they resent the attention the mother bestows on the child. This jealousy may lead to infidelity, separation and/or divorce. On the other hand, fathers may feel intensely involved with the child, and sometimes (rightly or wrongly) feel the mother cannot be trusted with him, may willingly (rather than dutifully) substitute for the mother when she is at work; or may be driven by their own feminine identifications or envy of the mothering role. But many young couples regard shared child care as natural, and see no distinction between the sexes in this respect. What Dorothy Burlingham said about this in 1973 is truer still today, when shared child care is taken for granted by so many young, working parents. Social pressures may, in this respect, have great force: today, some mothers even find it embarrassing to say they stay at home with their children. An example from my own practice is illustrative.

A woman of thirty-seven who had sought help for long-standing anxiety and mild depressive affect was the mother of a boy of thirteen and a girl of nine. Her husband was earning well, was very supportive of his wife in her mothering role. From the beginning, she had stayed at home to look after the children. She was very self-critical, and whenever either child had any of the expectable difficulties encountered in growing up she invariably regarded them as evidence of her "bad" mothering. Her social anxieties bordered on the phobic, and at any social gathering she feared any enquiry about her occupation. She would feel deeply ashamed on "confessing" that she was "only" a housewife: all her women friends had careers. Many of the factors underlying her anxiety were, however, deeper. They included strong but unspoken criticism of her own mother, who had always stayed at home but who never seemed able to meet her childhood needs. She was envious of a strong and powerful father, and masculine wishes – partly responsible for her envy of women who worked – were defended against by her maternal identification. There was no real evidence that she was uncaring or incompetent as a mother. Her husband, like her father, was strong but, unlike him, considerate and kind. This woman could not have tolerated an ill or handicapped husband, who would not have been able to provide for her *or* to undertake any care of the children.

A father's maternal attitude may play a part in his choice of partner; in such cases, an absence of *true* mothering capacities in the woman may be welcomed. Less happily, the father may interfere with the mother's management of the child, which in turn may lead to friction and marital disharmony. But many fathers who are neither resentful nor critical of mother's involvement take great pleasure in their relationship with the infant, take an active part in facial interchange, stimulate the child and enjoy the response. To begin with, there may be little difference in the way fathers treat a daughter or a son: as confidence grows, they bounce and tickle the baby irrespective of sex. Burlingham suggests that, at this stage, the infant, whether boy or girl, "is treated by the father as if it were a symbiotic addition to his own masculinity" (1973: 37). But Burlingham adds that this does not apply to other and later areas of interaction: male children are generally regarded as "replicas of themselves, whereas they relate to their daughters in more complex ways, influenced by their attitude to femininity in their [own] early object relationships and the feminine part of their own natures" (ibid.).

The stimulation and excitement engendered by fathers is generally much greater than it is by mothers. Mothers do not as a rule lift and swing their little ones, or toss them in the air, or pretend to let them fall before catching them. The father's freedom in handling the child increases and is often rougher as the child gets older and responds with delight and excited laughter. The mother may fear that the child may be hurt. Burlingham suggests that the child's whole body may symbolise a part of the father's body (the penis and its erection). With further physical development and increased motility, the child may initiate these activities and reverse the role of father and child. The child may tease and provoke in this new stage of reciprocity.

In a few instances vigorous paternal handling may have detectable consequences in adult life. Many people who love riding on roller coasters enjoy the combination of fear and excitement that they find in these thrills. In this connection I recall a patient who was afraid of riding on buses and other vehicles. He was terrified of fairgrounds, though this fear was of no particular consequence since it was so easily dealt with by avoidance. But he did tell me, one day, that, without any conscious intention, he had passed a funfair that morning and had suddenly realized – and marvelled at the fact – that many people paid money to experience something of which he himself was so fearful. Naturally, his symptoms had other determinants though, in other patients, fears of heights, of falling, and similar symptoms do not necessarily contain this element.

Very often, certain symptoms that *can* be traced to childhood experiences with the father appear *only in the transference and not outside it*. One of my patients felt as if the couch were swinging and rotating, an experience brought to an end by interpretation of the relevant childhood encounters with the father. Another analysand suddenly felt sick and dizzy in the session. When this was related first to a ride on a roundabout with her father when she was about four, the symptom disappeared. The *verbal memory* replaced what I have called *somatic remembering*, suddenly no longer needed with the restoration of recall in words. It was then possible to extend the interpretation to include the sexualisation of the episode in the transference (the experience occurred, after all, in the session) before leading the analysis back to childhood sexual fantasies about the father. We were soon occupied with the intricacies of the Oedipal complex. What is of special interest from the developmental point of view is the further finding, arrived at later, that earlier experiences of being held by the father while being swung by the legs had been carried forward to contribute to the *form* taken by the cover memory.

The infant's early tie to the mother is generally stronger than it is to the father, but there are many exceptions.[7] The tie to the father may be stronger when he substitutes for the mother when she is working, confined to hospital, or for any other reason that interferes with her own part in mothering. But where the tie to the mother is stronger, the father may play an important part in loosening it. As the child gets older, pleasure in the father tends to increase; his arrival home is awaited and greeted with excitement, and his presence becomes a move away from daily routine and may foster greater interest in the outside world.

One must beware of generalizations. An early preference for the father is not invariably linked with a perceived deficiency in the mother. Observations at Hampstead have pointed to instances when the father is preferred even in the presence of a mother who is well and willing to play her part in care and play. Closer study of such instances (which are not common) might be enlightening. But even in those commoner cases where the mother–child tie is initially strong, the infant may turn to the father for comfort when the mother is overly anxious or depressed. Some mothers do not cuddle their children, and here again the child may turn to the father to supply the deficiency.

Again, an example may be in order. One patient of mine could remember no display of affection from her mother – "not ever"; and although not everything patients tell their analyst is objective, it still expressed, for her, what we know as "psychic reality". At all events, when the patient started school she always found her mother in a drunken state, unable to talk to her. The patient once said to me: "Talk: say anything! I don't care what it is! I just want to hear the sound of your voice." This replicated the wish that the mother would speak to her. Not perhaps surprisingly, the patient had remained strongly attached to her father, turning to him for every kind of support and advice. But an excessively strong and unresolved Oedipal phase seemed to have been bolstered by earlier experiences, and the patient was in considerable personal difficulties when she first entered treatment.

Small children do not always respond pleasurably to fathers who are interested in them and want to play with them. Even a loved father may become the subject of eight-month "stranger anxiety" and be hurt if he fails to understand that this is a forward step in the growth of the capacity for differentiation. And, of course, inconsistency of handling, excessive roughness, bad temper, changes of mood, and quarrelsomeness may all have a deleterious effect on the father–child interaction. Naturally, unreliable behaviour may affect the mother–child relationship too. In any case, we have to remember that the balance between masculinity and femininity in any individual may profoundly affect parent–child relationships and point to the need to avoid sweeping statements in discussing the roles of fathers and mothers. Due weight, too, must be given to other personality differences and preferences, as well as innate qualities in the child. This said, we can perhaps agree with Dorothy Burlingham (who discussed such reservations with clarity) in her conclusions that "maternal care is more gentle, soothing, and comforting, while paternal involvement is more active, exciting, stimulating, and occasionally also arouses discomfort and anxiety" (1973: 45). And she adds that the infant is a rather more *passive* recipient of maternal care, while paternal care tends to produce more *active* responses. But again, generalizations are risky. That said, social changes occurring since Burlingham wrote are unlikely to invalidate these points, though the feminine inclinations of some so-called "new men" may affect the way they treat their children.

Nowadays we can see that the tendency towards similar roles between the two sexes in child care means that many of the distinctions described above have been reduced, though personality differences and the balance between femininity and masculinity are as likely as ever to make themselves felt. But, since Burlingham's time, the psychoanalytic literature on *paternal mothering* has expanded, and where this kind of "mothering" is prolonged, or replaces the care of the mother altogether, interest has been pronounced. It would go beyond the remit of this chapter to make any detailed comment on these studies, but the reader may be referred to papers by Pruett (1983, 1985, 1989) and Pruett and Litzenberger (1992); and to Chused (1986). Pruett's work has involved seventeen fathers – all members of intact families who chose to be primary caretakers. By the time of the 1986 report the children's progress had been followed for eight years. The method involved observations and interviews, and the nurturing was deemed to be successful. The women generally *wanted* to work, but in five instances the decision was based on economic circumstances rather than choice – e.g., the father had lost his job while the mother was still employed. Chused's sample of cases is hardly an adequate one on which to draw general conclusions; in any case, it may be worth bearing in mind what Chiland said at the conclusion of her paper:

> Women, in spite of the excesses of some feminist demands, which are covered by the French term *feminitude*, copied from *negritude*, have found in the contemporary culture means to overcome some secondary effects of penis envy. Men are in the process of acknowledging as valuable some aspects of the wish for femininity. Will the children benefit?
>
> (Chiland, 1982: 378)

She ends with a question, not a conclusion; and an answer cannot be found by observational and interview data alone. As Chiland had said earlier in her paper: "Until we have actually analysed children and adults whose early child care was shared by their mothers and fathers or who were raised predominantly by their fathers, we shall not be able to answer such questions" (p. 376).

Disability and the father's care

It is tempting to go more deeply into the question of the extent to which fathers can successfully take on a mothering role in early life; fathers and children differ and it is dangerous to generalize. If a father *can* do so – as he sometimes must – then his ability will only be impaired if, at the start of his child's life, a physical handicap interferes with his carrying out the necessary functions of motherhood. A mild limitation of sight could prevent his driving a car but leave him entirely free to offer the bodily and physical care required. An ocular disturbance that interfered with eye contact would hardly be an advantage. Facial disfigurements or ticks might interfere with his capacity to make effective face-to-face contact, and, depending on their nature, could make it difficult to respond appropriately to an infant's smile and return it effectively. Innumerable forms of bodily infirmity could make daily physical management difficult or impossible. Chronic illness could make it hard to meet a child's needs on an adequate day-to-day basis. A depressive illness or comparable mental disturbance would hardly affect mothering capacities any differently than it would do in a woman. In either case, the difficulty both in finding the necessary energy to look after the child as well as the capacity to display affection could have serious consequences for the child's development.

Psychoanalysts are well aware that there is far more to bringing up a child than the provision of physical care. It was, surprisingly, not until the Second World War, with the experiences of evacuation and its attendant increase in bed-wetting, eating disorders, and behavioural problems, that the principle of *continuity of care*, and the need to maintain it at almost any cost, was widely realized. Those pioneers in childhood mental health who witnessed at first hand some of the tragedies of evacuation (I. Hellman, A. Freud and D. Burlingham), and who saw the improvements that occurred when a child was returned to its parent (in those days almost invariably the mother), were instrumental in bringing about changes in policy. That principle would surely be just as applicable to fathers doing duty for mothers.

In an intact family that does not conform to the contemporary belief that mothers and fathers are interchangeable, the father, as a rule, is much less important in the earlier stages of an infant's life while bonding is proceeding and the early mother/infant interaction is laying a foundation for sound one-to-one relationships in later life. But once the father is more directly engaged with the child, he becomes an essential member of the family whose love (if he is able to give it) is returned by the child and plays a very significant part in the child's development. But physical ill-health, even more than a chronic disability which the father has accepted and to which he has become accustomed, generally leads to an increase in narcissism and leaves less energy, both physical and mental, available for the active interest in, and emotional engagement with, a child – let alone a capacity for play and games.

We are all familiar with the narcissism of old age, brilliantly if cruelly satirized by Wyndham Lewis in the prologue to *The Apes of God* (1930), but we have to bear in mind what Lewis so clearly depicted: that physical infirmity in the aged contributes enormously to the narcissism. In the case of the father of a young child, the narcissism may be just as pronounced. Yet everyone knows severely ill people, old and young, who somehow manage to retain an interest in others even at their own expense. This is particularly difficult, however, in the case of severe pain: anyone who has suffered from toothache knows how hard it is to keep his mind off the aching tooth.

Whatever else, physical health is normally essential if a father is to be able to take part in the more boisterous games with his child. But poor health or handicap may be of lesser significance if he is otherwise able to play an effective part in other kinds of interchange; and a child's feeling that he is loved by the father can, as experience suggests, make up for a lot of other limitations. A boy may want, and in the ordinary course of events expect, to play football with his father, but although he may miss the opportunity to do so he is unlikely to suffer detrimental effects from his deprivation. *Such effects are much more likely to follow the refusal of a healthy father to give his son this pleasure when he is well able, but unwilling, to do so.*

The problems that may be associated with handicapped fathers in intact families are unlikely to be confined to the relationship between father and child alone. Much depends on the effect of the handicap on the family constellation. A mother who despises a disabled father, *even unconsciously*, may affect the children by her attitude, and that in turn may partly depend on a child's relationship, conscious and unconscious, with her. Again, issues such as this are far too complex and various for generalizations. These remarks are necessarily selective, and as restricted in their general implications as they would be if made at random. If we think, for example, of the Oedipal phase, there are innumerable ways in which the outcome will be influenced by the personalities of all concerned, of their interaction, and of their introjections and internalizations. A mother whose hatred of the father is, at some level, detected by the child, may hasten a daughter's move towards the father, deter it, or increase her ambivalence to a point which makes normal developmental moves difficult or impossible; but unless one knew the intricacies of the family relationships, and both the internal and external conflicts of those involved, it would be all but impossible to predict which way this phase of development would turn out.

To this may be added a common problem affecting the girl's entry into the Oedipal phase – namely, her own attitude to the damaged father and its effect on the outcome of her castration complex. If she perceives him as castrated the forward move will, to say the least, be interfered with or seriously impaired. The normative wish to turn to the father as her primary sexual object may be seriously diminished, and the close pre-Oedipal tie to the mother prolonged. But if psychoanalysis has taught us anything, it is the unreliability of predictions and prognostic speculations, even when a great deal of analytic material is to hand.

A mother who was alarmed by her child's distress referred a six-year-old girl, tormented by free-floating guilt and by fears of punitive suffocation. The guilt stemmed largely from death wishes to her father who suffered from a chronic and incurable lung disease. The mother was very supportive of the father in his disability and, consciously, the child identified with the mother's caring attitude. It was not easy to uncover the death wishes of which, consciously, she would have profoundly disapproved, but their analysis in the transference brought about improvement. It is well known that aggression against close relatives and friends who are handicapped may be hard for the aggressor to bear. I am reminded of a child analyst who presented a paper to a group of colleagues. In the discussion it became clear that he had great difficulty in dealing with an aspect of the transference that stemmed from his female patient's hostility to her father in the negative Oedipal phase. Analytically, patient and analyst were stuck. A colleague recollected, however, that the analyst presenting the paper had himself been analysed by a severely disabled woman. Presumably, his own aggression

towards his analyst had been difficult *for his analyst* to deal with, and an unconscious complicity between analyst and patient may well have arisen. The
colleague was privately advised to seek a second analysis with a healthy analyst;
did so and became able to function much better in his own analytic work.

I was once asked, by a senior member of the British Society who played an
active part in the procedure for admitting applicants for training, whether I
thought it would be appropriate to accept a blind candidate. (I was asked on the
basis of my personal experience in the analysis of blind patients.) I replied that,
even where the applicant's credentials and suitability were otherwise evident, it
would perhaps be wise to bear in mind that some of the patients he would have
to treat might find it very difficult, if not impossible, to express aggression towards
him. I believe this advice was right.

I want to return for a moment to cases where a mother despises a damaged
father. A daughter (or son) may love the father in spite of his physical imper-
fections, identify with him, or be highly ambivalent towards him, depending
on many factors. He may be torn by a loyalty conflict in many ways comparable, and sometimes as intense, as some of the loyalty conflicts suffered by so
many unfortunate children who are victims of a divorce. The victim may find
his former love of the two parents is replaced by intense hatred *for the one or the
other*, and where the child, dividing his commitment between them, is obliged
to listen to cascades of hostile condemnation of the father by the mother and
vice versa. *The child is in an impossible position*; and though, in the case of the
handicapped father, family break-up may not be in question, the child may suffer
lasting harm.

Some years ago I discussed some of the ways in which people cope with
physical disabilities (Yorke, 1980a), and pointed to two very different but widespread methods encountered, with many variations, in clinical practice. One was
simply denial: the handicapped patient behaved (or tried to behave) as if he had
no disability whatsoever. The other attitude was to attribute every difficulty,
every misfortune, to the handicap. The deaf patient would believe that if only
he could hear all problems, whether related to the disability or not, would
disappear; the blind person would be convinced that all would be well if only
his sight would return. Often the first sign of improvement was the patient's
recognition that this was not the case; that his psychological difficulties were
only loosely related, if at all, to a deficient modality of sensory input. But I did
not address, at that time, the problems that arose in the family when either of
these methods was adopted by a parent. Yet these are many, and vary in character
with the relationships and personalities of those concerned. Thus, a father who
attempts boisterous play with a child when this is largely beyond his physical
capacity not only risks injury but draws attention to the handicap he tries to
deny. But denial may take the form of an apparent lack of interest in such play.
The denial, though unrecognized as such, is often maintained at the border
between the preconscious and conscious systems.

233

But children, too, use denial; it is, after all, one of the earliest of all defences and, depending on their level of development and psychic structure and function, can deny a father's disability, though when contact with other children makes them more aware of fathers without such disadvantages, may need to defend themselves against feelings of shame. Shame is an emotion with some very special features (Yorke, 1990); it is not easily forgotten and cannot be dealt with by the defence mechanisms used against other affects. The denial can therefore only be of the perception of the father's disability – in effect *disavowal* – and this is more likely to be at all effective if the incapacity is inconspicuous and has little impact on the routine family functioning. If the father has different meals from the rest of the family, or has to be pushed around in a wheelchair, denial can scarcely be operative.

A complex story, that raises some difficult questions, seems worth telling in some detail. It concerns a nine-year-old girl, Amanda, referred for assessment by her mother because she was bullied at school. With a possibly crucial exception, noted below, there had been no flagrant difficulties until the previous year or so, but Amanda, always of a shy and retiring nature, had been even more reserved of late. She was somewhat excluded and made fun of by girls from whom, nevertheless, she could not keep away, even though the bullying had become "vicious and nasty" and Amanda seemed unable to defend herself. At the same time, the mother thought she "looked for trouble". At any rate, she would return from school in a miserable frame of mind, lie on the bed, and say that her legs wouldn't "work" properly and that her head ached. Both parents felt that this behaviour had a histrionic quality.

The salient points of Amanda's past history can be stated briefly. Milestones were normal and there had been the usual childhood illnesses. Nursery School reports between the ages of three and four suggested a hesitant little girl who required encouragement to mix, but who was also intelligent, verbal and capable. Her behaviour at home had not given cause for concern, although, at the age of four, when parental disharmony was pronounced, she had been somewhat regressed and "had acted like a baby". This behaviour began to disappear as the parental crisis was surmounted. Amanda's school reports in the next few years were satisfactory, and her relationships with her peers were not untoward. But at times she could be watchful of other children, retire into a "dreamy" state, or "sit on the sidelines" and watch her schoolmates rather than take part in their games. Recently, before the onset of the bullying, she had improved, no longer seemed hesitant, and the earlier tendency to be diffident and somewhat tense had largely disappeared.

Her father suffered from a lifelong physical disability in one limb, and from epilepsy. His generalized seizures, invariably nocturnal, were sufficiently controlled by medication to ensure that they occurred not more than twice a year. Father was rather dominated by his wife, and accepted this with some degree of resignation and not a little passivity. From time to time he would flare up, to no great effect. The marriage had deteriorated when Amanda was four or five: father had failed to get a job in which he was seriously interested and expected to be appointed, and which would have offered considerable advancement. His wife made full use of this fact in outbursts of derogation, though these later became less virulent and more short-lived. At the height of the crisis the father had seriously considered leaving the mother. It is noteworthy that he had always been dominated by his mother and, in a number of respects, his wife was very much like her. The marriage had improved over the last few years, though the difficulties persisted in the background and the mother's bossiness towards him had in no way abated. He was rather a sad, unhappy man, with low self-esteem, and was self-disparaging. In interview he was "vague, conciliatory, and apologetic". But he was undoubtedly fond of his children and followed their progress with interest.

The mother was the dominant member of the family. She was active, hard working, decisive, opinionated and determined. With the children, her bossiness was more restrained, and she enjoyed trying to meet their different needs. Although she set firm limits, Amanda, like the others, was praised appropriately. All the children had, at the start of life, been bottle fed, since the mother "loathed breast-feeding" almost as much as she disliked housework and cooking. The father made himself responsible for most of these everyday household chores.

Amanda was the youngest of three children, all girls. The sisters shared a small bedroom, and the physical proximity seemed to intensify the quality of their relationships with each other – both positive and negative. Amanda, however, became victimized by the second sister, who resented the fact that the *eldest* child had changed schools. According to the mother, she "took it out on" Amanda. It was then that the bullying started. Furthermore, Amanda felt that the bullying was instigated by *two former friends who had turned against her.*

There was another feature of interest. Amanda had been asked to be discreet about her father's difficulties (his physical disabilities, as well as money problems made worse by his limited earning capacity), and this request may have fed into the child's existing preference for secrecy. It had long been evident that, in her periods of withdrawal, Amanda was silent and didn't communicate with the rest of the family. One of the discussants considering the case pointed out that, in this connection, Amanda's long-standing inclination to be a "private person" might have been reinforced by the degree of exposure to her sisters in the bedroom they shared.

For all the problems within the household, Amanda's difficulties were mainly evident outside the home; her relationships with the individual members of her family were generally warm, though she got on better with the eldest sister than with the other. She regarded her mother (consciously) as kind and considerate, and *especially warm towards her when she was ill*; but for all her reserve elsewhere, she had at least one close personal friend and one or two others with whom she was on good terms.

It remains to add a comment or two concerning findings from the stories she recounted during Thematic Apperception Testing (TAT). In one, a woman was featured who was somewhat in awe of her husband, who appeared in the tale as a somewhat idealized figure. Another story suggested Amanda's attraction to a "father figure" and a disparaging attitude towards a woman representing the mother. A number of responses to certain cards pointed to a difficulty with aggression. Lastly, a couch, beside which a boy was huddled and a revolver lay on the floor, was seen as a *bath*; the boy was seen as a man who had collapsed from working too hard.

I have selected here one or two points from the history that seem to deserve attention, together with a few observations that may help to give the story a certain life. The patient was not considered sufficiently disturbed to justify psychoanalysis, and more restricted help was offered to the family. The reader has therefore been provided with material only from initial interviews, reports, and psychological testing, together with a record of the presentation, based on Anna Freud's diagnostic profile schema, and the minutes of the discussion that followed.

The fact that Amanda did not come into analysis at that time is not, to my mind, a disadvantage for present purposes. True, it might well have provided answers for the kind of questions that can be asked at the stage of assessment. But it may be more useful to look at the questions themselves: fascinating though it may be to follow psychoanalytic clinical material in the hope of finding confirmation of provisional diagnostic formulations and answers to speculations. For the one thing that is certain about children's responses to damaged fathers is that *every case is different: generalizations have no validity*, and it may be more helpful to look at the kind of questions that arise when we are faced with any one instance.

Following the presentation of Amanda's profile, most discussants took the view that she had failed to negotiate the Oedipal constellation. If she were deeply in that first painful love affair, as most speakers assumed, did she fail to negotiate it, remaining arrested there, or did she come through it, regressing to it at a later date? The diagnostician was inclined to think that Amanda had never satisfactorily surmounted the Oedipal phase, and thought it possible that the lack of resolution gave rise to guilt and a need for punishment. The mother's sympathy, care and concern for Amanda's physical suffering was a significant secondary gain. If, on the other hand, Amanda regressed to an Oedipal phase at the time the *need to be bullied* declared itself, one would expect some common factor leading both to regression and to the symptom.

What part, if any, could the father's disabilities play in her Oedipal difficulties and/or in the bullying? The material points to a number of possibilities: the need for secrecy about his handicaps, instilled by the mother, suggests that *she* (the mother), was, at any rate to some degree, ashamed of him. (The fact that she married him does not run counter to this hypothesis: the limb disability was not conspicuous and was hidden when suitable clothes were worn, and the epilepsy would be unknown except to those whom the father chose to confide in. And as her attitude towards him was controlling and bossy, one could further speculate that the mother's attitude to the father, whatever the facts, meant that he was in no way a threat to her.) From Amanda's point of view, the mother's attitude, in this respect, did not seem particularly welcome, at least unconsciously; the response to the TAT card mentioned above reversed the parental roles as far as the issues of control and submission were concerned. The disparaging attitude towards the mother seen in another TAT response may be in accord with this. Amanda's inhibition of aggression was evident in pre-Oedipal stages, though death wishes at the later phase may have included and put to fresh use the impulses that she so strongly needed to keep at bay. In any event, the inhibition may also have signified a character trait that may have served abundant purposes.

As I see it, this whole developmental area is problematic. The Oedipal constellation was complicated by many factors. To begin with, it must have been in this phase (between the ages of four and five) that Amanda regressed and became temporarily baby-like. Furthermore, it was at this time that parental difficulties were at their height, and the father was thinking of leaving the mother. That would not, perhaps, be the best time to be struggling with Oedipal issues, death wishes towards the mother, and the separation a child both longs for and hates. And more could be said here about the damaged father: was he seen as castrated and a source of disappointment as an Oedipal figure. But, according to the mother, the father had been somewhat idealized in those days, and that might have redressed the balance. The response to the TAT in which the couch is seen as a bath raises the interesting point that epileptics are often at risk in the bath, and the rest of the card is scarcely conducive to anything other than doom-laden fantasy. But comments such as this are entirely speculative: what seems certain is that getting through the Oedipal complex, in the light of all the circumstances, was hardly child's play, even for a five-year-old.

Further points of interest arise when we consider the factors leading to Amanda being bullied. She was bullied by the middle sister at the time she suffered from bullying at school; and the fact that she seems to have sought out the insulting and antagonistic behaviour from her *two former friends* may be significant. What part did masochism play in these events? How important was it at the Oedipal stage and did it affect its outcome? Does the combination of headache and leg pains *following the bullying* point to an identification with the father both as a damaged and a masochistic victim, and, if so, does it reflect sympathy with him? Does it reflect disappointment in which identification replaces object choice and emphasizes features of a *negative* Oedipal phase? Or has it other implications that cannot as yet be guessed at? The questions seem endless, and I will only add that, out of the very many profiles[8] I have read or heard presented over the years, I have rarely found a provisional assessment so difficult to arrive at.[9]

Perhaps that is as well. It is vital to approach every case as unique, and that goes for children with damaged fathers as much as anyone else. So if no firm conclusions have arisen from this last somewhat meagre vignette, *that*, at least, is in line with the spirit of the chapter and the fact that its subject can never invite general conclusions, much less universal truths.

Notes

1 "His" (and comparably with "him", "himself" and other related words) is used generically throughout, and can, where the context allows, equally be read as "hers".
2 For example, Burlingham (1975, 1979), Colonna (1981), Curson (1979), Earle (1979), Kennedy (1985), Lopez (1974), Moran (1984), Radford (1973), Wills (1979a, 1979b, 1981).
3 I have discussed these changes and their effects on the practice of child care at some length in five radio talks for BBC Radio 3 in November 1995. The text was made available in *The Bulletin of the Anna Freud Centre* (Yorke, 1996a), and is currently being expanded for publication elsewhere.
4 A fashionable term, as we know. Chiland is by no means a victim of fashion, but I find the term misleading and far more political than scientific.
5 Some aspects of the subject had been discussed, in a more specialized way, by Neubauer (1960), *vide infra*, and by Leonard (1966).
6 This is still the position taken by "attachment theorists" and many experimental workers.
7 This statement will be challenged by many contemporary social theorists, even with the qualification I have included. It seems worth recalling a remark made by Charcot, and one Freud never forgot: "Theory is all very well, but it doesn't prevent things from happening." (See, for example, Jones, 1953: 228, who reports the original French.)
8 I have long been convinced of the value of Anna Freud's profile as a tool that assists provisional diagnostic formulations (Yorke, 1980b, 1996b).
9 There is a rider to this story. Four years after the events described, Amanda was again referred for assessment. The bullying, or the fear of it, had long since vanished. Amanda was now *afraid of leaving her mother*, and had difficulty in going to school on that account.

References

Arlow, J. (1976). Communication & character: a clinical study of a man raised by deaf-mute parents. *Psychoanalytic Study of the Child*, 31: 139–163.
Bene, A. (1977). The influence of deaf and dumb parents on a child's development. *Psychoanalytic Study of the Child*, 32: 175–194.
Burlingham, D.T. (1973). The pre-oedipal infant–father relationship. *Psychoanalytic Study of the Child*, 28: 23–47.

Burlingham, D.T. (1975). Special problems of blind infants: blind baby profile. *Psychoanalytic Study of the Child*, 30: 3–13.

Burlingham, D.T. (1979). To be blind in a sighted world. *Psychoanalytic Study of the Child*, 34: 5–30.

Burlingham, D.T. and Freud, A. (1942). *Young Children in War Time*. London: Allen & Unwin (1944). (Published as *War and Children*, New York: International Universities Press, 1944.)

Chiland, C. (1982). A new look at fathers. *Psychoanalytic Study of the Child*, 37: 367–379.

Chused, J. (1986). Consequences of paternal nurturing. *Psychoanalytic Study of the Child*, 41: 419–438.

Colonna, A.B. (1981). Success through their own efforts. *Psychoanalytic Study of the Child*, 36: 33–44.

Curson, A. (1979). The blind nursery school child. *Psychoanalytic Study of the Child*, 34: 51–83.

Earle, E. (1979). The psychological effects of mutilating surgery in children and adolescents. *Psychoanalytic Study of the Child*, 34: 527–546.

Freud, S. (1931). *Female Sexuality*. Standard Edition, XXI. London: Hogarth Press.

Freud, S. (1933). *New Introductory Lectures in Psycho-Analysis*. Standard Edition, XXIII. London: Hogarth Press.

Hellman, I. (1990). The war nurseries and follow up studies. In *From War Babies to Proud Mothers*. London: Karnac Books.

Kennedy, H. (1985). Growing up with a handicapped sibling. *Psychoanalytic Study of the Child*, 40: 255–274.

Jones, F. (1953). *Sigmund Freud's Life and Works, Vol. 1*. London: Hogarth Press.

Leonard, M.R. (1966). Fathers and daughters. *International Journal of Psycho-Analysis*, 47: 325–334.

Lopez, T. (1974). Psychotherapeutic assistance to a blind child with limited intelligence. *Psychoanalytic Study of the Child*, 29, 277–299.

Moran, G.S. (1984). Psychoanalytic treatment of diabetic children. *Psychoanalytic Study of the Child*, 39: 407–447.

Neubauer, P.B. (1960). The one-parent child and his oedipal development. *Psychoanalytic Study of the Child*, 15: 286–309.

Pruett, K.D. (1983). Infants of primary nurturing fathers. *Psychoanalytic Study of the Child*, 38: 257–277.

Pruett, K.D. (1985). Oedipal configurations in father-raised children. *Psychoanalytic Study of the Child*, 40: 435–456.

Pruett, K.D. (1989). The nurturing male. In S. Cath, A. Gurwitt and L. Gunsberg (eds) *Fathers and their Families*. Hillsdale, N.J.: Analytic Press, pp. 309–408.

Pruett, K.D., and Litzenberger, B. (1992). Latency development in children of primary nurturing fathers: eight-year follow-up. *Psychoanalytic Study of the Child*, 47: 85–101.

Radford, P. (1973). Changing techniques in the analysis of a deaf latency boy. *Psychoanalytic Study of the Child*, 28: 225–248.

Wills, D.M. (1979a). "The ordinary devoted mother" and her blind baby. *Psychoanalytic Study of the Child*, 34: 31–49.

Wills, D.M. (1979b). Early speech development in blind children. *Psychoanalytic Study of the Child*, 34: 85–117.

Wills, D.M. (1981). Some notes on the application of the diagnostic profile to young blind children. *Psychoanalytic Study of the Child*, 36: 217–237.

Yorke, C. (1980a). Comments on the psychoanalytic treatment of patients with physical disabilities. *International Journal of Psycho-Analysis*, 61: 187–194.

Yorke, C. (1980b). The contributions of the diagnostic profile and developmental lines to child psychiatry. *Psychiatric Clinics of North America*, 3: 593–603.

Yorke, C. (1990) (in collaboration with T. Balogh, P. Cohen, J. Davids, A. Gavshon, M. McCutcheon, D. McLean, J. Miller, and J. Szydlo). The development and functioning of the sense of shame. *Psychoanalytic Study of the Child*, 45: 377–409.

Yorke, C. (1996a). Childhood and social truth: five talks for BBC Radio 3. *Bulletin of the Anna Freud Centre*, 18: 47–74.

Yorke, C. (1996b). Diagnosis in clinical practice: its relationship to psychoanalytic theory. *Psychoanalytic Study of the Child*, 51: 190–214.

Postscript

CONCLUDING COMMENTS

Martin N. Baily

As stated in the introductory chapter, we trust that this book has shed some light on why the role and function of the father is important for the development of children. Social change occurs slowly, but it does appear that fathers are being recognized as important, as reported in the following study by M.N. Baily, R. Lawrence and K. Shaw (*Economic Report of the President* 1–2–2000 US Government Printing Office, Washington, DC). (No comparable statement has so far been found in the UK policy documents.)

The importance of fathers

Although the proportion of single-parent families headed by the father is rising, the mother has typically been the custodial parent in such families. For this reason, and because of the higher incidence of poverty in female-headed families, the discussion of single-parent families in this chapter focuses on single mothers. An important issue for such families is the link between children's well being and the absence of the father.

It is estimated that 36 percent of American children live apart from their biological fathers; about 40 percent of children in fatherless households have not seen their fathers in at least a year. Before they reach age 18, more than half of America's children are likely to have spent a significant portion of their childhood living apart from their fathers.

Yet there is strong evidence suggesting that the presence of a father matters:

- Children under age 6 who live apart from their fathers are about five times as likely to be poor as children with both parents at home.

243

- Girls without a father in their life are two and a half times as likely to get pregnant and 53 percent more likely to commit suicide.
- Boys without a father in their life are 63 percent more likely to run away and 37 percent more likely to abuse drugs.
- Children without father involvement are twice as likely to drop out of high school, roughly twice as likely to abuse alcohol or drugs, twice as likely to end up in jail, and nearly four times as likely to need help for emotional or behavioral problems than those with father involvement.

The absence of a father has effects beyond those on his own children: it can affect communities as well. About 4.5 million children in 1990 resided in predominantly fatherless neighborhoods in which more than half of all families with children were headed by single mothers.

We hope we have shown that the father is a necessary and not a contingent figure in the child's life and in society.

Index

245